Praise for *What*

"Evocative and clear-eyed . . . Just as *Eat Pray Love* and *Wild* inspired millions, this book will send countless readers on a different—yet no less life-changing or profound—pilgrimage, as it did for me."

—Samin Nosrat, *New York Times* bestselling author of *Salt, Fat, Acid, Heat*

"I freaking love this book. It's about so many things, but mostly love and loss, and how you can't let fear keep you from experiencing all the love—and pain and joy—in this glorious, heart-breaking, unpredictable world."

—Jeannette Walls, *New York Times* bestselling author of *The Glass Castle*, *The Silver Star*, and *Half Broke Horses*

"The best kind of breathless, propulsive, rollicking human story—it will surprise you, inspire you, break your heart, and make you laugh out loud. To say this book is impossible to put down is cliché, but true: I tore through it in one sitting. It's a life-changing lesson in healing from loss and trauma, and a master class in resilience. It couldn't have come at a better time."

—Rebecca Skloot, *New York Times* bestselling author of *The Immortal Life of Henrietta Lacks*

"A gripping, luminous story. Braitman teaches us how to stay open to life and love in a world we can't control, a world in which loss is inevitable but where hope springs eternal. It's a revelatory tale about using your past to create your own beautiful future. A must-read."

—Lucy Kalanithi, MD, Stanford School of Medicine and widow of Dr. Paul Kalanithi, author of *When Breath Becomes Air*

"Beautiful. Laurel proves to us that home is something you carry inside of you and, in it, there is room for every feeling—the great, the bad, and the cheeky. This book will tear you apart and then put you back together again—and it will feel so good."

—BJ Miller, MD, author of *A Beginner's Guide to the End*

"Gripping and gorgeous, this memoir is drawn from wisdom that only comes from life-altering loss. With breathtaking candor, Braitman sits us down by the campfire and shares a story that is relatable in its humanity but filled with the unexpected details that make for a riveting, mesmerizing tale. It made me understand my own childhood in a whole new way. *What Looks Like Bravery* is deeply, surprisingly healing."

—Kevin Kwan, *New York Times* bestselling author of *Crazy Rich Asians*

"Read this survivor tale. Braitman transforms a free fall into a soaring triumph. It's a little slutty, a lot brilliant, and you may notice the falcon that was always there, waiting for you to look up."

—Jillian Lauren, *New York Times* bestselling author of *Some Girls*, *Pretty*, and *Everything You Ever Wanted*

"After a spell of world traveling, earning a doctorate, racking up honors and achievements, and, most of all, enduring the ordinary griefs of life, the author has prevailed. One of her closing realizations is worth the cover price alone: 'There is no such thing as happily ever after. There is only happily sad or sadly happy.' An affecting investigation of loss, sorrow, and the search for meaning."

—*Kirkus Reviews*

"An inspiring memoir . . . Her prose is shot through with rigor and intellectual curiosity, resulting in a candid study of one woman's long path to emotional peace. This is perfect for anyone looking to heal a broken heart."

—*Publishers Weekly*

"Readers struggling with grief will identify strongly with Braitman's story."

—*Booklist*

100
YEARS
SIMON &
SCHUSTER
PAPERBACKS

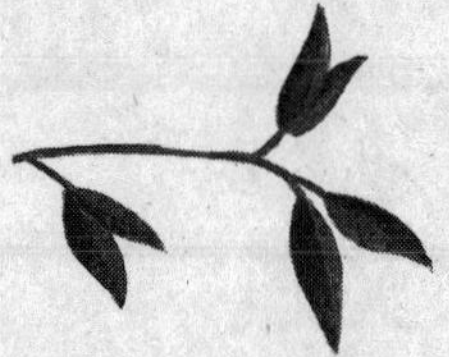

Also by Laurel Braitman

Animal Madness: Inside Their Minds

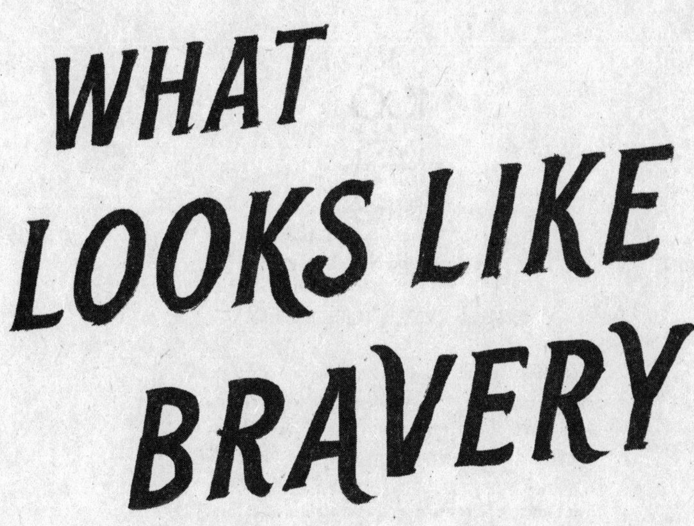

WHAT LOOKS LIKE BRAVERY

An Epic Journey Through Loss to Love

Laurel Braitman

SIMON & SCHUSTER PAPERBACKS
New York London Toronto Sydney New Delhi

Many names and some identifying details have been changed, whether or not so noted in the text.

An Imprint of Simon & Schuster, LLC
1230 Avenue of the Americas
New York, NY 10020

First Simon & Schuster trade paperback edition July 2024

SIMON & SCHUSTER PAPERBACKS and colophon are registered trademarks of Simon & Schuster, LLC

Simon & Schuster: Celebrating 100 Years of Publishing in 2024

For information about special discounts for bulk purchases, please contact Simon & Schuster Special Sales at 1-866-506-1949 or business@simonandschuster.com.

The Simon & Schuster Speakers Bureau can bring authors to your live event. For more information or to book an event, contact the Simon & Schuster Speakers Bureau at 1-866-248-3049 or visit our website at www.simonspeakers.com.

Interior design by Ruth Lee-Mui

Manufactured in the United States of America

1 3 5 7 9 10 8 6 4 2

Library of Congress Cataloging-in-Publication Data has been applied for.

ISBN 978-1-5011-5850-6
ISBN 978-1-5011-5851-3 (pbk)
ISBN 978-1-5011-5852-0 (ebook)

For Jake

my 9-1-1

I'm writing this story
with the pen my Dad gave me.

Prologue

Santa Paula, California, September 1994

It was a warm Saturday afternoon and the Santa Ana winds ruffled the tops of the avocado trees. I was at home with two good friends, all of us sixteen years old, draped like hormonal Dalí clocks over the living room furniture while we watched *The Bodyguard* on VHS and painted our nails.

I knocked over one of the bottles and went into my parents' bathroom to get the polish remover. I glanced at myself in the mirror, disappointed, as usual, by my wild hair, tight cheeks, and how little I looked like someone Kevin Costner might want to carry to safety. Kneeling down and reaching into the cabinet under the sink, I pushed aside the bottles of rubbing alcohol that Dad used to clean the stump on his amputated leg and the tray of stainless scissors he had brought home from his job at the hospital. I was moving a multipack of Dove soap when I saw it—a small, plastic pill bottle. It was strange, not labeled like everything else in the cabinet. It didn't look like the transparent orange prescription bottles that came from the pharmacy either. My body sensed danger before my mind did. Something clenched in my chest; my pulse started to throb in my face.

There was a handwritten note rubber banded around the bottle. I unrolled it carefully.

No one should have to do this for a friend, but here you go.

My throat went hot and dry as the winds outside. I steadied myself on the cabinet door.

It hit me. Dad had a suicide plan. And he kept it in the bathroom like a box of Q-tips or Mom's Velcro rollers.

Underneath the message was the name of a drug and dosage instructions written out longhand.

I had no idea how long the bottle had been there, or when he was going to use it. But I knew I couldn't ask or tell anyone about this, not even Mom. Or Jake. Not ever. I understood without being told that I wasn't supposed to know about this or that anyone had helped him or that his death was barreling toward us like a car whose brakes had gone out.

I let myself feel my pounding terror for just a few more seconds, and then I rewound the note and put the bottle back exactly where it had been. Standing up, I took a long breath, summoning every bit of power I had, and shoved my fear and panic down as hard as I could—burying them so deeply that for years I thought they were dead and gone. Only, you can't kill bad feelings.

Part I

A man who has not prepared his children for
his own death has failed as a father.

King T'Chaka, *Black Panther*

One

Santa Paula, California

It was 1985. I was seven years old and had one thing on my mind: saving my family.

I went to the library at Mesa Union, my public primary school surrounded by lemon orchards, and told Mary the librarian that I was done with my usual ballet books, Laura Ingalls Wilder, and the Tales from the Crypt series. Instead, I wanted stories about kids with dead parents. Or survival skills.

I remember her looking at me, curious, but she didn't make me explain. Mary, like my parents, did not believe in age requirements for literature.

"How about *Island of the Blue Dolphins*?" she asked.

I'd read it but took the book anyway. Then she gave me *Julie of the Wolves* and told me that I might not understand all of it yet.

After school that day I didn't do what I normally did: play with my dollhouse or stare at the swollen testicles and oozing rashes in the skin disorders book that was up in the loft with all the rest of Dad's medical textbooks. Instead, I read. Soon I was reading before and after school and every night after dinner. I read in the car waiting for Mom at the grocery store. I read outside, sitting on the big hill with our herd of half-wild donkeys, turning brown in the sun. And I read while walking around the ranch where we lived, looking up every once in a while to make sure I didn't walk into an orange tree. My favorite books were about orphan girls. Some could make fire using a bow and pocket lint. Others joined wolf packs to hunt for game. I read these books like they were manuals and I could study their tactics—all so I could do my part in case my younger brother, Jake, and I had to take up seal hunting to feed ourselves or build a shelter out of lemon bins. One day, I spent a few hours figuring out how long, realistically, we'd be able to survive on the ranch without any outside food or water. If we didn't mind scooping pollywogs out of the stagnant creek, or eating Midnight the pony, this would be a very long time.

What I really wanted though was something to protect us, especially Dad. I'd said goodbye to him once. But then he'd survived. Surprising all of us except, maybe, himself.

It started four years before, in 1981. Dad was forty-one. Mom was thirty-three. I was three and my brother hadn't been born yet. Dad's knee hurt. He thought he'd injured himself in a ski accident in Utah. He went to the emergency room there, still in his blue woolen ski sweater, but the on-call physician didn't see anything broken or torn on his X-rays. So Dad flew home, iced his leg, and went back to work as a cardiothoracic surgeon at our county hospital. But the pain got worse instead of better. During the day he hardly noticed it, but at night his knee throbbed so badly he couldn't sleep. The only thing that helped was walking, so he'd get out of bed, trying not to wake Mom, and pace the orchards. Up and down, he went through the rows of new baby avocado trees they'd just planted and the older, taller orange groves.

My parents bought the ranch in the spring of 1978. We were living in Camarillo then, a small town named for a Californio (a Spanish-speaking Californian descended from Mexican and Spanish colonizers) who grew lima beans, bred fancy white horses, and was famous for riding around town on a studded silver saddle. My parents owned a small house on a couple of acres with a vegetable garden and enough space for Mom's two donkeys, a flock of chickens, four aloof merino sheep, and me. Dad wanted more space to garden. More animals. More everything.

"What if we grew avocados?" Mom remembers him asking as he tamped down the tobacco in his pipe, one night after dinner.

"Jewish avocado farmers?" she asked.

"Ranchers. I don't know why but no one says 'avocado farming.' It's like they're raising cattle instead of fruit."

Mom was skeptical. They were not farming, or ranching, people. He'd grown up in downtown Baltimore, a few miles from Johns Hopkins where he'd later go to medical school. She was the daughter of an optometrist in Beverly Hills. But they loved working in the garden and having animals and they thought it'd be an interesting way to raise a kid.

I was born just before Valentine's Day that winter. Mom was worried about bringing me home because Dad didn't want children. At their last house, in Oakland, where he'd been working as a doctor in the navy, he planted New Zealand thorn trees around the perimeter of the yard like a barbed fence so none of the neighborhood kids would be tempted to kick a ball over. He eventually agreed to have a child, not because he wanted one but because he loved her. When he looked into my eyes for the first time, though, dark as his with eyebrows like quotation marks waiting for him to say something worth remembering, whatever thorn trees he'd planted inside himself were uprooted forever. We didn't know it yet but we were each other's becoming. Loving one another in direct proportion to how much we fought. A mutual crucible. To the death.

After Mom and Dad's ranching conversation, she started strapping me into my car seat in the afternoons and driving the long, straight roads along irrigation ditches through strawberry fields and lemon orchards where farmworkers in straw hats and canvas gloves picked fruit, looking for FOR SALE signs. She talked to agricultural real estate agents, called up commercial growers to ask advice, and scoured the listings in the local *Star-Free Press*. When she saw an auction notice for a fifty-acre citrus and cattle ranch in Santa Paula—the self-proclaimed Citrus Capital of the World, a small, mostly Mexican town with a sun-bleached main street home to a string of panaderías and vaquero supply shops selling crocodile boots—she drove straight there.

The ranch was named Los Perules, for the giant pepper trees that stood in front of the old farmhouse, their leaves like pale green ostrich feathers drooping toward the ground, hiding the papery pink clusters of peppercorns. The property stretched from the main road all the way to the lip of the canyon where the orchards gave way to purple sage and wild lilac, dotted with California live oaks and shot through with grassy meadows. As Mom walked under the old gray trees with scrabbly bark, she had visions of donkeys grazing on the long grass. A creek was the western boundary and it was lined with sycamores and noisy with frogs. There were corrals for horses and lots of room to ride, space for a chicken coop, and plenty of flat spots for vegetable and flower gardens. The view from the dilapidated house was of the entire canyon spread out like a citrus quilt and if you climbed to the top of the hill behind the house, you could see the ocean and ridges of the Channel Islands rising soft and dark through the sea fog.

Mom stood in front of an old water tank with me on her hip and decided this was it. She asked to use the old rotary phone inside the house to call Dad at the hospital. He told her to make an offer, as much as they could afford plus an extra five thousand dollars they didn't have yet.

Within a year my parents were in the middle of rebuilding the house, hauling away trash, tearing out a few of the ailing orchards and replanting them with younger orange, lemon, and avocado trees. Dad started a raspberry patch and Mom, the first of three vegetable gardens. They bought a few peacocks and let them roam free and installed the donkeys in the old corral. They built worm bins for compost and took classes in beekeeping before setting up their own hives.

For the next few years, whenever Dad wasn't at the hospital, the two of them were planting trees, digging holes, laying irrigation lines, spreading fertilizer, tending the beehives, and otherwise teaching themselves how to farm. While they worked I collected roly-poly bugs, snuck into the corral to touch the donkeys' springy fur, and pestered the barn cats who slept on the alfalfa bales. During one of our first summers there was a wildfire that came a little too close and the following winter, a flood that took out the bridge across the creek, but other than that everything was pretty peaceful.

Soon the local paper got wind of a couple rebuilding a ranch west of Santa Paula and dispatched a reporter to write a story. "Complex Couple Motivated by Simple Dreams" was a fawning profile of my parents, accompanied by a large photo of Dad bent over the operating table, his surgical mask splattered with blood. There was another of them with me—a toddler now, in corduroy overalls—approaching our meanest peacock, the one who liked to peck the peanut butter sandwiches out of my hands. Mom is kneeling next to me, her hair flipped and feathered Farrah Fawcett style against her denim shirt. Dad looks on, smiling at me, in worn leather work boots and a short-sleeved cowboy shirt with pearl buttons.

The reporter was clearly charmed by the way my parents finished each other's sentences and what he called their "unorthodox variety" of plants and animals. "Howard indulges me," he quoted Mom. "Some people get jewelry and furs. I get burros and one year I got a chicken coop." Later, as they led the reporter around, prompting him to look in the long worm bins they'd built, Dad said, "It looked like *Grapes of Wrath* here. The guy who sold it to us said the only thing keeping it together was all the termites holding hands."

If it sounds idyllic, the ranch and even how they talked about each other, I think it was. My parents were so happy it screwed me up a bit. Made all my own love stories a little pale by comparison. It's not like they didn't want to strangle each other sometimes or fight so hard and loud that every once in a while Jake and I fled into the oranges to wait them out. They fought about stupid stuff—like whether a housekeeper had stolen Dad's pants (she had not) and once, about how Mom made the lettuce pieces in the salad too big (she got up from the dinner table and didn't come back for a long time). Mostly, though, they got along in a way that made falling in love seem so easy that it happens over an evening or two, and then blooms, effortlessly, into a lifetime of compatibility. At least, that's what I thought I was entitled to because it was all I knew.

What we didn't know was how quickly it could change.

Two

Santa Paula, California, 1981

Dad's knee pain transformed from a dull whisper into a scream. Soon he couldn't walk it off no matter how hard he tried. He went to see a few different orthopedists but no one had any idea what was going on. Dad tried not to think about it, but back in medical school he'd learned that terrible night pain that improved with movement could be bone cancer. He was a healthy forty-one-year-old with no other symptoms but Dad wanted a CAT scan. The problem was that no doctor would order one. They didn't think it was worth the expense for someone so young and in shape. So in the end, Dad ordered the scan for himself.

His diagnosis, osteogenic sarcoma, a rare and aggressive bone cancer, blasted into our lives like a meteor, which is exactly what Mom says his tumor looked like on the scan he brought home and showed her, standing at the kitchen counter next to our baskets of avocados. A blazing ball of light at the base of his right knee. And it was a death sentence, especially in 1981. Chemotherapy for bone cancer was new and toxic, still in the experimental stage. If the cancer hadn't spread beyond his leg, he had a one in five chance of living five years. Dad did the math quickly. If he had no metastases, it was more likely he'd be part of the 20 percent that survived. I was three and a half years old then. If he could get five more years, I would be eight. That was half a childhood, he told himself. That was something. If the cancer had spread, well that was another thing and he wasn't going to think about it unless he had to.

Dad switched to research mode. He called dozens of his physician friends and colleagues and ordered stacks of printed journal articles to the house. At UCLA, where he first saw an oncologist, they told him the cancer had likely spread even though it wasn't showing up on a scan yet and to get his affairs in order. This was not an acceptable answer.

Seeing Dad research his own treatment options quickly became just another fact of my life. While I watched *The Smurfs*, he sat next to me combing through articles on guided radiation. While I drew mermaids on butcher paper, cross-legged on the living room rug, he was on the phone talking to oncologists working on new chemotherapy protocols. Dad said all the time that doing your own research and being demanding might be the most effective treatment of all. He wasn't shy about cold-calling experts. And when he went to see them in person, he didn't leave until he had the answers he wanted. He was also wary of any physician who could see him too quickly. He wanted doctors who were so busy that he might need to wait to be seen. He felt too that you should only have a procedure done by someone who'd done the same one thousands of times. And you should definitely make sure to ask what their outcomes were. If a physician got defensive or offended then Dad said to run, not walk, out of their offices. Good doctors, he was convinced, were delighted to talk about their experience and weren't threatened by your questions. "Good doctors," he said, "will only respect you more for asking."

For his first surgery, Dad chose the Mayo Clinic in Minnesota. A surgeon there who specialized in osteosarcoma said he couldn't save Dad's leg but hopefully he could save his life. My parents went to Rochester in November and tried to take as many walks as they could while Dad still had two feet. Not far from their hotel was a pond, with Canada geese, where they liked to go to shake off the day's appointments.

One afternoon, as they were walking there, Mom told Dad she was pregnant. She'd taken a pregnancy test while he was meeting with his oncologist. At dinner that night he made a little drawing for her on a napkin of a stick figure family: two parents, two kids, and a dog with a curly tail. "I promise it's going to be okay," he said, handing her the napkin like a contract. "I will make sure it's going to be okay."

I remember very little of that time. I stayed back at the ranch where Dad's mom and sister came to take care of me. The moments I do remember are hazy GIFs. Before my parents left, there is me sliding down Dad's bent legs like a slide, laughing the whole time. Then I can see him coming home after his surgery, with one leg. No sliding now. There were Mom's hushed conversations with my grandmother and aunt in the kitchen while I played nearby. I don't remember them being worried but I also know that these are my first memories and they must have been infused with it. A child knows what they know before they know it.

My brother, Jake, was born that May. By then, Dad had been back at work for months, standing for hours in the operating room on his still-bleeding stump inside a heavy wooden prosthetic leg. He was scared he would die before paying off his medical school loans, leaving Mom with an infant, a four-year-old daughter, a ranch to run, looming debt, and zero income. He booked more surgeries than he'd done when he was healthy. He was angry too.

While Dad was at Mayo his partner had done some research on his prognosis and decided to be proactive about giving Dad's patients away and finding another surgeon to replace him. Dad found out when one of his surgical nurses called him in his hospital room. He was furious that his partner and the head of the hospital had killed him off before the cancer had. He was going to prove them all wrong. His practice was booming.

Then Dad's one-year scan turned up a tumor in his lung. Mom says the news was like getting kicked in the heart. Dad's survival odds were now basically zero. He couldn't find anyone to talk to who'd beaten stage four osteosarcoma. No statistics to give him hope. Dad needed time. Time to figure out a plan. Time for new drugs and treatment protocols in development to improve. Time for the research to catch up to what he wanted: a life. To do this he needed his lung tumor cut out. But the oncologists at UCLA wouldn't do it; they recommended radiation and chemo, saying that more surgery before they knew the source of the metastases was a bad idea. This just made Dad angrier.

"The source was my leg," Mom remembers him yelling at his oncologist over the phone. "And it's gone. I want the lung tumor out before it has time to spread anywhere else. Then I'll do chemo and radiation." His doctors refused. So he called his friend Bill Plested, who had his own cardiac surgery practice in Los Angeles. They'd been chief residents together and still operated as a team on challenging cases. Dad trusted him.

"I need you to do me a favor," Bill remembers Dad asking.

"You know that's a pretty horrific surgery," Bill said. "The lung is so painful. And your docs are right, what if there are more mets? Are you just going to keep doing this?"

"If I listen to these guys and postpone surgery till after I do treatment, it would be months before I was ready. I may not have months. I may not even have weeks."

Decades later Bill would write me and Jake a letter in which he'd say that he was amazed by Dad's willingness to do anything. It was as if he were trading his body parts for time with us. The most sinister of fairy-tale pacts.

Bill hadn't wanted to do the surgery. "As a physician, I'm telling you this isn't advisable," he'd said to Dad. He thought going straight from surgery into chemo and radiation would be hellish. But he did it anyway.

Three

Santa Paula, California, 1986

Bill's lung surgery worked. Or maybe it was the chemo and radiation that Dad did afterward—treatments that, especially in the early '80s, were torturous. But Dad didn't complain. He was alive. And he stayed that way. Before we knew it, he made it four years without a recurrence. It was a miracle. Dad was now an N of 1, a single case study, an exception. There were no statistics, no map, no protocol for how to keep his disease at bay. No one else had been here before, at least as far as he could tell.

I was eight now, pigtailed, earnest, and constantly stained by the pomegranate juice from the fruit I ate off our bushes. Jake had grown out of the toddler phase seemingly overnight and was now talking up a storm about his favorite things: chain saws, Mom, and how much he wanted a pet tarantula. Life started to feel like something we didn't have to be grateful for every minute. Sure, Dad only had one leg but I thought that was cool and was always asking if I could take his prosthesis to school for show-and-tell. Sometimes he used it to club fish when we were out sturgeon fishing without anything else on hand to stun them with. And yet, at night alone in my room or in the cracks of the day when I had a quiet moment, I worried still. I knew that someone dying was a thing that could happen. To Dad. But also to Mom. Or

Jake. Or me. And once you know, you can never unknow. I didn't want to be surprised ever again.

It took me a year to work my way through all the survival books I could find, but reading didn't feel like enough. My friend Marisa was religious and once, during a sleepover, she told me that she knew Dad was sick but not to worry because Jesus loved me. This was interesting. Maybe there was help outside of the library. When her parents dropped me off at home the next morning, I came into the kitchen where Mom was pureeing bright orange persimmons for pudding.

"The birds are going to get all the fruit," she said. "Can you go get some more?"

"Do you think Jesus loves us?" I asked, heading out the door.

She sighed.

"Jesus was a nice man, Lar," she said, pouring the lava-colored puree into a bowl. "Jewish even. We just don't believe in him."

"Why not?"

She sighed again. "Let me be clear, he was most likely a real person, we just don't *believe* in him."

It wasn't like Jesus didn't exist in our house. He was mentioned occasionally just like other famous people, Mikhail Gorbachev, for example, or Ross Perot. Someone we should know about but not anyone to go to with wishes, hopes, and dreams. If we wanted something, my parents thought it was best to ask them for it, or better yet, ourselves.

We were Jews. This they made clear. And we should be proud of that. But religion was for other people. As a formality, they joined the only temple in town—Temple Beth Torah—and made Jake and me go to Sunday Hebrew school where we memorized Shabbat and Hanukkah prayers and learned how to make lumpy challah.

One afternoon I was at recess with my best friend, Cath. We were swinging full circles on the parallel bars, our palms squeaking against the metal. She and I were born three months apart, arranged into a friendship by our moms who met when they were pregnant with us.

Cath grew up on an avocado ranch a few canyons over from ours. We went to each other's houses every day after school.

"Do you believe in Jesus?" I asked Cath.

"I think so," she said, "Grandma Pink does."

Grandma Pink, Cath's dad's mom, picked us up at school sometimes in her big gray Ford LTD. Her golden curls were perfectly coiled, and she wore dark-rimmed glasses with colorful housedresses. She'd just taught me that cracklins were made from pigskin, proof that she knew a lot about the world.

"Have you tried praying?" Cath asked, swinging a full 360.

I hung upside down from my knees, letting my palms graze the gravel.

"Does it work?"

"I dunno. But I told God I wanted a 4-H steer and then Dad said I could get one next year. I'm going to name him Baxter," she said.

When I got home, I pulled all my Jewish books off the shelf to look for clues about God. I had a bunch about the Holocaust. *The Diary of a Young Girl* by Anne Frank was comforting because it meant you could survive in a secret compartment if you had to. I'd made Jake get into the small closet under our stairs to practice. My favorite book, though, was *I Never Saw Another Butterfly*, a collection of poems and drawings made by Jewish kids in a concentration camp outside Prague called Terezin. They wrote about bedbugs and black potatoes and watching the dead pile up in stacks. I paged through it looking for clues. It was confusing. Why would God let Anne Frank and the Terezin kids and their families all die, but give Cath a steer? How exactly was I going to get God to care about Dad? Especially since Dad liked to say he didn't give "one good god-damn about it" whenever I tried to bring up religion.

That night before I fell asleep I looked up at the wooden beams on the ceiling and came up with something. A kind of prayer. If I listed all the terrible things I could think of, saying each one of them out loud, they wouldn't happen.

Car breakdown, I said to the ceiling.
Flat tire
Car accident
Hit by car
Broken arm
Broken leg
Broken neck
Bad fall
Stitches
Heart attack
Holocaust
Any other illness I don't know about
Cancer

I did this every night. For at least two years. I always whispered *cancer* quieter than the other things. And sometimes I avoided saying *cancer* altogether, just in case I was wrong, and my words were a conjuring.

Four

Douglas County, Oregon, 1986

Mom and Dad started to unclench their jaws and we started to fly again. They'd gotten their pilot's licenses a few years after getting married, racing to see who could finish all their qualifying hours first. They bought an old Cessna with blue and red racing stripes and rented out a mint-green hangar at the Santa Paula Airport, where the runway was surrounded by citrus orchards. They loved being pilots together and on Dad's rare days off we packed small bags of clothes and books and stuffed animals and flew somewhere for a few hours or a weekend.

On one of our family flights we landed in the town of Roseburg, Oregon. We left the plane on the tarmac, rented a rusty blue station wagon, and headed for the coast, where we spent a few days exploring the tall sand dunes, chilly beaches, and shops spelled *shoppes* that sold saltwater taffy and novelty mugs. Our roadside motel had a bed that accepted quarters just like the rides in front of the grocery store. Jake and I begged our parents for change. When we slid the quarters into the little metal box by the headboard the frame quivered and shook, like angry Jell-O. Mom and Dad started to laugh, and Jake and I hopped up and down on the mattress, making the bed growl louder. Mom and Dad laughed harder then, so hard their laughter was more like wheezing. Mom held her side, both of their eyes watered. It lasted forever. When I think of them now, it's like this. Laughing so hard they clutch themselves. No matter how scared we ever got, we still laughed hard enough to cry. There was always something more ridiculous than terrifying, more funny than sad. A therapist might call this a coping mechanism and maybe it was, but it's also the result of paying attention to the most incongruous things, the moments in which you can hold two feelings at once.

The next afternoon we turned inland at Reedsport, following Highway 38 along the wide green Umpqua River. We pulled over at a sign that said ELK VIEWING STATION, because that's not the kind of thing my parents drove past. Neither were rock shops, covered bridges, blackberry patches, boat dealerships, bookstores, diners, and tackle shops.

At the viewing station, elk were standing around in a big green meadow like tan horses in elaborate hats. We marveled at them, at the lush emerald forest and the towering firs. A bit farther on, the river was still wide but narrow enough to swim across—Mom was wondering how warm the water might be when she suddenly pointed to the opposite bank.

"Howard, look at that little log place!"

Dad whistled. We could see a cabin painted gray, like a bleached set of Lincoln Logs, with bright white chinking and a wood-shingled roof covered with soft green moss.

Dad drove straight there to check it out. No one was home, and when we looked in the windows we saw that even though the cabin was small, it had tall ceilings crisscrossed with logs, a stone fireplace, and a rustic stairway up to a second-floor loft. Walking around the back side, Jake and I found a short wooden gate and through it, a set of stairs, lined with blackberry bushes, down to a white wooden dock that reached into the river. We grabbed a few handfuls of dark, juicy berries and ran back up to the house to ask if we could swim.

The cabin was for sale, listed at sixty thousand dollars. This was a lot of money, my parents decided, for a house that was a fourteen-hour drive from home. What on earth did we need a second house for, anyway? The ranch was so much work and gasoline for the plane was expensive. "It's a beautiful fantasy, Howard, but enough, let's go home," Mom said, as we drove back onto the highway. But they didn't stop thinking about it. Or at least Dad didn't.

And so, a few weeks after we got home, my parents were lying in bed talking after the ten o'clock news. I'm not sure if Dad really knew in the beginning himself, but the cabin would become a big part of his plan. It was, or at least it became, a place to store as many memories of us together and having fun that he had time to make. A little log house he could use like a tool to teach us what we'd need to know to live without him.

"I think you should go back up there," Mom remembers Dad saying. "And get a guide. Go fishing. If you catch a steelhead, we'll get the place." She thought this was ridiculous but went anyway, to humor him. And she caught a huge fish. We have almost no family photos anymore, but I remember it. She was standing in her waders, holding up the big silver steelhead, smiling at the camera, but really she was looking through it at Dad.

He'd always wanted the women in our family to be excellent fishermen. He decided, probably when I was still an infant, that if I could bait a hook and land something impressive, not only would I never starve, but I'd surprise any man who dared underestimate me. This was very important to him.

Sometimes, when we went fishing as a family he'd hang back and let Mom and me wander over to a popular hole together, waiting for the moment when the men fishing there would ask, officiously, if we needed any help. When we started pulling in more than they did, they'd shoot Dad curious, appreciative looks. I loved outfishing the men around me. It became a feeling I craved. Seeing Dad's pride in my ability to do something he loved. It happened slowly but inexorably, in that way that our parents' hopes for us become so tangled up with what we want for ourselves that eventually it's impossible to tell the difference. The hurling line, the plunk of the lure or the fly, the hope of pulling a living darting thing up out of a mystery. The better I got, the more I wanted to do it. Most of what Dad wanted for me was like that. And as long as I was excelling—at reading about infectious disease or at a barrel roll fly-cast—we didn't talk about it. But *best* was a silent one-word half command, half incantation that he instilled and expected. If he'd been the kind of man who approved of tattoos, which he wasn't, he would have had it inked on the back of my hands.

Five

Santa Paula, California, Winter 1989

I'd just turned eleven years old and was halfway through fifth grade, when Dad came banging through the door from the garage, exhilarated, in the middle of the afternoon. He'd gone another two and a half years without a recurrence and had been busier than ever in the OR. He was almost never home this early.

Mom and I were in the kitchen. I was reading aloud from my social studies textbook about the glory of the California Mission system. "Genocide," Mom said. "That's what it should say."

Dad looked confused as he sat down at the counter next to me.

"Lar's homework," Mom said. "It's lies." She put down the wooden spoon she was using to stir cheddar cheese sauce on the stove. "Why are you home?"

"I quit," he said. And smiled. "I told the head of the hospital to go screw himself. I'm done."

Dad had been saying for years that the hospital administrators were more interested in profits than patients. He fought the administration all the time about patient care decisions. He liked to do the occasional free surgery for people who needed it and sometimes accepted weird presents in lieu of payment: rare seeds or bottles of whiskey even though he never drank hard liquor.

That night, I remember Mom and Dad went out for dinner at a

sushi place in Ventura. The next morning they made an announcement. Dad was going to join Doctors Without Borders, but before that, he needed more training in plastic surgery. It was too hard to take cardiovascular surgery on the road, he said, but he could learn to fix cleft palates and other procedures that wouldn't require so much assistive technology. Mom wanted to go to graduate school for landscape architecture. Their idea was to eventually take us to a country where Dad would do surgeries and Mom would learn about plants. Jake and I would enroll in whatever schools were there and learn a new language.

Mom had wanted to go back to school for years. She'd met Dad the summer she turned twenty-three. They were living in the same apartment complex in West LA. She'd been interning at the Nixon White House but moved back to California after she called off an engagement to her boyfriend, another White House intern who refused to stand up to his overbearing mom. She'd met Dad one night while heading to the trash. He was smoking a pipe, standing in front of his apartment. He asked where she was going, and she explained she was looking for newspapers to cover the floor while she repainted her dining room table. Dad said she didn't need to go through the trash.

Before she could answer, he'd disappeared inside and reappeared with his arms buried beneath weeks of unread issues of the *New York Times* and *Wall Street Journal*. He offered them to her and asked if he could walk her back to her apartment. She thought he was handsome. He was well over six feet tall, with short, thick hair, strong eyebrows, and big hands, wearing a pressed shirt and a tweedy sport coat with what looked like expensive leather shoes. He told her he was thirty-one but he looked older. It occurred to her that he might have been on his way to a date.

He was but he didn't tell her that. Instead, he explained he was from Maryland, had grown up in a working-class Jewish neighborhood of Baltimore, and had two sisters. He'd just gone back there and taken some photos of groundhogs in his mom's garden that he was excited to show her. While he was talking, he noticed how pretty she was.

Everybody always did. Mom was five-five, with brown shoulder-length waves, a delicate face, and high cheekbones. Beautiful in a way that made it hard to be her daughter. By the time I was in junior high my friends asked all the time if she modeled (she had) and as far back as I could remember, men stopped her at the gas station or in the shoe section at Macy's or really anywhere at all. Sometimes these men would bend down to tell me how pretty she was and then wink at her before turning away. Once, in the early days of cell phones, a man in a BMW convertible chased her down the 101 freeway, honking and waving his brick of a phone in the air until she pulled over, thinking it was an emergency. He wanted her number.

When they got to her door Dad explained that he was the chief resident at UCLA. He barely had time to sleep, let alone read the paper. But he couldn't stand thinking about all the news he was missing, so he was holding on to them just in case he had time to catch up someday. He said he wanted to be a heart surgeon. He wasn't even supposed to leave the hospital, but he wanted to have dinner with her. Would she give him her number?

He called an hour later to ask her out. She canceled a date with the comedian Albert Brooks, whom she'd dated in high school, to have dinner with Dad. She wore a pair of white vinyl boots and a fake Pucci minidress with long sleeves and pink paisley swirls. Dad chose the restaurant, with white tablecloths and thick red votives. She told me they spent the date debating whether welfare was a public good (Lynn: pro, Howard: con).

By the time dessert arrived she knew she wanted to kiss him good night. He knew he wanted to marry her. He hinted at it that night but waited a week to tell her. Mom remembers every detail of their conversation, sitting on the dark leather couch in his apartment.

"But you don't even know me," she'd said.

"I do. And I know who you're going to be. And I know you're going to love me more and more and I'm going to love you more and more."

They got married three months later, in late November 1970, standing in Mom's parents' living room in Brentwood. She wore baby's breath tucked into her loose chignon and a high-necked lace and brocade dress she'd bought from a shop on Sunset Boulevard that repurposed old drapes. Dad wore a striped wool suit and black leather wingtips. In the only photo we still have, Mom is grinning and Dad is smirking.

Six

Santa Paula, California, Spring–Summer 1989

After he quit his job, Dad accepted a position with a group of plastic surgeons affiliated with Harvard Medical School. They offered to pay him to do a fellowship in facial reconstructive surgery and would support his plans to travel as long as he eventually returned to practice in Boston. Mom started to fill out applications for landscape architecture programs. Jake and I weren't excited about leaving the ranch, but we didn't have a say in the matter. And then we went to Boston on a scouting trip to find somewhere to live. While we were there, my parents were happier than I'd ever seen them. Dad even talked to strangers in a restaurant one night, something he almost never did. And I got my first wool sweater, a red turtleneck. I was walking down the sidewalk admiring myself in it when Mom pointed to the T and told me that it was a train that teenagers were allowed to ride by themselves.

My parents found a rental house quickly—two stories with green wooden shutters and a long carpeted hallway that Jake and I loved. We never imagined we'd live in a house with carpeting, let alone a sidewalk out front. I started dreaming of taking the teenager train by myself. Jake was most excited about the idea of snow. Maybe, I wondered, I'd find new friends here who also did *Anne of Green Gables* reenactments and liked reading about Ebola (I'd abandoned survival skills for epidemiology). I was still playing with Barbies too but as a fifth grader, I knew that this was not something I should talk about.

On our last night in Boston, Dad's knee started to hurt. The one on what he called his "good leg." He figured it was all the walking around—too much for his stump pinned inside the tight wooden socket of the prosthesis and probably for the other leg too.

We went back to California, where Jake and I finished up the school year. We weren't planning on moving till July or August, so Mom signed me up for beach camp in Ventura. Probably so she could start packing up the house in peace.

The morning of my first day at camp Dad walked into the kitchen while I read the funnies and ate my cereal. Jake poured me some milk from the ceramic cow pitcher.

"Lar," Dad said, "I'm taking you to camp this morning."

For some reason, this set off a quiet alarm bell that kept dinging softly inside me as we got into the silver F-250 ranch truck and it kept going, below the crackle of 1070 AM news on the radio, till we pulled into an open parking spot at the beach. The air smelled like ocean and cut, wet grass.

Dad turned off the ignition, rolled down the window, and reached through to knock the old tobacco out of his pipe against the mirror. I looked at his face—tan with deep laugh crinkles around his eyes. He looked serious but healthy. From the cup holder between us he pulled out an envelope of Schippers tobacco and started to tamp it into his pipe.

"I want to tell you something," he said. "I'm going to die, Lar. This cancer is going to kill me. And it's probably going to be soon."

Maybe he was just making his usual point about how we couldn't take anything for granted? I held myself so tight hoping that was it, I could feel my teeth grinding.

"I'll do everything I can, for as long as I can. But when I can't enjoy life with you, your mom, and your brother, I'm going to die."

I knew this already. Had heard it before. So. Many. Times. Just let me go, please, I willed him silently. I wanted to bolt from the truck. But I didn't. Not crying and not bolting felt important, like the kind of thing I'd have to master to get a wolf family if things turned out badly. He folded the tobacco pouch, put it back in the cup holder.

"I went in for a CAT scan to confirm my knee pain was nothing to worry about, but I have a tumor in my good leg. I'm going to do what I can."

"Surgery?" I asked.

"Yes," he said. "My surgeon wants to remove part of my femur along with my entire knee, and he's going to replace it with a titanium one."

"Oh."

"I'm also going to do chemo and maybe some radiation."

"In Boston?"

"No. We're not going to go to Boston anymore."

"Not for treatment or not, like, ever?"

A shadow passed over his face, so dark I felt it too, and then it was gone. He looked resigned.

"Once I do this, I don't think I'll be able to stand without crutches. I might have to retire."

I sat there silently, trying to understand what he was saying. The cancer was back. All the way in his other leg. And there was no more Boston. We didn't have to move! We could stay at the ranch! I felt a pang of happiness and then immediately, a wave of shame for finding something good in this. Why had I stopped saying my lists every night?! Dumb. Dumb. Dumb. I shoved my hands under my thighs and rocked lightly back and forth. He was going to die. He said it would be soon? What was *soon*? I didn't say any of this. Instead, we listened to the squawks of gulls and happy screams of kids on the pirate ship swing set in the park nearby. I felt a thousand years old and also like I might disappear.

"Lar, I love you. And I am so proud of you," his voice cracked.

"What are we supposed to do afterward?" I said quietly.

"After what?"

I couldn't bring myself to say the words.

"After I die?" he asked.

"Yeah."

He tapped the tobacco down in his pipe again, looked over at me, and smiled. I think he honestly liked the question, thought it was funny.

"Have a party."

I raised my eyebrows and waited for him to say what he really thought. But he didn't say anything else. He was serious, looking through the windshield dotted with crusted-over peacock shit, the wipers buried under dry pepper tree leaves from the trees that shaded the driveway. We sat there like that for a few moments and then he said, "Time to go."

He leaned over to hug me, smelling like pipe smoke and coffee, and pushed the passenger door open.

I glanced quickly in the side mirror to make sure I was still there.

I saw the fat, round cheeks I hated and my tight ponytail. I looked like a kid.

I slid off the bench seat and he pulled the door shut as I walked across the parking lot. I didn't want to keep going. I wanted to run straight back to the truck, sobbing and howling, and make him take me home with him or out to the Santa Paula airport for waffles and whipped cream. But I knew I couldn't. I felt like a grown-up with a job. Even if that job was, right now, to seem like any other eleven-year-old camper.

When I got to the top of the little dune I turned around. Dad was still there, parked in the truck with the engine off now, watching me. He'd lit his pipe, the smoke trailing out the window in lazy blue clouds. Before I could lift my hand, he waved.

Seven

Santa Paula, California, Fall 1989

Dad called the plastic surgery practice in Boston and told them he wouldn't be coming. Mom threw out her landscape architecture applications. Their dreams had evaporated in the time it took Dad's oncologist to read the scan of his left leg and were replaced by question marks, so big they cast shadows over the whole ranch. It felt like there shouldn't be enough light for the trees but they bloomed anyway, everything ripening relentlessly on schedule. The tomato vines erupted in thousands of tiny red globes, the apricots turned juicy and orange on the trees, and the plums fell in such thick carpets the yellowjackets descended en masse, their *zzzzushing* so loud you could hear them before you turned the corner into the orchard.

Dad went in for surgery and came home stormy, tubes draining fluid from either side of his new titanium knee.

Now I wonder what was worse—the bone pain, the queasy drives back and forth to chemo infusions in Los Angeles, the fear of not knowing if any of this would work or for how long, or the knowledge that his life as a surgeon was over.

Dad had been feeling better, good enough to finally take a shower. He was standing in the stream of water in my parents' bathroom when his new knee suddenly gave out, sending all six foot three inches of him crashing onto the Mexican tile floor. I wasn't home but Mom told me it was terrifying. He screamed. And I don't think she'd ever heard him in pain like that. The bone pain from the cancer was horrific but this was something different. Sharper. And in the few seconds it took for him to collapse, he must have realized that this was it. This titanium knee wouldn't be strong enough to hold him up. His career was over. A surgeon needed his hands and he couldn't operate if he had to use them to hold on to crutches.

He was fifty years old. He'd done four years of university at Cornell, then sixteen years of training: medical school at Johns Hopkins, internship and surgical residency at UCLA, more surgical fellowship in New York City, and then a few years of surgery in the navy. Then he'd practiced for thirteen years, done hundreds of open-heart surgeries, bypasses, and other procedures. He'd only recently paid off hundreds of thousands in medical school debt. He had at least three more decades left of doctoring ahead of him and now he had to give it all up. It was another amputation.

That September I started sixth grade at Balboa Middle School, a big public junior high sandwiched between walled-off lemon groves and a crappy shopping plaza. Balboa didn't have cops on duty or mandatory metal detectors yet, but the gray fencing, cracked concrete, and squat, square buildings with cloudy windows made it feel like a juvenile detention center. One afternoon I saw a seventh grader get beat up with a length of chain by a kid from a rival gang. Girls attacked each other in the bathroom. Once, I got caught in there with Bubbles, a sixth grader with crunchy bangs, thick eyeliner, and a shiny LA Raiders bomber jacket that I lusted after. She pinned me against the wall when I tried to sneak out and told me she'd cut me if she caught me in there again.

This was rare because I didn't stand out enough to be bullied much. Mostly I was invisible, camouflaged in jean shorts with flower-printed ruffled hems, matching socks, and color-coordinated scrunchies. The only place I was really hassled was on the bus. Our ranch was at the eastern edge of the school district so I was picked up last and dropped off first. The only other stop near mine was ag worker housing, a cluster of stark wooden houses in the middle of a lemon orchard. The kids who lived there waited for the bus in the sun at the edge of a dusty road. I waited at the end of my family's long paved driveway, between blooming stands of matilija poppies buzzing with honeybees, our big wooden farmhouse visible in the distance. I spent most mornings pulling unopened poppy blossoms off their stems and hurling them into the creek while screwing up my courage to pretend that I didn't care when the kids on the bus called me "vaca gorda."

One afternoon a few weeks into September I came home from school and the house was empty. Alone in the kitchen, I ate a few mint Milano cookies and then I went outside to look for my family.

They weren't in the garage, or up by the worm bins, or with the donkeys. Maybe they were off on the ranch somewhere working on the irrigation? I slipped between the aluminum bars of Poppy and Durango's corral and touched their wooly necks. My parents had started with the donkeys early on in their marriage, when they still lived in Camarillo, but Mom's love for them expanded to fit the bigger corrals at the ranch. One day Dad had seen a notice in the *LA Times* for California's new "Adopt-a-Burro Program" run by the Bureau of Land Management. There were more wild donkeys than the state felt the California desert could support and so they wanted to thin the herds. If someone came to one of the state-sponsored roundups with a trailer, they could bring home as many animals as would fit. So my parents drove out to Death Valley where they chose two burros out of a dusty, swirling herd, not knowing that one of the donkeys was pregnant. Then they went back again. And again. Occasionally, someone would hear that there was a local couple who would take in a donkey in trouble and so we'd get them that way too. At peak donkey we probably had twenty animals roaming through the oaks and nibbling down the wild grass.

"Lar!" Mom called when she saw me, wiping my hands of burro dust, as I turned the corner toward the garden. "How was school?"

Her voice was muffled because she was wearing a bee suit with a head net. Dad and Jake were wearing them too. Jake held the smoker, puffing blue clouds into the air. My family looked like a hazmat team crowding a chemical spill.

"Jake," Dad said, "stop it! The smoke is for the hive."

"We're almost done, Laurel, don't come any closer."

In front of them, a stack of white wooden bee boxes was raised off the ground on a little wooden platform. The top of one was off and bees were swarming in big clouds.

"I think they're angry," Jake said.

"The smoke will calm them down," Mom said.

"Happy bees are better bees," Dad said through his head net. "They have an easier time beating infections and are more resilient."

The two of them were always going on about bees. Mom loved to talk about their dances and how complicated and smart they were. Dad liked the fact that honey never spoiled. Jars found in Egyptian tombs were still delicious thousands of years later. Honey, he told us, is a natural antibiotic, and was used in a third of ancient Egyptian prescriptions.

Dad became a beekeeper because he loved this history; also, it was a new thing to learn and the pollinators would be good for our trees. Then, as time went on and his illness came back for good, I think beekeeping became something else. He wanted to go out, in some way anyway, like the pharaohs he loved reading about. And the white five-gallon plastic buckets of honey he was stashing away in the shed would last forever. Or at least till Jake and I were grown. There would be enough to stir into our tea till we had kids of our own. And maybe till they had kids themselves. A great-grandson or -granddaughter might one day taste the dark avocado honey made by a man they'd never met who nonetheless imagined them. It was a lifetime supply of medicine to treat the gaping hole we'd have without him. An impossible prescription.

Eight

Santa Paula, California, 1990

Dad had a scan every six weeks now. And more often than not, it turned up something. First there was another lung tumor and then another, then a third or fourth tumor in his back, more in his leg. No one can remember the specifics and his medical records were destroyed. I do know that Dad was doing regular radiation and chemo at UCLA, Sloan Kettering in New York, and Mass General Hospital in Boston. Some of these treatments required long periods of isolation in a room where he'd receive full-body radiation behind a heavy metal door. He'd found a radiation oncologist named Herman Suit at MGH who was the first to use proton therapy for the treatment of hard-to-reach tumors. Dr. Suit also implanted beads for targeted radiation along Dad's spinal column. At UCLA Dad did more chemo. In New York, he had surgeries.

Mom and Dad would fly back East for a few weeks at a time, renting a tiny apartment near whatever hospital they were going to. They left Jake and me with a babysitter we couldn't stand who crocheted pastel blankets while sitting in Dad's chair, ate Little Debbie cakes she wouldn't share with us, and told us that we were spoiled while she watched soaps. Then my parents found someone we loved. Mrs. Gold was a kindergarten teacher who taught me to sew and liked make-believe and didn't think I was weird for spending most of my time in imaginary worlds. She was our own fairy godmother who waved her wand to help us forget about what was going on with Dad even if it was just for long enough to watch a rerun of *The A-Team* or bake cookies or sew Halloween costumes even though it wasn't Halloween.

Sometimes the intervals between Dad's trips for treatments and surgeries were monthslong. He learned to walk everywhere on crutches and whenever I saw him without his shirt, I noticed more tiny blue tattoo spots that guided the radiation beams, and more scars running up and down his torso like pale railroad tracks. He stayed in the hospital as little time as possible post-treatment or post-surgery. He was convinced the hospital was the most dangerous place to be—because of antibiotic-resistant bacteria—but more so, I think, because it kept him away from us.

It's sort of shocking to think about now, but in all the years he was sick, through more than a dozen surgeries, and thirteen years of outpatient and inpatient treatments, Jake and I never once saw him in a hospital. We were simply not allowed to visit. And when he came home, it wasn't what he wanted to talk about.

"I don't want them to see me as a patient," he told Mom whenever she brought it up. He didn't want us to think of him as someone with a disease, no matter how much it shaped our lives.

And yet, we did notice things. Dad could only wear his wooden leg till the late afternoon and then he'd have to go into the bedroom, take it off, and lay down for a while. When he came out he wore nothing but his plaid bathrobe and a pair of dark blue Jockeys, his naked, hairy stump still dusted with talcum powder. We knew without having to ask that if his leg was off we weren't allowed to have friends over, and if someone showed up unexpectedly he got pissed and crutched loudly back to the bedroom, refusing to come out till they'd gone. We saw a lot of his pain and some of his resentment that he was losing his ability to do what he loved but showing him empathy felt too much like weakness. Something he abhorred in himself and others. To this day, seeing Mom sad makes Jake and me pretty uncomfortable. I think it's a remnant of all those years when acknowledging suffering was a form of betrayal, ever so slight, of Dad's invulnerability.

His closest friends, Phil Weinstein and Jake Gillespie, stayed his close friends because they knew to call Dad not to discuss his health but to talk politics, and tell stories of their escapades in downtown Baltimore as kids lighting firecrackers in people's mailboxes. Dad wanted to talk about computing, geology, fisheries science, Middle Eastern politics, volcanoes, astronomy, the CIA, the history of medicine, and photography. He didn't want to waste time talking about anything he didn't think was interesting.

Now that he had new metastases again, Dad was even more focused on preparing us for a time he wouldn't be here. It seemed like every day was a new lesson: how to squish a man's eyeballs if I was ever attacked, how to change a tire, fix a carburetor, take apart a camera for cleaning, shoot pool, make a good espresso, read a map, properly plant watermelons, and understand the Dewey decimal system. He quizzed me on the reasons that leaves turned colors in the fall, member nations of the UN, American state capitals, the scientific names of various species of moss. All the while, new jars of deep-brown avocado honey filled the shelves in the pantry and new buckets stacked up in the garage. Like a promise, or a bittersweet plan.

And then one afternoon, he picked up Jake at school in the ranch truck and told him they had a job to do. I didn't know anything about it at the time. But Jake remembers it perfectly. He was around eight then, I must have been twelve, in the thick of junior high, studying for a bat mitzvah that I delusionally hoped would make me less likely to be bullied on the bus.

"Where are we going?" Jake asked.

"All will be revealed."

This wasn't strange. Dad and Jake had lots of projects. They were always building something or taking something apart or coming up with an elaborate plan that included playing tricks on Mom or me.

That afternoon they stopped at McDonald's for my brother's favorite after-school snack, two hamburgers with absolutely nothing on them, and then they got on the 126 freeway heading east to Santa Paula.

When Dad pulled up at the Mill Jake was ecstatic. It was a farm supply store in an old wooden building by the train tracks that also sold animals and smelled like cracked corn and sweet alfalfa. We often left shopping trips there with an animal peering out of a cardboard box on the back seat, wondering where it was going. I'd been agitating for a pig.

"What are we going to get?!" Jake asked.

"Something for your sister."

Jake's face fell.

"But you're going to be in charge of it."

He perked up.

"Is it a chain saw?"

"No."

"Backhoe?"

"No. We're at the Mill, Jake."

"Chickens?"

"Closer."

By now Dad was crutching through the main door and Jake hurried to catch up.

"Dr. Braitman! Great to see you. How can we help? How's Lynn?"

"Everyone's fine. I need doves. White ones."

"Oh, okay. How many?"

"A few dozen."

"I might have to order . . ."

"There's no rush."

"May I ask what they're for?"

"My daughter's wedding."

"Congratulations!"

"Oh, no, it's not like that. She's twelve."

I'm guessing the man looked back and forth from Dad to Jake, confused, as if the eight-year-old eating the dry hamburger could explain. But Jake just grinned; he'd learned what his job was. Now they just had to build a coop.

I found out about all this when I came across the two of them up by the garden going through a scrap woodpile looking for good perches. Rolls of wire were piled next to them on the ground. For now, a half dozen doves were cooing and blinking inside the chicken coop. The hens were keeping their distance, looking annoyed.

Dad put down the scrap wood when he saw me and wiped his hands on the front of his work pants.

"I'm not going to be here for your wedding, Lar," he said.

What? I lost feeling in my face. My chest hurt.

This wasn't a surprise, but it still shocked me to hear him say it. Or maybe it was the sudden knowledge that there were new levels of pain I hadn't known were possible. I didn't want to cry. I couldn't. This was my end of the bargain. If Dad told us we were fine, then we needed to be. I tried to smile.

"Jake is going to take care of the birds after I'm gone," he said, "and one day, when you get married, you will release them and I will be there with you too."

Nine

Santa Paula, California, 1991

I distracted myself from Dad's new tumors, and my parents' regular departures, with sex. Not actual sex, but Barbie sex. I was thirteen now, too old to be playing with dolls. But I couldn't help myself. I came home from school or softball practice, shut the door to my room, and orchestrated group sex in the plastic pool, or two of them doing it in the Barbie Jeep. They pulled each other's hair back and had sex doggie style on top of the plastic picnic table, knocking the tiny orange bottles of soda onto the floor. In between sex sessions they went to work at their jobs as magazine editors or lawyers and came home to make elaborate picnic lunches that they ate while windsurfing. When they talked, my Barbies sounded like Melanie Griffith in *Working Girl* or the blond lady reporter in *Crocodile Dundee*. I'd begged Mom for a Ken doll but she said no. Later she told me that she was worried I'd make my Barbies have sex. I guess it didn't occur to her that girl Barbies could have sex with each other. I cut off the hair of a few and colored over their blue eyeshadow with brown Pentel pens. I dressed them in the most masculine clothes I had—bright yellow shorts, baseball caps, and tiny white T-shirts—and tried to ignore their feet molded into high-heel position. Soon, I could have filled every stool at Barbie Dyke Bar with horny, choppy-haired butches. I named every one of them Skip.

When I was done playing I carefully untangled their limbs, undid the elaborate beach houses and corporate offices, removed their nylon shorts and hats, took the tiny hot dogs off the tiny plastic plates, and buried all of it deep inside a big blue trunk in the corner of my room.

I think this lasted so long because my Barbie world was controlled, like a sexual terrarium, where nothing happened without my say-so. And that was pretty much the opposite of the rest of my life. Also, the Barbie bodies were hard and sleek and impossible to embarrass, while mine was becoming a battleground.

The more Dad seemed to be losing control of his limbs and internal organs, the harder he tried to do something about mine. I was chubby, with thick thighs and arms. Dad didn't like it and he wasn't shy about saying so.

"You don't want to be overweight, Laurel," he said. "It makes everything difficult."

I didn't want to be overweight either, but being skinny felt like something that happened *to* you, not something I had agency over. Dad glared at me when I reached for a second piece of garlic bread or asked for vanilla ice cream on my cobbler. I felt hot shame every time. It was just another way I was disappointing him. We fought constantly. Partly, I think, because he was teaching me to fight for myself by fighting with him, but also because he had a near-delusional belief in my abilities. He saw anything less than a stellar grade as proof that I was slacking, not that I wasn't capable. This enraged me. We were one set of fears yelling at another. And now my body and how I ate were just added to the pile.

Mom heard about a diet from the mother of another girl at temple. Apparently it had helped that girl lose twenty pounds. For weeks I ate chicken breasts that tasted like hamster bedding. I didn't lose any weight. And denying me the food that the rest of the family was eating only made me want it more. I sat on the toilet and counted my stomach rolls with dread: One, two, three. One, two, three, four. Until Jake needed the bathroom.

One afternoon I came home from school starving and sat down at the kitchen counter to eat a frozen French bread pizza. I could hear Dad heading into the kitchen, the loud clanking of his crutches on the tile always preceded him. When he turned the corner he looked down at me disapprovingly.

"You've got to deal with this now, Laurel. It's not going to get easier," he said.

I burned with humiliation and anger, taking slow, deliberate bites of my pizza but I couldn't taste anything but my own thick tongue.

I wanted to be beautiful, not just to my family and the other kids at school, but to myself. My beauty icons were Elisabeth Shue from *Adventures in Babysitting*, Jessica Rabbit from *Who Framed Roger Rabbit*, and the woman who inspired the song "Lady in Red," whoever that was. The only time I felt even remotely desirable was when I played with Barbies alone, hung out with the burros, or paged through *The Clan of the Cave Bear*. I'd found *The Mammoth Hunters* first, on a shelf in the cabin at Thanksgiving. Dad read it right after it came out and then left it there, between a copy of the *Roadside Geology of Oregon* and his favorite book, *Crossing to Safety* by Wallace Stegner. Reading it I felt dizzy and hot. And then I went through all the books one by one, scouring the pages for sex scenes in caves.

I wanted to know how it worked so I could make my doll sex as realistic as possible. For a long time, I'd thought sex was a medical procedure. Bob and Mike, twin tennis players I hit the ball around with after school sometimes, told me that a man's penis was inserted into a woman's vagina. This sounded a lot like surgery, something I was familiar with—body parts being moved around or exchanged. Plus, babies were born at hospitals. It seemed natural that they'd be made there too. This theory of mine was punctured eventually. And once I knew sex wasn't a clinical procedure, it started happening in my head all the time, only it was Barbie sex. Real people were too stressful. They could judge you for your fat upper arms. Or die.

Threaded through this period of lurking terror was a campaign by my parents to ward it off with fun. Mostly they played jokes on each other or on us. Friends who stayed overnight found plastic dog poop on their bed, or a fake fly in their ice water at dinner. Once, after discovering that Jake's pet tarantula had molted and emerged in his new skin with an extra leg, Dad took off his clothes and laid down on the floor in the hallway with his eyes closed, waiting for us to discover him. After a moment of panic that he'd fallen and was hurt, we watched him open one eye and tell us to come back later after he'd crawled out of his old skin and gotten his leg back.

One Saturday night I invited a friend for a sleepover. We woke up early the next morning and went to the kitchen for orange juice. As we got closer, I noticed Mom and Dad were awake and sitting at the table. Jake was there too—standing in the doorway looking confused. I felt a spike of fear. Was there something wrong? But I didn't sense the crackle of danger in the air. Also, I couldn't be sure, but it looked like Mom and Dad were naked. My stomach lurched.

Before I could turn and flee with my friend, Mom saw us.

"Surprise!" she yelled. "Welcome to Breakfasts of the World!"

I took a few steps closer, avoiding eye contact with my friend, worried about what her face might be doing. Mom and Dad were indeed mostly naked, wrapped in what looked like bright colored dish towels.

"Come on in, Lar. Welcome, Lar's friend. This morning you will be taken on a journey to the beautiful island nation of Tahiti. You will learn about the food, the culture, and"—at this point Mom dissolved into her loudest donkey-snort laughter—"the traditional dress."

Dad laughed too. So hard I could see tears forming in the crinkles of his eyes. His big round hairy belly was heaving above the scrap of purple fabric that covered his lap. Jake smiled because they were laughing so hard. Too young and dumb to be embarrassed, I thought.

Mom walked past me and as she walked I saw a flash of her upper thigh. I prayed desperately that my friend wouldn't notice. I still hadn't met her eyes. When Mom reappeared, she was holding our biggest wooden cutting board piled with fishy-smelling green packets.

"In many Pacific Island nations, people eat fish for breakfast, steamed in banana leaves. So that's what we're having!"

She put it down on the table, covered in more colorful fabric, next to five coconuts and a plate of sliced bananas.

"I picked the banana leaves from our yard," she said conspiratorially to my friend.

Dad set the atlas on the table and opened it to a field of blue dotted with tiny green specks of islands.

"We went to Tahiti on our honeymoon," Mom said. "That's where we purchased this fabric. Tahitians call this a sarong. Your father's is a bit small." She laugh-snorted again. "Imagine it larger."

That's all I wanted to do. Imagine it so large that I could throw it like a sheet over this whole affair as if I was putting our pet parrot to bed.

"Do you do this every Sunday?" my friend said.

I shuddered. But her voice wasn't mean, she sounded excited. Was she actually enjoying this? Oh god, what if she told people about it?

"This is the inaugural Breakfasts of the World. We're going to keep doing it until Laurel and Jake learn world geography but it's always going to be a surprise. We're thrilled you could join us," Mom said.

So that was what this was! A few weeks earlier, they'd suddenly gotten very worried about what we were learning in school when Jake had asked Dad what "an Indonesia was." Dad had started spinning the globe after dinner and asking me to name the countries he was pointing at.

After Tahiti, there were more Breakfasts of the World. I don't remember how many exactly. But I do remember the last one. I walked into the kitchen to find Dad shirtless, in a brown leather vest he'd bought in the seventies, his chest hair spilling out over the top, wearing a large plastic Viking helmet with horns and blue athletic shorts. We were in Norway. We ate fondue. And waved little red, white, and blue flags while the peacocks yelled outside. My parents laughed so hard whenever they looked at each other in their Norwegian getups that they could barely breathe. I gave in and laughed too. I wanted to be in on the joke rather than pressed up against the outside of it pretending not to care. The sand was sifting through the hourglass and there wasn't any point in pretending it wasn't.

Ten

Spring 1992

On our next school vacation, my parents took Jake and me to Hawaii. We went snorkeling for the first time and I was blown away by the busy underwater cities of parrotfish, wrasses, and brain coral. We stopped at honor farmstands to plunk money into empty coffee cans for ripe papayas and hands of apple bananas. I spent the trip in a kind of daze, mesmerized by the beauty of the place and how it smelled like flowers even at the airport. Halfway through the trip, though, Dad's throat started to hurt. He went home early to get himself checked out. It turned out to be a new metastasis, this time in his larynx. The first oncologist he talked to said the only real option was to get a laryngectomy. Dad would be left with a hole in his neck that he'd talk out of using one of those boxes that make people sound like Darth Vader. He told the surgeon he was willing to do it. But when he talked it over with Mom, she put her foot down.

"I told him it was a step too far," she told me when I asked her about it. "Talking out of a box like a robot."

"So you were more willing for him to die than have a laryngectomy?" I asked, incredulous.

"It's just, we kept losing these parts of him. I didn't want to lose his voice. It seemed like too much."

He didn't get that surgery, but he went looking for a surgeon who was willing to go in and get out the met. Most doctors he approached said no because it was too risky, but eventually he found a surgeon at Sloan Kettering who told him he'd be willing to try. We flew back East as a family and Mom and Dad left Jake and me with his mom and sister in Baltimore.

That spring I'd expressed some interest in wood carving. This was one of Dad's many passions, in addition to orchid rearing, lawn maintenance, coffee, aquatic plants, mechanical engineering, and us. He was building a few things at the ranch and had set up a woodshop in the garage. I thought the wooden boxes and chairs and such he was making were cool but I was more interested in duck decoys for some reason. Probably because if I could have, I would have flown as far away from Balboa Middle School as possible. But also because I'd seen a book about carved ducks somewhere. On the cover were a bunch of birds bobbing in a stand of reeds while a brilliant sunset fanned out behind them. I remember thinking it looked like paradise, being a duck. Years later, in graduate school my classmates would tell me about duck syndrome. It described the way that students often looked like they were floating along just fine but under the water they were paddling wildly just to keep up. This too was me even though I never could have articulated it back then.

As a gift, Dad signed me up for carving classes at a woodshop near his mom's house so I'd be busy while he was getting his surgery. Afterward, when Dad was cleared to leave, he and Mom drove straight there to pick me up. I could see the fresh stitches across his neck. His voice was so hoarse he could hardly talk. I hugged him and Mom and then handed them the carved wooden ducks I'd labored over, day and night, for weeks, my heart pounding. They looked at the birds, with their folded feathers and twinkling glass eyes, then back to me and my teacher. Both of them started to cry then. I would have too, but I was scared to let on that I was having feelings like theirs. I felt like I'd lose my job. So I just let them fawn over the ducks and I let myself feel as proud as the birds looked, glossy tails lifelike but frozen.

I needed that moment because my life was about to change. My parents had decided I should have classes that kept up with my curiosity, so they took me around to a few private schools in the area. I'd never been to private school, let alone considered living at one. But I fell in love with Thacher immediately. It's a sprawling boarding school in Ojai, California, about a half hour from the ranch, where students are required to take care of a horse their freshman year, learn to do gymkhana (competitive horsey activities like ring spearing and barrel racing), go on mandatory camping trips, and study really hard. The school, and the town itself, are a lot fancier now, but in the early 1990s the place was rustic. I loved that it was dusty and smelled like home, orange blossoms and sage, and was still close to my family. Also, when I toured the campus I saw lots of kids reading under oak trees and spreading sycamores. They didn't look embarrassed at all. Maybe it was a nerd mirage but I didn't care. I wanted to dive in like my life depended on it. When my parents said I could go, I was thrilled, though my desire was counterbalanced by pounding guilt at leaving my family, especially considering Dad's new tumors.

By August, his voice had come back to the point that he'd begun to sound like himself again. We were at the cabin then, fishing and swimming. Every day I went for a walk by myself down the road and silently begged the sky, the blackberry bushes, the asphalt, and the scurrying chipmunks to keep Dad safe. I'd given up on the God I'd learned about in Hebrew school but just in case there was some sort of power in the fir trees or the river, I wanted to cover my bases.

One afternoon a packet arrived in the mail from Thacher with the list of supplies I needed—for my dorm room and for the required weeklong camping trips at the beginning and end of every school year, when the whole campus emptied out into national forests and deserts across California. All freshmen went to the Sierras, to the school's camp called Golden Trout near the base of Mt. Whitney, and then broke off into small groups to go backpacking for four or five days. I was nervous. For all the time my family spent outside doing things like digging holes, I had no experience camping.

"Jews don't camp," Mom said when I asked her recently why this was.

"But some Jews sturgeon fish and rescue donkeys and start avocado ranches," I said.

"Yes, but we had to draw the line somewhere."

The first required item on the school list was hiking boots. So we made a family trip to REI to look for a pair. A salesperson pointed us to a display of expensive boots with tags that read Danner, Merrell, Salomon. These sounded like names of square-jawed boys who wouldn't want to kiss me, or maybe Labrador retrievers, who would. I wondered if Thacher would turn out to be just another place where I'd be both odd and unremarkable. Thankfully, Cath, my best friend from childhood, would be going too, so I'd at least know one person.

"Lar, this is going to be a great adventure," Dad said, his eyes shining looking at all the outdoor gear around us, the backpacks and jackets brightly colored as tropical birds.

I grunted, more worried by the minute. That I'd look ridiculous in all this stuff. Or that if I left home, something bad would happen to him.

But Dad was so happy. And the truth was that I felt happy too. Underneath my fear was something else. Hope, maybe, a river of it, as wide as the Umpqua. Perhaps none of this would work out but I needed to try.

I don't remember what I said to him while we stood there. I just remember his excitement, standing in front of the shoe display with me, and the feeling, gaining in my chest like a tide, that I had to wear these boots for both of us. That maybe I always would.

Eleven

Ojai, California, 1994

Thacher turned out not to be a mirage. I found friends, real ones, who did think I was a little weird but who liked me anyway. I loved riding horses through the sage-covered mountains behind the school and camping with my teachers and classmates. I found adults, who weren't related to me, who believed I wasn't an idiot, and lots of places where I could read in public and no one would judge me for it. And then, somehow, it was September 1994, my junior year. I was sixteen years old, and still, Dad hadn't died.

I was spending a lot of time thinking about boys who didn't seem to notice me, painting watercolor landscapes, and eating raw cookie dough in the thick plastic tubes that my friends and I called "donkey dick" and passed around the dorm after 9 p.m. check-in. I wanted to hook up with someone exactly as much as I didn't. The desires didn't cancel themselves out, they just swung back and forth like a pendulum, dozens of times a day. My friends were talking about blow jobs. Those scared me, less than cancer but more than bad grades, which was saying something. I worried about choking or getting mouth sores. All I really wanted was for someone to touch my tits and think I was beautiful. I still wanted to be skinny too. Or just more streamlined, like a dolphin. I thought a lot about Hollywood movie transformations where the girls came back from summer vacations with glossy hair, tight thighs, and boyfriends who looked like River Phoenix or Denzel Washington in *The Pelican Brief*. I wasn't that heavy, but I was fat for Thacher in the way that isolated groups of kids can make subjective things into facts. I hid my body inside green or blue scrub bottoms that I bought for two dollars at a thrift store near the hospital in Ventura. I wore these with the cream-colored sweater sets Mom bought for me at Ann Taylor and blue and white slip-on Adidas athletic sandals. My style, if you could call it that, was medical receptionist on her way to a swimming pool.

One Saturday I came home to the ranch with my friends Stef and Brooke. We planned to spend the weekend on the couch, eating Mom's homemade chocolate biscotti and watching *Philadelphia* or *The Bodyguard*. At some point Stef asked if I'd like her to paint my nails. My cuticles were ragged and bloody because I'd been picking at them. But before she could finish, I spilled some of the color. I went to my parents' bathroom to get the nail polish remover Mom kept under the sink. I pushed aside the bottles of rubbing alcohol and talcum powder that Dad used on his stump, the multipacks of soap and toothbrushes from Costco. And then there it was: what I wasn't looking for at all. The pill bottle. Quiet, white, waiting. The note wrapped around it with a rubber band.

In a fraction of a second that bottle taught me it was normal to get news that can flatten you, another piano falling out of the sky when you've finally stopped scanning for it. When was he going to do it? How long had this been here?

No one should have to do this for a friend, but here you go.

Below that was the name of the drug, which I don't remember. And dosage instructions.

Fear started spinning, tornadolike, inside me. I could barely breathe. Here was his plan to die how he wanted to.

I wouldn't cry. I couldn't. My feelings didn't live inside my body then because I didn't live inside my body yet. I could fake it or feel real sadness about things that didn't really matter—like the fact that Peyton didn't want to go on a walk with me down to the lower soccer field and kiss my neck even though he clearly wanted to with the other girls in my class. I just couldn't let myself feel the things that threatened to really level me. I let the cold of the tile seep through the knees of my cotton scrub pants and pushed the buzzing, throbbing feeling down so hard I knocked it out.

Carefully, I wound the rubber band back around the bottle, grabbed the nail polish remover and a handful of cotton balls. I could not tell anyone about this. Not my friends, not anyone in my family. Physician-assisted suicide was illegal in California, would be for another twenty years, and plus, Dad would have gotten mad at the word "suicide." He said all the time, that "When I can no longer enjoy life with you and your brother and your mom, I'm going to die." I'd thought he meant this in some unspecific way but now I realized he'd been telling us about his plan for years, I just hadn't realized it.

I took one last look in the mirror, trying to arrange myself into a facsimile of a teenager who could sing along to "I Will Always Love You," and walked back into the living room with the polish remover, plopping down onto the couch next to Stef and giving her my hands, palms up, like an offering.

Twelve

Ojai, California, Winter 1995

Months went by and the pill bottle stayed untouched, as far as I could tell, in the cabinet. I let myself relax a little bit. At least as much as I could, which wasn't much. If Thacher was a mountain, I'd crawled to the top and was now looking for other peaks to bag. Not because it made me feel good but because it kept me from thinking about everything else. I was on so many committees, it felt like mainlining the drug of adult approval. I fed meals to the elderly in Ojai, sang in chorus, talked my way into AP English, History, Biology, and Art as a junior, managed the boys' lacrosse team so I could get extra practices in, and planned to become a prefect, senior class president, and varsity lacrosse captain. I was also one of the busiest tour guides for prospective students, the co-president of the Thacher Gourmet Society, and had passed advanced trials in knot tying, stove repair, and map reading so that I was now certified to go backpacking with other advanced campers—unsupervised without faculty members.

My favorite activity, however, was Judicial Council. I think we were supposed to serve for a year, but I did it for three—a campus record. Thacher prided itself on its honor code. Our rooms had no locks on the doors, and it was drilled into us that honesty was the most important thing in all situations. The Judicial Council was the on-campus enforcer. When students occasionally got into trouble for doing things like smoking weed at the outdoor chapel, they went in front of a group of five students and a faculty advocate of their choosing. We would hear their case like a jury, discuss the details, and then give the headmaster a recommendation for punishment that ranged from expulsion to work crew to community service. Then we'd make a presentation about our reasoning to our fellow students at each dorm after check-in.

Brooke nicknamed me Moral Laurel. I pretended to be embarrassed but I loved it. Policing made sense to me—I knew all about it from constantly doing it to myself.

When I wasn't judging anyone, I was writing. Not just for classes but for me. Journal after journal, mostly about boys and hiking but also about Dad. I wrote down my fears of what was ahead for my family, things I wished I was brave enough to say out loud. And whenever anyone asked what I wanted to do one day, I said I wanted to be a writer. The first time I'd admitted it was at Temple Beth Torah when I was thirteen. It was during a meeting with the rabbi, a few days before my bat mitzvah. I remember looking at his full bookshelves, his expectant holy face, and the yarmulke sliding so far back on his head I worried it might fall off, and decided to tell him the truth when he asked what I wanted to do when I grew up.

"Write books mostly, but also maybe for *National Geographic*. And I want to write about animals. And travel. Nonfiction basically."

The winter of my junior year, a list of exchange schools appeared in my mailbox at Thacher. These were places students could go to for a few weeks or months and study special topics. I tore through it. Then I brought it to my parents on my next weekend home. They asked me where I'd like to go. I had only one place circled: the Rock Point Community School, part of the Navajo Nation in Arizona.

At dinner that night, after I finished laying out my case for why I should go, Dad raised his eyebrows and asked to see the description of the school.

"It says here you'd be living with a family that has kids your age and you would go to high school with them. And that the school is a Navajo school. I think that means the classes are in Navajo."

"Yeah, I know."

"Well, it's a beautiful place," Mom said, getting a faraway look. "Remember when we used to fly out there? And that time we went to Canyon de Chelly?"

"You mean when we almost died?" The engine of our Cessna had stalled for a few terrifying seconds while we prepared for a crash landing somewhere near the Four Corners. Dad flicked some switch though and got it going again.

"Maybe this time I could go on a big plane like a regular person?" I asked.

"Who says you're a regular person?" Dad said.

I am extraordinarily privileged in nearly every way, but what I'm most grateful for now is my parents' belief, passed down like any other inheritance, that there's more beauty in the world than horror. That if you take reasonable risks, everything will probably work out okay. For all their fears, their parents' fears, and their parents' parents' fears of everything from pogroms and genocide to head lice, Mom and Dad didn't see a problem with their teenage daughter getting on a plane and going somewhere where they didn't know a soul, had no forwarding address, or phone number they could use to contact me. All we'd have was an assurance from the receptionist at the Rock Point school that my host family would have my flight information and would meet me at the Farmington airport and that there was a pay phone at the school I could use to call home.

This optimism gives you license. It's a kind of audacity and it can work like an all-purpose key to the locked doors of your dreams. "Why not you?" it whispers. Some people get there anyway, like my best friend Samin, who learned to try out all the locks herself without a dad telling her she could. Still others get there precisely because people tell them they can't, picking the locks as a kind of rebellion. But I'm not sure I would have gotten there on my own. I did it because Dad was insisting over my shoulder that I could, that I should, that I would . . . be fine. And that he'd be waiting on the other side to hear all about it.

Thirteen

Tsé Nitsaa Deez'áhí, Arizona, Winter 1995

I was in Rock Point for a month or less, but it changed nearly everything for me. I lived with a big family, the Benallys, and went to high school with their daughter Gloriana, where it was immediately obvious that I would not be invited to prom there either. Instead, I learned to weave (poorly), say "Diné" instead of "Navajo," tagged along to powwows, ate a lot of mutton, tried to come up with clans to research in history class even though I had none, helped shear sheep up on the mesa out of town, and discovered that even though it sounded like an herbicide we'd use at the ranch, *Anglo* meant white person, and it was definitely not a great thing to be. At least according to my weaving teacher.

I was also howling lonely. Since I couldn't speak Navajo and I was not Californian enough to be exciting (my love for botanical illustration, not surfing, bewildered Gloriana and her friends), I spent most of my time with old people or by myself, writing in my journal. Eventually I found a few friends. Mostly girls who were back home from college on spring break and wanted to talk to me about books and boys and teach me a bit about Diné spirituality. Michelle, a talented softball player, even invited me to spend the night at her house where her dad, a medicine man, showed me his loops of drying peyote, his fans of eagle feathers, and explained that the birds carried prayers to the heavens where they could be answered.

On my last day, my host mom, Gloria, gave me a turquoise and silver pin. Michelle had told me that the stone symbolized good things to come. I took it and said thank you about four hundred times. I was so grateful and didn't want to leave. I loved it there now. I'd learned a bit of Navajo. Not enough to make me popular, but enough to haltingly communicate with Gloriana's grandma, who taught me to make fry bread. I'd also discovered that TLC albums were universally beloved and that if you are patient and make eye contact, someone will come sit with you at lunch. Even my weaving teacher eventually approved of my little rug.

On the plane home I thought about how, without even trying, I'd forgotten about all the moments I was spitting lonely and even the small plastic bottle in the cabinet back home. Maybe this was proof that the world was bigger than it felt in the tightest, most worried places in my chest. That beyond the borders of what I already knew, there were strangers who could stop being strangers. Loneliness, and then something after loneliness. I wanted more.

Mom, Dad, and Jake picked me up at LAX and I asked them to stop at the grocery store on the way back to the ranch so we could get flour and lard to make fry bread like Gloriana's grandma had taught me. Mom helped me cook the dough at the big black range in the kitchen, dropping the stretched bits into hot grease while Dad and Jake sat at the counter across from us listening to me talk about looking for lost goats, finding a scorpion in my shoe, my classes, and the prom (that I'd gone to by myself). All of it scrubbed of any pain, embroidered instead with the thrill of telling them about it.

We ate the fry bread hot, with honey from our own bees, sitting and standing at the counter. When we were done, I gave them the little rug and sash belt I'd woven and showed them my silver pin, hoping with every raging cell of my body that the turquoise would work.

Fourteen

Ojai, California, Spring 1995

I think we were driving the back road to Ojai when Mom told me that Dad's doctors had found new tumors in his hip and two more in his lungs. They hadn't wanted to tell me when I was in Arizona. The two of them were leaving in a few days for Mass General so he could get surgery. Right after Jake's thirteenth birthday.

I slid the pin into a drawer in my dorm room, disappointed it hadn't worked. But then, a few weeks later, Dad's surgeries did. Or maybe that was the turquoise's way of bringing good things to us. Either way, he didn't have any more recurrences for six months. And then one Sunday morning I was home for the weekend and woke up to the sound of Mom begging Dad not to die, to not take his pills. I didn't have to hear which pills. I knew.

He was worried the new tumors in his spine were going to paralyze him and he didn't know when. But I could tell, eavesdropping anxiously from my room, that when she asked him to wait just a little longer, that he was listening. And he didn't take them. Not that weekend and then not for weeks after. And then not for months after that.

He went back to Boston to talk to Dr. Suit, his radiation oncologist, about possible treatments, and we combined that visit with a college trip for me during which he and I fought more than we ever had before. He felt like I should apply anywhere and everywhere I was interested in. But my high school college counselor was convinced I didn't have a prayer of getting into the schools I liked. He'd taken one look at my list (Cornell University at the top of it) and told me it was futile. Dad was furious. He'd crutched into the man's office and bellowed that it wasn't his place, or anyone's, to tell his daughter what she was capable of. "What's the worst thing that could happen?" he said. "She gets rejected? Let her get rejected. At least she'd have tried." He thought the counselor was trying to protect students' feelings, or the school's college placement statistics, he couldn't tell which. But either way, I should not listen to anyone who tried to set the bar for me before I'd had a chance to set it for myself.

When Dad said stuff like this, I knew it wasn't just about college. If he'd listened to the physicians he'd seen at his diagnosis, he wouldn't be here to argue with the counselor, or with me. And if he'd believed what he'd been told about what was possible after his amputation, and again after his knee replacement, he never would have continued doing surgery, or ranching. Instead he'd done all that and more. Seeing him sitting on the ground in the orchard, fixing broken emitters on the irrigation lines, muddy and happily focused, his prosthesis splayed out straight, his metal crutches tossed to the side in the dirt, was normal to me now. So was seeing the piles of extra legs under my parents' bed that smelled like wood and talcum powder. Instead of changing his shoes like everyone else, he changed his leg. Each prosthesis wore its own shoe. This way, he could get ready as quickly as possible. He only had to tie one set of laces. And he was always getting ready for something: heading out to visit a new specialty nursery, driving the orange Kubota tractor around the ranch, building something out of hardwood in his workshop in the garage, teasing Mom, digging holes in the lawn to aerate the grass, teaching Jake to whittle, researching new espresso machines, moving bee boxes, or reading the latest James A. Michener novel while puffing on his pipe.

He hadn't just survived, he'd lived.

But his conviction that anything was possible also made me angry sometimes. I worried my counselor was right, and I didn't want to let my parents down. On that college trip, Dad wanted me to see all the schools, not just the ones I might get into. One morning he pulled over on Massachusetts Avenue, right in front of MIT. I looked up at the big rotunda, the imposing stone stairs, and thought about my bad grades in Physics and Algebra, and said that there was no way I was getting out of the car. I didn't even like science and math. I would never get in here and I would never want to go.

"Don't say no to yourself before someone else does," he said. "Just hop out for a quick sec and look at it. I'll stay here. Won't even park."

This was too much. I refused. And he got angry. "Dammit, Laurel," he growled. And we sat there, Mom beseeching me to just run up the stairs, to humor him. Me, stone-faced, arms crossed in the back seat, taking a stand.

Eventually, he slammed his hand on the steering wheel and pulled back into traffic, muttering about how there are versions of ourselves that we have not met yet and why on earth couldn't I just take the long view.

Now I think it's because the long view didn't have him in it. A few days earlier, Dad's oncologist had told him there were no treatments left to do that didn't risk paralysis. The tumors were too close to his spinal column. I didn't know he'd gotten this news yet, but I did know that if he was well enough to fight with me, then he wasn't dead.

He might have been at the end of his road, but I was at the beginning of mine. And I didn't want to set off without him.

Fifteen

Scottsburg, Oregon, Summer 1995

After stopping all his treatments Dad felt okay. Good, even. At least for a while. I finished up my junior year, Jake finished seventh grade, and we went to the cabin for the summer. Our last one together, a fact we all knew but no one actually said. Mom made lots of blackberry cobblers and we ate them, sitting around the table laughing till our sides hurt and Mom snorted, or watching *A River Runs Through It* on rented VHS from Bob's Market. We fished for bass and canoed up and down the river and had lots of friends come stay. Dad taught me how to nymph, a fly-fishing technique that uses wet flies instead of dry ones, going for trout underwater instead of on the surface. And he got me a backpacking fly rod so I could hike out to good fishing spots on my own. In July, I left for a month to work on a trail crew in Montana and came home fit and strong and full of stories about digging pit toilets and the mountain goats who liked to chew the salt off my sweaty backpack straps.

After Jake and I went back to school in September, Dad took Mom up to the cabin again, just the two of them to look at the fall leaves. He surprised her with a chocolate cake and a green Jeep with a bow on it, going big for his last gifts to her. He wrote a card that said *Just because . . .* There wasn't any reason to bother finishing the sentence. They knew. After that, Jake had his bar mitzvah at the ranch, a big party where we served tri-tip grilled by a cowboy from Santa Maria on a big open rig in the driveway. Friend after friend came over to Dad to pay their respects. You could feel the goodbyes in the air, like a drop in barometric pressure. In November, Mom and Dad celebrated their twenty-fifth wedding anniversary and I started my college applications. To say that Dad was focused on seeing me finish them would be an understatement. "Did you get them in yet?" was a constant refrain with him and it was driving me nuts. I'd decided to apply to Cornell early decision and hope for the best.

The day before Christmas vacation I was about to start getting ready for formal dinner when a sophomore girl knocked on my door and told me I had a phone call. I rushed to the airless little phone booth on the first floor of the dorm. I needed to hurry or I'd be late to dinner. The receiver was hanging off the hook by its long metal cord.

"Hi, Lar," Dad said.

"Oh hey."

"Have you finished yet?"

He knew I'd turned my Cornell application in already.

"We talked about this," I said, annoyed.

"What if you don't get into Cornell?"

"It's very possible I will NOT get in there," I said, "like a snowball's-chance-in-hell level of possibility."

I had nearly perfect SATs and lots of As, but only in the subjects I liked. This drove him nuts. It was the same fight we'd had forever. He didn't understand why I couldn't just do well in all my classes, even the ones I thought were pointless.

He sighed, exasperated.

"Well, what about the other schools?"

I looked at my watch. I had only fifteen minutes to finish getting ready and still needed to shower. I was sweaty from back-to-back lacrosse practices. A bunch of us had made All-American and we were looking at a spring of traveling to games on both coasts. I'd become a team captain too, just like I'd planned, and was managing the boys' lacrosse team so I could practice even more—taking their shots in goal because I was hoping to be a Division I goalie if I got into college. How could Dad not understand?

"You can't procrastinate with this," he said.

"I KNOW, but break starts tomorrow and I'll have plenty of time. I don't know why you're giving me such a hard time about this." I was angry, trying to sound cutting, authoritative.

"Dammit, Laurel, I'm trying to help you. So is your mom. This is a big deal."

"You think I don't think it's a big deal? I KNOW it's a big deal. It's a bigger deal to me than it is to you, I promise."

But even as I said the words, I wondered if it was true. I couldn't stop now though. How could he not see I was worried about getting in somewhere? I hadn't had time to do any of the other applications, with all my lacrosse practices, serving on the JC, being a prefect. I was also senior class president, and had been busy studying for end-of-semester exams. Starting the very next day I'd have two weeks at home with nothing else to do but write my dumb applications, why didn't he get it?

"The deadlines are a few weeks away, okay? Leave me alone about this for God's sake. I promise I will go to college . . . Jesus."

I waited for him to argue back, for his own fury, white-hot as mine, but he just said, "I love you, Lar."

I was angry though. I couldn't tell him I loved him back. He needed to know he was being unreasonable.

"I gotta go," I said, my voice sharp.

I slammed the receiver down, comforted by the solid *click-ca-chunk* of the plastic hitting the cradle.

Sixteen

Santa Paula, California, December 1995

Mom called the dorm at least three times the next morning telling me to come home as soon as I could. No dillydallying. And would Leyla, one of my best friends, give me a ride?

I don't remember the drive through Upper Ojai and then Santa Paula, past the old walnut and apricot orchards, the fields of yellowing grass, and then the careful rows of citrus, only that it took us forever to leave campus because girls kept stopping us to talk about where good parties might be over break and Leyla needed to find the pair of soccer cleats she'd lost. I was looking at my watch, worried I was going to get in trouble. It was noon by the time Leyla left me in the driveway in front of the garage at the ranch. I came banging through the kitchen door into the house and then I knew.

Mom was sitting on a stool at the counter, folded in half. Her head collapsed on her arms. She looked like a broken bird that had flown too fast into the kitchen window. When she heard the door slam she looked up, her shoulders hunched, face wet with big messy streaks, her skin puffy and red.

Oh no. No.

No.

He was dead. Or dying?

Not someday. Today.

Now.

"My best friend," she said. "I'm losing my best friend."

And then she sobbed, long and hard, and put her head back down. She looked like my mom but she wasn't. Her grief was a walled room. And inside it, she was no one's mother. "My best friend," she said again.

What had I missed? I'd just talked to him last night. We'd fought about my applications.

Wait.

We'd fought.

He'd called me to make sure my applications were turned in.

He'd known.

Bile rose up from my stomach and burned my throat.

I could hear my voice—tight and angry on the phone with him the night before. He'd said he loved me.

I'd hung up on him.

This was why Mom had said I needed to get home. And I was late. Late. Late. Late.

Had I missed him? Was he gone?

I went totally and completely numb. A big sucking vacuum swallowing me whole.

I walked over to Mom and set my backpack on the tile floor.

"I'm sorry," I said softly. Then I smiled. A batshit smile, loopy, strange.

"Why are you smiling?"

"I don't know," I said. I didn't. I couldn't control my own face. I tried to give her a hug but my body was rusted metal.

"Where is he?" I asked.

"In the bedroom."

"Can I go see him?"

"Yes."

Of course he'd planned this for my first day of Christmas break. I knew without anyone needing to tell me. I'd have two weeks and then would go back to school without missing a single day of class.

I picked up my backpack and walked past the doorway to the den. I could hear the sound of the TV and figured Jake was in there, watching Nickelodeon, but couldn't stop. Did he know Dad was dead or dying down the hall? If not, there was no way I could hide it, so I kept walking. Past my bedroom and through the old wooden doors Mom and Dad brought home from Mexico in the back of the old ranch truck when they were rebuilding the house. I stopped in the doorway to their bedroom, not sure what I was about to see. Scared now. There was no chance though that I wasn't going in. "Go," I told myself.

Light poured through the skylight, leaving shifting shadows on the floor, filtered by the branches of the sycamore tree. Out the window I could see our rows of lemons and the oak forest on the opposite side of the canyon. I could hear the wind in the avocados.

It's too beautiful to die today. For him to die.

I made myself look at their four-poster bed.

He was laying in the middle, not on the left side where he normally slept. Their comforter was pulled up to his waist and I could see he was wearing a new Champion navy cotton T-shirt. Had he bought a new T-shirt to die in? That seemed like something he would do. Did he put on shorts or pants even though he only ever wore his Jockeys to bed? I could see he'd gotten a haircut and shaved. How like Dad to take care of himself in order to die.

It felt surreal, like I was watching myself watch him. Like we were together in someone else's story, with no idea what came next. I realized I'd forgotten to breathe.

Then I saw his chest move.

He wasn't dead. At least not yet. His chest rose and then fell. He was breathing. My eyes burned but I would not cry. Not now. Maybe not ever. I knew he wanted me to be strong. To be okay. So I had to be, even if it was pretend.

I walked over to the edge of the bed and put my backpack on the rug by my feet. Then I got on my knees and unzipped it. That fall I'd taken a class with one of my favorite teachers, Mrs. Lin. It was called Stories My Mother Told Me, and it had changed my life as much as my time on the Navajo Nation had, turning on a light in a dark room I hadn't known could be lit up. She'd assigned us books by Leslie Marmon Silko, Maxine Hong Kingston, Louise Erdrich, and Sandra Cisneros. She told us it was okay not to write like all the famous white men we'd been made to read in school till then, that it was encouraged even, to write in our own voices about stuff we'd seen ourselves. Our final project had been to make our own book, of all the stories and poems we'd written about our families all semester. I'd kept it a surprise and was planning on giving it to my parents as a Hanukkah present. I'd glued a photo of Mom, me, and Dad on the cover, the same one from the newspaper article so long ago. In it, I'm holding out a piece of bread to a particularly mean peacock of ours. Dad is looking at me and the bird as if he'd do anything to protect us.

Mrs. Lin gave me an A and I'd tucked the sheet with the grade and her comments inside the front cover. Now, I set the book on the edge of the bed and looked at Dad's face.

Was his breathing slower than it had been a minute ago? I couldn't tell.

If only I'd packed my stuff up faster. If only we hadn't taken forever to say goodbye to everyone at school. If only Leyla hadn't lost her cleats. If only I hadn't thought just about myself.

Late. Late. Late.

I felt like I'd been punched.

"Dad," I said, "I'm so sorry." I choked on the words.

This was the only goodbye that mattered. Why hadn't I sensed it on the phone call when he hadn't gotten angry with me? This was the only goodbye that would ever matter. I tried to push the thought away. I concentrated on the thick dark hair on the back of his arms, the cotton sleeves of his T-shirt. He was so heavily real. Still tan, he must have worked outside this week, despite the pain he was in.

"I wrote something for you," I said quietly. I didn't want to wake him up. The thought of that terrified me. I knew this was his plan and I didn't want to wreck it.

He didn't move. This definitely wasn't sleep. It wasn't death either, but it wasn't life. Dad was on a train already pulling out of the station and I was going to have to speak loud enough for him to hear me before he was too far away. I was going to have to speak like that forever.

"I love you, Dad. And I'm so, so sorry. I'm going to make you proud of me, I swear."

I wanted to hug him but was scared I'd hurt him. What if he was in pain?

I opened the book and flipped to the last page. I'd written him a poem. About us and the cabin. I'd spent the better part of the last two weeks on it, writing and rewriting, trying to make it perfect.

I started reading. Hoping my voice would hold and that he could hear me. If not with his ears then with his heart.

As the moon rises over the river
I sit
back to the stairs
chest to the water
thinking of you.
You want more for us
than we want for ourselves.
All we want is you.

I paused and looked up at him. He was still breathing, the muscles in his face were relaxed. I tried to catch my breath and kept going.

Like the rivers of scars
across your back and down both legs,
you teach me to be hard
like the slick rocks underwater.

You will fight forever
but the twist of the scalpel
will never extricate the smell of the dying shad.
It's that time of year.
The moon calls and the river answers,
quietly over the banks
tugging at the blackberry brambles.
As you struggle upstream with the salmon
Towards the tug of the tide
And the tail-dancing sturgeon,
I watch for you
and grow stronger.

There was too much fish imagery. It was heavy-handed. Sentimental. But it was me. The best I could do. And when I got to the final line my eyes were blurry. I didn't want to cry in front of him. I would be strong just like I promised. Today and every day. Till I died myself.

I closed the book and put it back in my backpack. I looked at him one last time, trying to burn the sight of him into me, knowing this was the last time I'd ever see him. And then I stood up and backed out of the room. I would not turn my back on him. Not ever.

Seventeen

Santa Paula, California, December 1995

The rest of that day and night is hazy. I know Mom kept checking in on Dad, and Jake stayed in the den, watching cartoons. I avoided both of them because I didn't want to say anything about Dad's plan. And also, I didn't go back in to see him because I worried I might wake him up. I remember going to bed early and staring at the ceiling making a list of all the things Dad was not going to be with me for:

My high school graduation
Jake going to high school
Me going to college
Me graduating from college
Me getting married someday, if that even happened
Jake getting married someday
Levi, our dog, getting old

Everything I added to the list was another punch in the chest.

And then I fell asleep. The next morning I woke up to the sound of the brass hinges squeaking on our front door, the one we never used ourselves. We came through the garage instead. Who was here? I walked down the hall to see what was going on. Mom was holding the door open as Dad's mom and two sisters walked toward the house from the blue and yellow Roadrunner Shuttle, still parked in the driveway. The three of them had close-cropped brown hair and were wearing dark knee-length skirts that swirled over the ground as they moved. My grandmother's bifocals swung in front of her soft chest on a gold chain. They looked like benevolent Jewish witches. They must have taken the red-eye, I thought. Did they know in advance? My grandmother didn't say hello, she just looked at Mom with a question mark in her eyes and Mom pointed them toward the bedroom.

He must still be alive, or whatever he is now.

I let them brush past me. And I stayed there at the door, looking out at the front lawn and the stand of agapanthus. We were irrigating and I could hear the *chit-chit-chit-chit* rattlesnake sound of the sprinklers, smell the water in the air, the tang of new fertilizer. Mom called Levi to his breakfast of Costco kibble in his brown plastic bowl.

The next thing I remember is a wail. From one of my aunts. It was so loud and long it sounded like an alarm. He must have been waiting for them to say their goodbyes. And now he was dead.

Inside me something tight and still snapped like a dry twig. I could feel it in my chest and behind my eyes. Here it is, I thought, the thing I could barely hold on to, and now I can't do it anymore. But I can't let it go in the house.

Must. Get. Out. I stuffed my feet into the shoes sitting by a chair in the hallway and ran through the open front door, still in my plaid flannel pajama bottoms and one of Dad's gray T-shirts. I sprinted down the tiled front stairs with the blue swallows painted on, past the lemons lining the driveway, past the corral with the donkeys dumbly chewing their morning alfalfa, and the coop full of my wedding doves cooing and preening, oblivious. I stopped to catch my breath at the Kubota tractor, bent at the waist, holding on to one of the giant wheels, gasping.

Late. Late. Late. Bad. Bad. Bad.

I stood back up and pushed off from the dirt and crunching dry avocado leaves. I ran, heaving, past the apricot trees, the still-green plums, and ducked through the barbed wire that bordered the wildest part of the ranch. I felt my hair and shirt catch on the fence but didn't stop. My T-shirt tore and a knot of hair ripped but I kept going, panting up and through the stand of wild oaks and into the scrub.

Purple sage scratched at my legs and sprays of burrs snagged up and down my pajama bottoms. Up, up, up the hill I ran. Birds skittered out of my way under the bushes. My lungs burned, just like I wanted them to. If I could have lit myself on fire, I would have. A match to the hair, till I caught and flamed up and out, my own wildfire. I wanted to set myself free of my body, all the pain my skin was trying to hold in. I wanted to outrun this new world without my favorite person in it.

Finally, I scrambled up the steepest part of the hill where Mac, our grouchy miniature donkey, liked to stand and look out over the canyon. When my calf muscles cramped too much to keep going I stopped next to a thicket of sage and crumpled to the ground, my back to the hill. I was nearly at the top and could see the whole ranch and the ribbon of road down the canyon spread out below me. To my right I could see the mountains that separated us from Ojai, soft hills of oaks and grass and chaparral. They'd be green soon with rain. I hated all of it.

I pulled my knees to my chest and wrapped my arms around myself, feeling the rocky ground through the thin fabric of my pajamas but I couldn't move. If only those rocks were sharper. Pain burst through me and out of my eyes. I started to sob, tears down both cheeks and onto my chest, onto my knees, and onto the dirt. It felt like a waking dream of falling. The ground was gone. Not the real one, that was here, smelling good and normal, but I hated that too.

What had I done? What would we all do now?

Sobbing, my head hot and heavy, I stayed in the bushes watching the road for I don't know how long. An hour? Maybe two? I know I was still there when a tiny, distant dark car appeared at the mouth of the canyon, passing the turnout where Dad used to pull over and ask

Jake, starting when he was three years old, if he wanted to drive the rest of the way home. He always said yes. Dad put him on his lap, where he would steer while Dad used his good leg on the gas and the brake. They drove all the way home like that, about a mile and a half, up the canyon, into our driveway, and then over the wooden bridge across the creek to the house, where Dad would take the wheel back to park.

It was a hearse.

He was gone. And I hadn't said goodbye.

Eighteen

Ojai, California, June 1996

Six months later was my high school graduation. As class president, it was my job to lead everyone across the lawn on that brilliant Ojai morning, two by two, like a frizzy-haired Noah, to our rows of white plastic folding chairs where we'd sit for the ceremony. The headmaster called us up one at a time, read a few sentences about each of us, and then handed us a diploma tied with green and orange ribbon. When it was my turn, I stood there sweating pit stains into my ugly linen dress cut like an apron while the headmaster said words like "uncommon common sense" and "unmitigated optimism." It felt like a eulogy for someone good. Definitely not me.

At the end, we sang the school song one last time, cheered, and then I looked around for Mom and Jake. I found them next to Mom's parents, standing under a pepper tree.

"I'm so proud of you, Lar," Mom said. "Everything they said about you, it's true."

"She's right," Jake said, nodding at Mom.

I looked at him, surprised, and then down at my feet.

"Thanks," I said, trying to believe them but I couldn't. I wouldn't. The person the headmaster described wouldn't have hung up on their dying dad, that person would have said "I love you."

Next to me, some of the boys in our class were knighting each other with their parchment tubes. I saw Brooke and Leyla talking to their parents and when they saw me they waved and rolled their eyes. Everyone was trying to extricate themselves as quickly as possible from their families because we had a senior party to go to. That night was the school-sponsored one at Cath's house, and the next day we were going to a classmate's cattle ranch in Santa Maria where we'd camp in his barn and drink warm beer. His parents said we could do whatever we wanted, provided no one drove anywhere. I was nervous, hoping desperately that a bookish boy I liked named Jack would give up on liking Cath, who didn't like him at all, and kiss me as a consolation prize. I didn't want to have to go to college without being kissed. I scanned the crowd for him or anyone else I thought I might be able to convince to kiss me, my crush a green sweep of radar pinging pointlessly. Mom was now digging for something else in the straw purse she used for special occasions.

"This," she said, pulling a small square box wrapped in the flower-printed gift paper she kept under her bed, "is for you."

I pulled off the wrapping and found a white cardboard jewelry box with a square of cotton in it. Underneath the cotton was a gold and silver bracelet. My graduation date, 6-8-96, was engraved next to the clasp.

"Thanks, Mom," I said, fastening it on my left wrist. It was smooth, elegant, like something she would wear. A bracelet for a grown woman I didn't want to be yet and wondered if I ever would. Then I felt guilty for thinking this. Why couldn't I just be grateful?

"I love it," I said, hoping she wouldn't notice I was lying.

She looked down at her bag again and pulled out another present. This one was rectangular, a little bigger than the other, wrapped in the same paper.

"This one," she said, "is from Dad."

Jake shifted his weight from foot to foot, watching a group of boys who'd stripped off their sport coats and were now tossing a basketball in the parking lot in front of the freshman guys' dorm.

"Open it," Mom said, handing over the box.

I wanted to hurl the thing into the bushes next to the stone stairs up to the dining hall or take it back to my dorm room and stuff it in the bottom of my hamper under my dirty mesh shorts. Opening this present would make it real that Dad was gone, more real somehow than just his absence did. Back when he was still working, there were lots of times he had to miss one of my games or school plays because a surgery took longer than he thought it would or he had to do a last-minute consult with a patient or fellow physician. Without even being aware of it, I think I'd convinced myself that Dad wasn't at my graduation because he had somewhere else to be. And somewhere else, despite all the evidence to the contrary, still wasn't dead. But opening this present, the last one he'd ever give me, meant he really wasn't coming back. Not ever.

Mom and Jake were looking at me expectantly. I glanced away and saw my good friend Nancy hugging her parents on the other side of the lawn. Her dad was wiping happy tears from his eyes, looking at his eldest daughter with such pride that it made my whole body ache.

I tore off the paper.

It was a bright blue box, about eight inches long and narrow.

Mom motioned to the side where I noticed two tiny golden hinges.

I tipped open the lid. The box was lined with bright yellow satin. A folded piece of paper was tucked into the top.

"Here," she said, reaching out her hand for the box, "I'll hold this while you read."

I unfolded the paper and saw that the note was in Dad's handwriting: angular, messy, forceful.

Dear Laurel,

This is to sign your first book someday
Or a mortgage or a marriage certificate

Love you, Dad

Mom angled the box toward me and lifted a tab of yellow satin. Underneath was a gleaming black and gold pen. It looked like jewelry. I noticed the old-timey tip.

"It's a fountain pen," Mom said. "A nice one."

As she turned the box, it caught the sunlight. I swallowed and looked back at the note.

I could tell by how he'd written it that he'd probably meant to just write the part about the book but maybe Mom looked over his shoulder and reminded him that I was seventeen and most teenagers didn't end up with the professions they dreamed of in high school. "But some do," I imagined him saying, "Why not her?"

I lifted the pen from the box. It was cold in my hand and heavier than I expected it to be. For a moment my fear of no one ever liking me back, of leaving Thacher and my family for a future I couldn't fathom, of being late to Dad's death, of fighting and then hanging up on him the last time we talked, of his disappointment—it all quieted for a second. I looked up at the mountains behind the school, craggy and covered in chaparral, and wondered if Dad was right about me. Maybe I would use this pen to sign my first book one day. Or at least write down some of the things he'd so badly wanted me to know—that more was possible than I thought and to hurl myself into life like I was the fishing line and also the prize.

I wasn't ready. But I couldn't figure out how to stop any of this. The train pulling out of the station now was for me. I hugged Mom and Jake goodbye and set off across the lawn to my friends and the beginning of something else.

Part II

You've got to understand your limitations. It's your limitations that make you the wonderful disaster you most probably are.

Nick Cave

One

Sausalito, California, 2015

Ninety-five miles per hour. Ninety-seven. Ninety-nine. I pushed down on the gas till I could hear the engine strain and feel the steering wheel shake, the car shudder. Harder now. One hundred and one. One hundred and three. My eyes burned. We were going south on the 101, way too close to the center median, past the first Sausalito exit, gunning it up the hill toward the Golden Gate Bridge. My sinuses ached from crying and my cheeks were hot and sticky. The heavy feeling in my chest pushed me against the seat. Cedar was in the far back of the VW wagon, looking out the windows I'd paid to have tinted darker than was legal.

Through my tears, I looked at him in the rearview, at the soft fur of his pointy bat ears. He was the closest thing I had to a life partner now. The last person I spoke to at night and the first one I spoke to in the morning. Because I worked for myself, and from home four days a week, he was also the pacemaker of my day. Wake up, breakfast, walk, work, walk, dinner, out for a bit, bed. Dogs were easier than people for me.

Me: Dr. Laurel Sara Braitman. Thirty-six years old. I'd spent the almost twenty years since Dad died methodically working my way down the list of things he'd hoped for me. Running not toward something but away, trying to use achievement, and all the good feelings that came along with it, as an analgesic on the pain I couldn't even admit was there.

Now, if I wanted to, I could tick off my accomplishments like an insomniac counting sheep. It was obnoxious and it started back at Thacher: Class president. Team captain. Dean's list. Honor roll. All-American lacrosse player. Excellent SATs. Cornell University. Two different Division I college sports (at least till I stopped getting my period due to overexercise). College Scholar. Dual major. Summa cum laude. Excellent GREs. TED speaker—not once but thrice. *New York Times* best-selling author. Book reviews in the *NYT* and the *New Yorker*. I'd even gone to MIT for my PhD, walking up and down, hundreds of times, the very same steps I'd fought Dad over so bitterly back in high school. There were so many fellowships and awards, grants and residencies, that if I added them up it would have been enough to buy a house, but instead I'd spent it all on the work itself. And now, I had a job at one of the top medical institutions in the world—Stanford University School of Medicine, where I was a writer-in-residence and becoming a professor, teaching writing and storytelling to medical students and physicians, leading workshops and classes, and where, dream of dreams, I could spend as much time as I wanted at the hospital taking it all in, just like I had as a kid when Dad would occasionally let me come on rounds with him.

It had taken me barely a decade to do most of these things. And that wasn't counting the stuff I didn't mention on a résumé: the grueling backcountry routes I'd hiked through the Andes and the Himalayas, the time I spent studying grizzly bears in Alaska or doing stream ecology research in Venezuela and the Amazon basin. There was marriage and divorce, a half dozen cross-country moves. A few great dogs and many donkeys, the last of which, Mac, had just died back on the ranch at twenty-eight years old.

I would never list any of this out loud, that would have been mortifying (even typing it makes me cringe and feel exhausted), but sometimes I repeated it all back to myself like a bulwark against self-doubt, something to keep stocked and ready in the pantry like nice crackers in case anyone stopped by you wanted to impress. For years now I'd been the person friends called for career advice or recommendation letters, the one asked to meet with floundering nieces and nephews, an emergency contact for not just medical emergencies but for life. It's not that I wasn't proud of what I'd done, I was. And I didn't regret any of it. But the accolades hadn't come with what I hoped they would: self-worth, or a feeling of safety. I was, I realized as I tasted the salty tears running into the side of my mouth, a ship about to splinter on the rocks.

"I'm sorry, Nu," I said over the radio.

"Nu" was my nickname for Cedar, or rather it was Connie's nickname for him, but it had stuck for both of us. "I know you love her," I told him, catching his eye in the rearview mirror and waiting for him to cock his head in listening mode. "I do too. It's just not gonna work." More tears ran down my face and mixed with snot. I wiped both on the sleeve of my green plaid shirt. It felt like something inside me was cresting its shores, spilling water onto everything downhill. A muddy landslide.

Connie was my girlfriend. Or had been till about an hour ago. The first woman I'd ever dated. The span of our problems had emerged inch by inch, just like the bridge I was speeding toward, appearing through the fog. We tried to fix everything for a while but we were different in the worst kind of ways. I resented her big messy spirit, for the same reasons I'd first been attracted to her. Once, when I refused to sing in the car, she'd accused me of not being free. She'd lost three iPhones in the last six months. She had anxiety and sometimes cried after sex. Other times she peed in jars she kept next to her bookshelf because she didn't want to have to go to the bathroom in the middle of the night. Instead of taking the sheets off her bed, washing them, and putting them back on like the rest of us, she'd wash all her fitted sheets at once, and then put them all on the bed. Taking off a top layer every once in a while when they started to feel sandy.

The biggest problem though wasn't hers. It was mine. I'd realized it one night, a few months after we'd started dating.

We were sitting on the wide brown couch in the living room of my houseboat apartment, anchored off a creaky dock behind a floatplane tour company, a few hundred yards off the 101 in Sausalito. That night, Cedar was splayed on top of Connie's lap, his front paws crossed elegantly over her thigh, his soft nose resting on a tan velvet throw pillow. I could hear the raspy caws of the night cranes hunting in the mud outside.

We'd been eating Puerto Rican food and arguing about the fact that I was stonewalling her. She said I was in a bad mood, I said I wasn't. She asked me what was bothering me, I said "Nothing" and changed the subject. She dug in her heels.

"Dammit, Laurel," she said, "give me a break here."

I wasn't doing it on purpose. I didn't have anything to tell her. Sure, I didn't feel great, in fact I felt a dark bubbling somewhere south of my chest and north of my knees, but I didn't see the need to dig into it. Plus, I couldn't put my finger on anything wrong. I was fine. Better than fine—I was excellent; a well-resourced white woman in America with her dream career. I even had a good dog and a supersmart, long-haired butch girlfriend who looked just like Peter Pan if Peter Pan had been half-Chilean with freckles and perfect tits and liked to sing Selena songs and dance salsa. I did not deserve to be unhappy.

"Really?" Connie said. "You're not going to give me anything?"

I shrugged.

"Laurel—I mean this nicely, sort of, but something is wrong with you."

I felt my chest prickle.

"You're thirty-six years old but you can't ever describe your feelings. It's like you don't know what's happening with yourself in real time. That means I can't help you. You don't know what you need."

I turned my back to her, facing my overstuffed closet, and scanned myself for the source of the trouble—where was the tight-sweater feeling coming from? I'd had this feeling often enough. It was like my insides were too big for my body and my skin was stuffed into a rough wool sweater five sizes too small. It vanished almost as soon as I started paying attention to it. But where was it coming from now? And when would it go away?

"Can I tell you tomorrow? Or, like, the day after tomorrow?" I said.

She smiled, despite herself.

Before Connie, I'd only been with men who asked me what was wrong as a kind of formality, like when a cashier asks if you're having a nice day and then startles if you answer honestly. I never answered honestly. Not because I was hiding anything, but because I was never sure what to say.

Connie was different though. She had a black belt in karate but might as well have had one in emotional jujitsu. There was nothing she liked more than a gut punch of an emotional conversation. I think it was all the years she spent gay and closeted in South Texas that made her an emotional spelunker, curious about other people's hidden places. Her mom is a proper Chilean lady and her dad a survivalist and marine biologist who rescued stranded dolphins. Before Connie fully realized she was queer, before she left home to join a group of artists called the Floating Neutrinos who taught her how to build and sail ships, captaining a boat made of trash the length of the Mississippi and then across the Adriatic, she worked as a Pepsi girl on the beaches of South Padre Island. Walking up and down the sand in a blue and white string bikini, giving soda samples to Mexican families and white Texans lounging on bright towels. Her own kind of survivalist.

I loved her desperately but stopped wanting to have sex with her a while ago. She felt like my friend, like my family. I wondered if maybe we just should have been just friends all along. But I couldn't bear losing her. We'd been together a year and a half now, but it felt long enough to break me in two. And then there was Cedar. He was Connie's dog too because he had decided he was. I brought him along on our first date. Connie had invited me to a surprise double quinceañera she was throwing her brother, Brian, on his thirtieth birthday in Guerneville, up on the Russian River.

Connie and I tailed each other through the bars on Guerneville's main strip, laughing, eating tacos, and drinking bourbon while admiring her bearded brother and his bearded boyfriend in the thrift-store ball gowns she'd brought for us all to wear. Eventually, she and I lay down next to each other in the house near the river a friend had lent us for the weekend. Cedar curled on our feet at the end of the bed.

"Are you even gay?" she asked, while we watched the darkness of the night sky turn gray with morning light through the pines outside the window.

"No?" I said. "Yes? I have no idea. Does it matter though? Don't the kids say we're beyond labels now?"

She snorted.

"Maybe I'm gay but just for you?" I said. She looked skeptical. I didn't yet know how much of an asshole thing this was to say.

"You're not some sort of experiment. I'm too old for that," I said.

We'd kissed the next day, back at the houseboat.

But now I wondered if I'd been wrong. Maybe thirty-six wasn't old enough to really know yourself at all. And I'd hurt us both. I felt a familiar maw in my heart gape open. I pressed down harder on the gas. This, I struggled to count, was my tenth breakup in four years? Or was it my twelfth? I had a routine. I'd meet someone so interesting, so different from me, that I'd get drunk on curiosity, always confusing it with passion. I wanted to dip below the surface of their lives, hold my breath, and look around. Some of these people were good and some were dangerous. Mostly, though, they were a drug I took to manage my restlessness and treat a longing I couldn't name yet.

Jake teased me about what he called my "YMCA" dating period—a rotating cast of professions that called to mind the costume section of a Halloween store. Cook. Biker. Hacker. Rock star. I approached dating like I did a good dim sum brunch. "What's that being rolled past on the cart? Oh, great . . . never had that one before. I'll take it." The more unique the offering, the more likely I was to try it. I was making up for lost time. I'd spent the Thacher years and most of college doing everything I could to stay outside of my body since that's where my pain lived. I didn't have sex until I was twenty. It happened in a tent in the Alaskan wilderness with a goat hunter whose parents were homesteaders. The feeling I'd had was more relief than pleasure. Though that could have been because it was peak salmon season and a ton of hungry grizzly bears were around. Still, I'd married my first real boyfriend and stayed with him for nearly a decade. We got divorced the year I turned thirty. I decided I needed to catch up. My post-divorce life started out well enough. I tried to say the word *divorcée* any chance I got—it felt ridiculous, preternaturally aged, and a little risqué, as if I were Elizabeth Taylor drinking spritzes on a patio in Capri between husbands. For years I'd been embarrassed by my lack of experience and avoided oral sex entirely out of fear of failure. But when I got divorced, I was in the second year of my PhD program and did the only thing I knew how to: research. I ordered lots and lots of books about sex. My favorites were *The Ultimate Guide to Fellatio* by Violet Blue and *Nina Hartley's Guide to Total Sex*, the latter of which suggested switching out all the bulbs in your bedroom for flattering pink ones (which I did immediately). Then I got into a three-and-a-half-year relationship with a Portuguese contemporary artist. We were in love and the relationship was glorious until it wasn't. Eventually we both cheated on each other and that's when the YMCA period began. It was wild and also, eventually, wildly exhausting. Quite a lot of the people I dated were unavailable but tried to seem otherwise or didn't try, but I pretended not to notice. Looking back on it, I think I was dating as a form of resistance to growing up and having to choose a lane. Not just romantically, but in my career, and even geographically. Some of these relationships lasted months, though usually they only lasted a few weeks. If someone started to fall in love with me, I was more likely to end it. If you'd asked me then, I would've said that I was sad these affairs crashed and burned. And I had been sad. But I didn't want a relationship. As evidenced by my choice of dumplings. I just couldn't admit it to myself.

By 2015, though, it was going on six or seven years, long enough to stop being a phase and become more like a lifestyle. I tried to tell Jake that I was worried something might be wrong with me, going person to person like I was interviewing for a job position I never planned on filling. But I didn't know how to explain. Not to him, not to me, not to anyone. Had I had the words maybe I would've said that what I wanted wasn't another person, it was to figure out who *I* wanted to be. Dating was my way of trying on potential selves like clothing at a sample sale. Did I want to live in an artist's loft or commute to work on the back of a motorcycle? Could I handle living in a hand-built home without a kitchen? How much God was too much God? Was being perennially on tour something I was cut out for and was I savvy enough to help run a merch table? There was also the much bigger factor, that I would not have admitted: If I never really loved someone again then I would not disappoint them and they definitely wouldn't die.

Driving down the road, away from Connie and our life together, in pain and snuffling all over myself, I hoped that in a few weeks the wound would be cauterized. I'd throw myself back into dating and tamp down the terror that I was too big, not beautiful enough, too old, too hard . . . too much to be loved. I hoped I'd have new stories for my married friends who turned to me at dinner parties like a streaming service of dating programming, jostling each other for the chance to flip through my Tinder, Bumble, or whatever new dating app there was now with yet another infantilizing name that offered up Bay Area men and women who liked brunch and worked at tech companies that sounded like kids' toys. Once I'd made out with a guy on the street in downtown Oakland who said he was a senior executive at something called Weebly. It sounded like a joke till I saw the big lit-up sign on a tall building off the freeway.

I was just past the second Sausalito exit when, at the edge of my vision, I saw a sliver of darkness. I blinked, but it didn't go away. It felt painful. Foreign but also familiar.

I'd described it only once, to my friend Rebecca, a few years before. We were on a road trip through the desert, to attend a concert at an abandoned drive-in. I remember looking out at the sandy hills, thinking about water.

"It's like a lake and the lake is both inside me and outside me," I said, hoping I didn't sound as unhinged as I thought I might. "And it feels like I can't even dip my toe in it or I'll drown. I think it might be full of sadness but it's confusing because I don't actually feel sad."

The lake scared me. Not just because it was pain but because the pain seemed tinged with a darkness I didn't understand.

I was just north of the bridge when something on the radio caught my attention. It was a *This American Life* episode. One of the show's contributors, Jonathan Goldstein, was talking about a center for children in Utah called the Sharing Place. Apparently it was for kids who'd experienced the death of someone close to them. I turned up the volume.

A girl named Eve, whose dad had died two years before, said, "Usually with me, it would hurt in the throat and kind of in my stomach. It's like something that needs to come out."

Then the founder of the Sharing Place came on.

"We need to let people know that children grieve," she said, "and help them when they grieve so it's not stuck inside and comes out when they try to have a relationship later."

Somewhere deep inside my chest a bell started ringing, slowly and then louder and sharper till the car, the road, my hands on the steering wheel receded. I'm not sure how long I stayed that way—seventy-five miles per hour and then slowing, my foot off the gas. I wasn't in my body but somewhere above it.

And then, there was Dad. Sitting in his brown leather chair, wooden leg propped up on the ottoman in front of him, winking at me over his burlwood pipe, smile curled around the black plastic mouthpiece. He was wearing a dark blue cotton T-shirt and khaki pants. It was a decades-old memory but it felt urgent.

Someone behind me honked, loudly, and then honked again. I was in the middle of the southbound 101, between two lanes. Without hitting my turn signal I swerved toward the Spencer Avenue exit, coming to a loud, gravelly stop on the shoulder.

Cedar popped to his feet, the thick curve of his tail wagging against the plush roof of the car. I turned off the ignition.

"When they start to get intimate," the woman at the Sharing Place said, "they cannot bear it, and they go off. And they don't know why."

The segment ended and I typed "kid grief San Francisco" into Google on my phone. Could there be something like the Sharing Place around here? Just below the hospitals and hospices in the search results was something called Josie's Place. I clicked on their contact page, found their number, and dialed. It went straight to the voice mail of a person named Pat Murphy who said she was the director.

"Hi, um, my name is Laurel Braitman and I'm a writer based in the Bay Area and a, uh, professor at Stanford Medical School. But I'm not a doctor. Or, um, I do have a doctorate, I'm just not a physician. I'd really love to talk to you . . . about your work."

I meant to just leave my number and hang up, but I kept going.

"I think I'm a bereaved kid. I mean a grown-up. I mean I'm a grown-up now." Long pause. "I'd really love to talk to you."

I hung up, ashamed of my message. Was I really a journalist? What on earth was wrong with me?

Two

San Francisco, California, Fall 2015

Pat Murphy and I met in person a week after I'd left my bumbling phone message. We chose Borderlands Books, a fantasy bookstore with a small café inside of it on Valencia Street in San Francisco. Pat looked to be in her early fifties, tall with long, wild, curly hair, and reminded me of a gray-haired Glinda, the good witch from *The Wizard of Oz*, if Glinda wore Clarks and wide wale corduroy pants.

"My motto for Josie's Place," she said, "is that we're all naturally creative, resourceful, and whole people. It's just that sometimes things happen and we become less whole. Everyone can heal though." She tucked a long gray curl behind one ear.

"So you help kids after someone close to them dies?" I was thinking about the fact that my parents never would have sent me to someone like Pat. Or into a group setting in which you talked about your own bad feelings. This would have been their idea of hell.

"The kids help each other, really," Pat said. "A lot of children in San Francisco haven't met another kid who's experienced a death of someone they love yet. So just introducing them to other kids who've lost someone is helpful. Even if they never talk about it. They play tag, do crafts, or even wrestle; regular stuff, but being around each other normalizes what they're going through. They feel less alone."

I thought about the years I said my obsessive-compulsive lists in the dark, all the times Jake let me pretend-hide him from Nazis under the stairs (inspired by Anne Frank), my walks around the ranch carrying a big stick and looking for threats. Protecting my family had been my responsibility. Not because anyone asked but because there'd been no one to tell me that it wasn't.

Pat said that parents and kids all attend the sessions, but the parents meet with a facilitator in a separate room from where the kids meet. She'd started the organization because she'd lost her own mom when she was a kid, and then her stepmom when she was a young adult, and there'd been no support for her at all outside her family.

"Pat," I said, choosing my words carefully, "I guess this might sound odd, but I'd like to sign up for your program."

"Fantastic. We need more facilitators. We like to have one volunteer for every two kids."

"Oh," I said, "I don't mean like that. I'm not trained as a counselor or anything. I meant I want to come as a kid. My dad died. A while ago."

Pat stared at me.

I continued on in a rush: "I've called a few grief support programs for kids and asked if I can enroll. I know it maybe sounds a little weird, because I'm actually thirty-six years old but . . . I just think it's something I need to do. But, they all said no. I honestly think they thought I might have been a little creepy."

Pat looked down at her latte. I wanted to sink below the table.

"Most of our facilitators have experienced an early loss too," she said carefully. "I'm afraid I can't have you come as a child, that would be too strange, but I'd love you to apply to be a facilitator."

Embarrassed, I took the paper application she slid across the table and stuffed it in my bag.

"It's really just about companioning," said Pat. "And kids are hyperaware of their parents. Sometimes they won't grieve unless they see their remaining parent or caregiver go through the process and come out on the other side. They're delayed mourners. They won't do it until they know they're safe."

I thought about the injured or dying elephants I'd written about in graduate school, who left the herd, walking off alone into the forest to suffer by themselves. And I thought about myself, how I hadn't cried in front of anyone else in years. Decades maybe.

"What if they never feel safe?" I asked Pat, trying to keep a poker face.

"Well, I guess they grow up and start grief support programs for kids," she said and laughed.

Three

San Francisco, California, Winter 2016

Josie's Place met every two weeks in the basement of a Catholic church in the Sunset District of San Francisco, a few blocks from Golden Gate Park. When I arrived for my first training session, the side door of the pastel two-story stucco building was propped open with a bucket. Inside, off a short corridor was what looked like a large, mostly empty storage room. Pat was there, standing next to a woman with short, blazing red hair, taping blank sheets of paper to the wall. "I'm Andrea Bass, the co-leader," she said. Her smile was turned up on one side. I got a good shiver.

One by one the rest of the trainees showed up. We were all women, between the ages of twenty-five and forty-five or so, from different countries. Most of the group was in social work school or getting master's degrees in psychology. We put on HELLO MY NAME IS stickers and then Pat and Andrea asked us to sit in a circle in metal folding chairs in the center of the room.

"You should know that really young kids don't understand the concept of death," Pat began. "A person is gone, then a person is there. When a person is gone and then still gone and then still gone, a child may grieve at each moment when he or she feels the person's gone-ness."

"Everyone deals with this differently," Andrea continued. "Some children act younger or regress. They want the care and attention they received when they were littler. Some freeze out of fear and become withdrawn. Some act out, being naughty, angry, or belligerent."

"Others," Pat said, "react by becoming overachievers."

"Oh God," I said, hoping no one heard me. I looked at the door and tried to gauge how long it would take me to slip out. But there were too few of us. Everyone would notice. I'd have to sit here and listen even though I suddenly didn't want to.

"These children are overachieving in an attempt to contradict their own feelings of helplessness," Pat went on. "They may do everything 'right,' even to the extent of parenting their parents. Some children exhibit exaggerated displays of power while playing to counteract their fears and this may take the form of superhero manifestations."

For nearly a year when I was five or six I'd refused to wear anything but my Wonder Woman Underoos, a kind of underwear set printed like her costume that was popular in the eighties. My parents' friend Roberto gave me a length of rope I called my Rope of Truth and I used it to lasso visitors, the donkeys, Jake. If Mom tried to make me change I pitched a fit so loud it made the peacocks call outside. The only time I took my outfit off was for school because even I knew that you couldn't go to class in your underwear.

I don't think this was just my doing. Dad had wanted to name me Thor after the Norse god of thunder and lightning. When I was born a girl, he tried to do it anyway, but Mom said no, so they'd named me after a tree they both loved. By the time Jake was born Dad had given up on the name, if not the idea, of us being extraordinary. Maybe this is what a lot of parents want for their kids, but Dad was as committed to making this happen as he was to everything else. His illness only turned up the heat. The high expectations, I think, were a key part of his plan to make us okay without him. He didn't talk about it like that, it's just that there wasn't any room for failure.

• • •

One day, while scrolling Instagram, in between ads for pointy flats made of recycled cups and photos of my friends' goofy kids, I came across a Bruce Lee quote: "I'm not in this world to live up to your expectations and you're not in this world to live up to mine." The rightness of this hit me in my calluses, the ones I'd gotten from running so hard after what Dad wanted for me. It's our own expectations for ourselves that should matter the most but knowing this intellectually isn't nearly enough to change the way you live. It took me years to understand that Dad had expected himself to be superhuman and, by extension, me too. He'd survived the craziest of odds. And he didn't just want to keep Jake and me from thinking of him as sick. He wanted to be powerful, not pitiable. If we acknowledged our own pain or suffering, we'd have to acknowledge his. Which was a kind of treason.

If another parent at soccer practice or some other well-intentioned acquaintance ever expressed anything approaching concern for him, like "I'm sorry about what you're going through, Howard," or "it must be really tough," he would actually get angry. "No one is going to feel sorry for us," he said often enough that I'd learned to think of pity as a useless gift foisted on you by soft-spined people who didn't understand that bad things happened but that we were just fine, thank you.

Sitting in the circle at Josie's Place I could finally see this more clearly. Or I was beginning to, anyway. Dad didn't have to choose between being vulnerable or powerful. He could have been a hero *and* still been in pain. The best heroes are. He might have known this in the beginning but as his disease showed up more often and stayed longer, I think he lost his way a bit. And since I was following so closely at his heels, I got lost too.

Four

San Francisco, California, Winter 2016

At one of my first Josie's Place sessions with the kids, our activity was to make paper shields. The idea was to draw things on the shield that make you feel protected. Most of the activities were like this, metaphors so obvious they may as well have been flashing neon signs, but I couldn't roll my eyes or the kids would see. So, I was forced to do them, and it was actually fun. We turned shoeboxes stuffed with newspaper into "scream boxes" that we took home and screamed into whenever we wanted, the sound deadening in the box so no one could hear. We smashed little ceramic hearts with hammers and then glued them back together to make sculptures of our own shattered and reconstituted hearts. We did lots of drawings—of our grief personified, of maps of our bodies. It was the epitome of earnestness and I loved it. That night, everyone was getting a piece of stiff paper that one of the facilitators had cut into the shape of a shield, just like a knight would use to fight dragons.

It was a big crowd for Josie's Place. There were twenty-one of us, including two new families. One of the families was a man named Philip and his daughter, Maria. Maria was eight, small for her age with long brown hair, serious eyes, and pale skin. Her mom had died only two weeks before, of colon cancer. Usually kids didn't come until a month or two after they'd lost a parent. Pat told us it was because those first few weeks are so busy—there are family visitors and memorials to plan, people are constantly stopping by with food, and everyone is still pretty shocked. But Philip told Pat that Maria's mom, his wife, had been sick for a while and they'd discussed Maria coming to Josie's Place before she died.

When I plopped down on the floor next to Maria with my blank shield and a box of pens, she was quiet. Sometimes with the kids I got the sense that I shouldn't look at them directly but just sit nearby, doing the same thing they were, waiting to see if anything happened. I took a Sharpie out of the box and started drawing Cedar. I'd just taken him to In-N-Out for his birthday with his best dog friend, Connie's chihuahua mix named Kim. We sat, just the three of us, at an outdoor table. The two dogs gamely wore metallic green birthday hats and devoured their hamburgers in seconds, tails wagging.

When I finished drawing Cedar, I drew the door to Josie's Place, a donkey, and a fishing pole. I drew books, the mountains across the river from the cabin, and then I drew the cabin itself. I also drew a cooking pot, a wooden spoon, and garlic. Because cooking always makes me feel better. And my laptop because writing helps too. Maria was still staring at her paper and the box of pens. I asked her what made her feel better when she was sad and she just looked at me as blankly as the paper. I felt bad for asking. Her mom had just died. Did she even know how to make herself feel better yet? It was going to take years. Forever maybe. Why was I pestering this innocent child?

But then she spoke.

"I think I want to draw when my mom and I went to Yellowstone," she said. "Is that okay?"

I nodded, worried that if I spoke too enthusiastically I might spook her. She started drawing grass at the bottom of the shield. Then she drew a cabin and a girl. She was incredibly talented; the images were very nearly real. She colored a wash of yellow sunlight at the top of the shield.

"I really like how you drew paws," she said, pointing to my approximation of Cedar's feet. Then, apropos of nothing, she said, "My dad woke me up in the middle of the night to tell me my mom died."

"What was that like?" one of the other facilitators asked.

"I wasn't sad," she said, and we nodded.

"Sometimes you're not sad till you have time to miss someone," I said.

I couldn't tell but if I had to guess, I'd say Maria was a little bit nervous that she was supposed to have been sadder but was working it out by telling us that she wasn't.

"Are you sad sometimes now?" I asked.

"Yes," she said, still not looking up from her drawing.

"What is that like?"

"Well, I just try to let myself be sad," she said. "My dad says that the worst thing that you can do is try not to be sad."

She was so damn wise. I wondered what my life would have been like if I'd met someone like Maria, or her dad, when I was her age. I'd circled the planet more than once, trying to outrun my own particular kind of sad. I think my running away from discomfort often looked, to other people anyway, like making myself more uncomfortable. But I knew the truth. Nothing was harder than feeling the depths of my own heartbreak.

When I was in fifth or sixth grade Dad bought me a little freshwater aquarium that I got to keep in my room. Unlike fishing, when I'd inevitably have to dig a hook out of someone's soft mouth to set them free or knock them dead with a club to eat later, the aquarium was more similar to what my Barbies had been. A space that was hermetically sealed off from my own life. The fish had their own concerns, of course, I just didn't know what they were. And soon, fish-keeping became another passion Dad and I shared. We filled the tank with a bunch of small tropical fish and learned about nutrient cycling and freshwater plants and dissolved oxygen levels. These were pets, but I didn't bond with the tetras or the angelfish. I got close to just one, a small brown armored catfish with old-man whiskers whom I named Harold. He listened to me, or at least I pretended he did, and that was enough back then. He also kept the tank walls clean of scum. He lived for years but by the time I went to high school he'd been buried under the big oak trees as a kind of fishy annex to my hamster cemetery. I'd nearly forgotten him until college, when I got a job in the Cornell Ichthyology Collections, a year or so after Dad died. It was a way of staying close to fish without having to skip class to go fishing. I loved the neatly labeled specimens, the deeply rational organization, the quiet, tall shelves holding creatures I'd never seen before—leaffish and stickfish and lots of other fish named for things they weren't. Once in a while I'd come across a sleepy-looking fruit bat in a jar or a stingray, its eyes open and staring. But it was unpacking samples sent in by professors doing fieldwork around the world that was my favorite part of the job.

One day I came in to find a big cardboard box from Venezuela, sent by an ecology professor named Alex Flecker. These boxes were surprises, like fish Christmas—I never knew what'd be inside. I started unwrapping—removed the padding and a few random plant samples till I got to what I wanted: the final mummy layer of preservative-soaked gauze around the fish. Scientific name: *Ancistrus sp.* An armored catfish with whiskers. Harold! Or someone who looked like him. It was thrilling to see him again, to find out where he'd come from: the Orinoco River Basin.

A few months later, a sign appeared on the fish collection bulletin board from Dr. Flecker. He was looking for field assistants for a stream ecology research project in Venezuela. My heart rate sped up just reading the sign. The closest I'd been to South America was Breakfasts of the World. I applied that same day and when he hired me, I took leave from Cornell and went to work for him for six months in the dry tropical forest. I loved the rivers full of catfish and electric eels, the noisy howler monkeys in the tree canopy over my tent, and the homemade hot sauce we ate on arepas stuffed with salty scrambled eggs for dinner. Even though I got anal worms that itched so badly I couldn't sleep for weeks, I came home only to find enough grant money to go back again. This time farther south, to the Amazon. I wanted to follow the path of aquarium fish from where they were caught in the flooded forests of Colombia, Peru, and Brazil, all the way to pet stores in the US where people like Dad and me bought them and took them home to listen to our problems. I wasn't sure how I'd do it, but I went anyway, and eventually I befriended an aquarium fish exporter who helped me secure hammock space on a boat heading upriver where I hung out with fishermen and their families and went on collecting trips in beautiful handmade canoes.

I saw a lot of the Amazon during that time, mostly from hammocks on a long succession of riverboats. If I counted the tiny streams that flowed into the channels that flowed into the bigger tributaries that finally emptied into the main river, then the Amazon basin rivals only the human circulatory system in complexity. It's the big wet heart and lungs that breathe for the world. I wished I could tell Dad about it. Without really noticing and certainly not on purpose, most of my life had become like this. Country by country, mountain range by mountain range, river by river, ocean by ocean, I went to all the places on the globe that Dad had once quizzed me about.

When I eventually came home, lots of people told me how brave I was to be doing all these things by myself. Especially because it all started before I was old enough to buy beer. But by then I knew the truth. The Amazon, and everywhere else I went that required special vaccinations, was just someone else's hometown. And, sometimes, what looks like bravery is just us being scared of something else even more.

Five

Portland, Oregon, Summer 2016

I'd been volunteering with Josie's Place for about a year when I heard about the Volcano Room. Pat told me about it: a padded room full of pillows and punching bags where kids could erupt, banging and hurling themselves around, without anyone telling them to calm down. It sounded amazing and I dreamed of installing one in my houseboat apartment. The room was inside the Dougy Center in Portland, Oregon. A kind of mothership of kid-grief support where Pat had done her training.

By now, I knew not to call the place and ask, point-blank, if I could just be locked in the Volcano Room for a little while or join one of their sessions as a geriatric teenager. Instead, I emailed from a rest stop off the I-5 and asked for a tour and to interview the senior director, an author and thanatologist named Donna Schuurman, and the program director, Joan Schweizer Hoff. They'd both been working with grieving kids and adults for more than twenty years. Donna had written a book called *Never the Same* and I read it at the cabin, sitting in front of the fire with Cedar. "Time does not heal all wounds," she wrote, ". . . Without proper care and attention, wounds fester, get infected, remain painful and leave scars. I believe this is as true for emotional wounds as physical ones."

This made me wonder if I had a secret infection. Connie and I were friends again now, had been for more than a year, and she hadn't stopped asking me about my feelings. I'd tried to explain the lake of pain to her, and the occasional twinges at the base of my spine that scared me to death. I wanted a CAT scan that would show me the aberrant cells I was convinced were there, waiting silently in my lumbar spine for the right moment to turn into cancer. This is what pain always was. Even a sprain. I would try to tell myself I was catastrophizing, that for most people minor aches weren't the first sign of terminal disease, but I was too good at arguing otherwise, sliding down the greased track to worst-possible outcome. Donna's words about festering wounds, though, sounded clinical enough to be interesting. Maybe the pains that scared me most weren't future-cancer but old wounds I hadn't known were there.

That night I walked down to the end of the road from the cabin. It was low tide, and I heard a few geese winging by overhead. The sun was still out but barely. Everything was blue except the tops of the ridges, shafts of gold light hitting the tallest Douglas firs. I was thinking of nothing in particular when I had a memory so clear it felt more like a vision. I remembered walking past this exact spot, with my family, late in fall, just after a rain, when the leaves on the road shone, and Jake and I moved the giant slugs off the pavement and onto the shoulder with sticks so they wouldn't get squished. Dad was walking without crutches so it must have been before the cancer came back for good. Our dog, Levi, trotted along beside us. Dad wore a plastic rain cover on his Stetson and was puffing on a pipe. Mom was smiling from under a dark green rain hat and talking to Jake. It reminded me of something Andrea Bass had told me when I was doing Josie's Place training.

I'd gone to see her on my own in order to hear a bit more about her work. For years now, Andrea had been a youth bereavement specialist at a Bay Area hospice organization and done art therapy with teens and children with terminal illnesses. I asked her how she helped these kids and she said that mostly the kids heal themselves with their own imaginations, a kind of superpower. Children use play, she explained, to reenact some of their hardest experiences. Only this time they're the ones in charge. They can also act out different endings from the ones they've gotten in life. She told me about one five-year-old girl she'd worked with whose brother had just died. The girl spent weeks playing with a plastic bear she said was sick. One by one she had all the other toy creatures come see him and offer medicine but none of it worked. And then one day she announced that the bear was healed. "How?" Andrea had asked her. "His tears," she said. "His tears were his medicine—he just didn't know it."

Other kids grew wings and flew back to the scene of a car accident to swoop in and grab their parent before it was too late, or invented other ways to time travel and hang out with people who had died. "They're closer to the imaginal realm, fantasy worlds where they believe anything can happen," Andrea said.

Now, picturing my family, alive and together, out on this walk with me in the fading light, I wondered if I could do it too. If I was doing it already.

Instead of imagining every night pain as osteosarcoma, every headache as glioblastoma, or every date as someone who might disappoint me one day, perhaps I could use my imagination to spend more time with the people I loved, even the ones I'd lost. This had always been Dad's plan, anyway. To be so singular as to be unforgettable. And to be so opinionated that we'd never, ever wonder what he might say or think in a given situation. It wasn't his pharaonic honey that would make him live forever, it was our most vivid memories. Simple, obvious maybe, but true.

The next afternoon I pulled up to the Dougy Center, a Craftsman-style building set back from the street, with bright white trim and gray wood siding. Warm light shone from the windows. I pushed open the wood front door and walked over to the reception desk. Joan appeared a moment later, striding down the stairs, wearing a floaty scarf over a light green shirt and brown Danskos, the official shoe of the helping professions.

We said hello and I followed her past a large tree sculpture into a curving hallway. As we walked, I looked more closely at the walls. They were painted bright yellows and greens, but it didn't feel like the forced cheer of a children's ward or retirement home, where people apply color like cologne over a bad smell. Here the walls felt authentically welcoming. Painted across them were quotes about the importance of play. I was trying to write them all down when Joan motioned to me to follow her into an open doorway.

"This is the Littles Room. We call it that because it's where the youngest groups meet."

Following her inside was like tumbling into another universe where suddenly Joan and I were Gullivers and the three-foot-tall inhabitants had left. All the objects in the room were miniature—the tables, the chairs, even the coatracks. There was a bathroom off the main room that had a tiny toilet, a tiny sink, a tiny hand dryer. There was a slide that landed in a pile of stuffed caterpillars and little nooks to climb into. It was a gorgeous, soft cat tower for small people in pain.

"They love to hide and then be found again," said Joan. I nodded, thinking of the kids at Josie's Place, who liked to bury and unbury things in pillows. All of us were just trying to get lost only to be found again by the people we missed.

The Volcano Room turned out to be as great as I hoped it would be. The walls were covered in bright teal vinyl. On one, a giant purple volcano spewed orange and red lava. The floor was covered with stuffed animals and beanbags. I could see the hills and valleys where the kids had last thrown themselves in. I wanted to be left alone in there. Instead, I tried to be professional and asked if doing all this fun stuff really helped kids deal with loss.

"Play is their work. That's not just a quote on the wall," Joan said.

At the next doorway she paused.

"This room is actually my favorite. Most adults get really uncomfortable and don't want anything to do with it, but the kids run right in."

She opened the door and I gasped.

It was a hospital room. With a real metal hospital bed made up with a quilt, sheets, and a pillow. An IV drip trailed from a rolling cart next to the bed. A side table held a cordless phone, a box of Kleenex, extra blankets, and plastic gloves in small sizes. On the wall behind the bed a heart rate monitor was painted so realistically that I could almost hear it beeping.

And then I was gone. Back at Community Memorial Hospital with Dad. Sometimes, I'd been able to go with him on rounds, when he was checking on his patients pre- and post-op, or talking to folks admitted for chest pain or difficulty breathing. He'd pull back the curtains around their beds and they'd smile at him and then down at me in my white hat and pinstripe blue dress with puffed sleeves and Peter Pan collar. Over the dress I wore a white pinafore with a big red cross and a silver pin that read NURSE in red letters. Sometimes Dad left me at the nurses' station where they'd ooh and ahh over my badge, pretend to page me, and let me use my stethoscope on them. I felt like part of a team, and they offered me little paper cartons of ice cream that I ate with a flat wooden spoon while I waited for Dad to finish up. I couldn't know then that I'd spend half my life trying to get back to those nurses' stations, the beeping ICUs, and the bright ORs where he'd saved everyone but himself. Now here I was, in another one.

Joan walked over to a hospital curtain hanging from the ceiling and pulled it in one sweeping motion down the track so that it closed the bed off from view, making a metallic roller swish. "We've found that the sound is really important in making this room feel real."

She was right.

"So many of these kids either know their person died in a hospital or spent time there. And they had no control over what happened," she said. "Now they can come in and be in charge."

I looked at a whiteboard sitting on top of a file cabinet. It had blank spaces for patient names, the names of an attending physician and nurse, and a space for goal of care and treatment. "Your nurse is: Dr. Sparkle," it read. "Your ed tech is: Nurse William." The goal? "Fix arm, eye test, tooth." Treatment: "cotton balls."

There were child-sized blood pressure cuffs, bottles of hand sanitizer, and a stack of patient "files" in manila folders with actual blank hospice forms the kids could fill out. The form on top had no name but the allergy section had been filled out: "Enoying Cildren" in purple pen.

"Is this where kids save the people they love?" I asked Joan. "The people they couldn't help in real life?"

"Absolutely," she said. "It works."

I was heading back to my car when I saw a flash of red in the play area behind the center. What was back there? It hadn't been on the tour. I ducked around the corner and saw a miniature firehouse, probably twenty feet tall by fifteen feet wide. Bright red with white trim and a lovely gray door. Through the windows I could see a fireman's pole, a few child-sized fire hats and uniforms hung on hooks along the walls. It was the emergency-responder version of the hospital room inside. There were no children playing right now but I could picture kids sliding down the pole into their small boots, rushing to their imaginary engines to flip on the sirens.

Jake.

He'd trained as a paramedic as soon as he could and then went into the fire academy. Jake had been a firefighter paramedic now for more than a decade and was on his way to becoming an engineer and, ultimately, a captain. He was the exact kind of person Dad loved best. A human Swiss army knife who could make or fix anything with quiet competence, good with his hands but not at the expense of his mind. Sometimes, when Jake emerged from the garage wiping oil off his hands on the front of his work pants or when he gasped with laughter after cracking a joke about me, I'd see Dad in him so clearly it was like a form of mourner's déjà vu. And it came with a chaser of sadness that Dad couldn't see what I was seeing. This good grown man who was so much more than the sum of his parents.

"Play is the highest form of research," I'd seen painted on one of the walls inside. Albert Einstein said it. I pictured myself in my nurse's outfit eating vanilla ice cream in the cardiac ICU and Jake pushing his toy fire engines around our old rust-colored rug at home. Both of our identities were inextricable from the loss of Dad, and from the desire to undo or redo something we didn't have the power to change when it was happening. I had a real hospital badge now, could buy my own cafeteria ice cream whenever I wanted, and had learned to write in order to, possibly, make up better endings than the ones we'd been given. Jake, more nobly, was roaring off in his engine, lights flashing, to save other people's moms and dads—everyone but the one person he probably wanted to save the most. If play was research then it was an essential kind, practice for the day we might be able to rescue the people who need us most, even if it's ourselves.

Six

Oakland, California, December 2016

Adam (not his real name) popped up in my Bumble app late one night while I watched *Orange Is the New Black*. He was a tall, dark-haired guy who wasn't particularly attractive, but there was something about him I liked. His profile said only "Californian living on the east coast. 6' 1"." We matched, and he told me he taught at an Ivy League university but was out West for a few weeks visiting friends and family. He asked me out for a drink and we decided to meet at a tiki bar I'd been wanting to try.

I got there first and busied myself with my phone, trying not to seem like someone waiting for a stranger. I was dressed in what I call my professor costume since I'd come straight from teaching at the medical school—a camel wool blazer and white button-up shirt, turquoise necklace, black jeans, and scuffed black leather boots. The professional version of my Calamity-Jane-meets-Charles-Darwin style ethos. I was teaching a lot more now and running the Storytelling & Writing Program, working with hundreds of clinical students and physician faculty at Stanford and beyond, helping them write personal essays, op-eds, and do the occasional radio piece. Mostly, though, my work involved helping people articulate their innermost thoughts and feelings so they could put their application-writing voice aside for just a little while in service of communicating more meaningfully with themselves and others about what they were seeing on the wards, with their patients, or at home with loved ones. In so many of these healthcare professionals, I saw my own fears and anxieties reflected. The medical school was a magnet for overachievers, a whole institution of people who believed in excellence as an analgesic, just like I did, just like Dad had. I wanted to help them tell their own stories because, in a field in which vulnerability can be punished, being yourself is a radical act. I knew from experience that this was way more complicated to do than it sounded and if I learned to teach others, maybe I'd figure out how to do it for myself too.

On my nonteaching days I did my own writing and a lot of stories for *Pop-Up Magazine*, a Bay Area phenomenon that was a little like a podcast, but live, onstage. We toured the shows around the country, nearly always to sold-out crowds, and some of my best friends were regular contributors. I did stories on everything from Colin Kaepernick's pet tortoise to the scientific reasons we like to listen to sad music when we're sad. I'd also started giving a fair number of talks about my work in medicine or about animals and mental health, the subject of my last book. Life often felt like one long series of packing and unpacking suitcases with breaks to do laundry, make soup, and swipe through dating apps.

I sipped my too-sweet drink and daydreamed about a long-distance relationship between New York and San Francisco. I always did this, even if I knew the date was probably not going to lead anywhere serious and wouldn't have wanted it to. The daydreaming was the thing that got me to stop at a bar after a long day of work, when I could be at home soaking in my bathtub, listening to true crime podcasts and talking to Cedar. I wasn't attracted to people I couldn't picture dating. Fantasizing about the future was part of the allure, even of a short-term relationship. It's a little like looking at real estate listings in a town you have no intention of moving to. The fantasy was always my motivation, especially internet dating, because wild hopefulness was the only thing that made meeting a stranger bearable. There was a 90 percent chance, at least, that within the first three seconds I'd realize I didn't like how someone moved their hands, or that their voice was too mousey. Or even more likely: that they'd be perfectly kind and attractive but for the life of me, I just couldn't imagine kissing them.

There were exceptions. I'd had a great brunch with a retired Major League Baseball player, a fascinating few months with a guy in a famous motorcycle club, and was currently messaging back and forth with a professional cowboy who had three horses and two dogs.

I was almost done with my painkiller cocktail when Adam walked in wearing a waxed canvas jacket. He was hard to read. At one point, when I mentioned that my family was Jewish avocado growers, he breathed in loudly and said, "This is me swooning. Can you tell I'm swooning?" I couldn't.

He was fluent in multiple languages and asked me to teach him how to fly-fish. He said he'd just ended an eighteen-year marriage. Maybe I should have asked more about this but I didn't want to. Having been married so long made him seem safer somehow. We ordered another round of drinks and when we were halfway through he swiveled to face me, put a hand on each of my knees, and leaned in to kiss me. It was good.

Oddly enough, like me, he was going to Ventura County for the holidays. We'd both be there for a week. We made plans for him to come to the ranch. I pictured us walking through the orchards, picking blood oranges for juice.

"Want to get out of here?" he asked.

I did. But I didn't want to sleep with him. I just wanted to make out and then have him call me the next day.

We walked toward the bar bathroom and he pressed me up against the palm-covered wall and kissed my neck.

"I'm not going to have sex with you. I just want you to know that," I said. I meant it. This guy had potential. I wanted to try something new.

He raised an eyebrow, smiled, and said he understood.

I got in my car and followed him to the pretty Craftsman cottage where he was staying. We started making out and before I knew it, he'd gotten most of my clothes off. I told him no a few times. Couldn't we just wait? But he begged me, and I was still playfully suggesting alternatives when he pushed inside of me.

"Adam," I said, "don't you have a condom?"

"No," he said. "I'll pull out before I come."

Whether or not this was assault did not occur to me till much, much later. In the moment, instead of yelling or fleeing, I dove into mental calculations gauging my risk. He'd been married for eighteen years, I told myself, so odds were he didn't have any STIs. But a more insistent voice throbbed underneath. *If he's having unprotected sex with you, someone he just met, he's doing it with other people too.* I told it to shut up. I wanted this guy to like me. I wanted him to be boyfriend material. The idiocy of this makes me furious now.

Afterward he rolled over and said, "I really hope I didn't mess this up."

I assured him he didn't. I was totally drunk. Not on alcohol, but on fantasy.

He apologized again on the front porch, as we said goodbye. And instead of screaming at him, I told him not to worry. And then I did what I'd practiced for so many years. I slammed my fears and any hint of anger down so hard that I knocked them completely out. It was as if they didn't exist. If you'd asked me that night if I'd had a good time, I probably would have said yes.

The next morning I picked up my phone but there were no new texts. He's probably just sleeping in, I figured, but I sent him a quick note that I'd made it home so he wouldn't worry. And then I fell back asleep.

The next night was the last Josie's Place meeting before the holidays.

It was also the winter solstice. Pat had sent us an email about how hard a time this was for the families and asked us to please make sure we'd be there. Since the night was special, we'd meet parents and kids, all together, at the beginning.

When I arrived I saw there were twice the usual number of mismatched floor cushions arranged in a circle, each with its keeling stuffed animal—a beady-eyed penguin, a small teddy bear with fuzzy white angel wings that seemed to be sleeping upside down. Soon the parents and kids filed in and we settled onto the cushions. The kids tried to swap stuffed animals, roughhoused loudly, and kept asking to get started. Finally, Pat asked a girl named Imani to turn off the overhead lights and then we began.

"Does anyone know what the winter solstice is?" Pat asked.

"The longest night of the year!" Cora shouted.

"Yep. It's also the first day of winter. The word literally means 'sun standing still.'"

A kid named Marco hurled an owl across the circle at his brother, Alex. Alex yelled and I tried to quiet him. But it only made him talk louder.

"People in the past," Pat continued, "were afraid that the sunlight wouldn't return unless they kept watch and had a celebration. There were feasts and schools closed."

The kids sat up straighter. Marco hissed, "Yes!"

"This might be the longest night but it also marks the return of light," Pat noted. "From here on out, every night of winter will be shorter. For me, that's a little like grief. Slowly, over time, everything gets a little bit lighter."

I heard one of the parents sigh.

Pat asked who wanted to start with the talking stick.

I shifted on my cushion. I wanted to check my texts. Adam hadn't gotten in touch all day. But now my phone was off and in the other room. Maybe he'd written back. I felt unmoored. A little panicky. Anticipatorily sad. I had a bad feeling.

I told the other facilitators I had to go to the bathroom but instead I walked quietly to the back room where we left our things and pulled my phone out of my bag. Nothing.

Against my better judgment I quickly tapped out, "Are you ghosting me? Lol."

As if the "lol" made me chill.

I went back to the kids. Everyone was starting to make luminarias. "To light our way through the darkness of the holidays," one of the facilitators had explained. Another achingly literal activity. But the luminarias were going to be beautiful. I helped a few of the kids cut circles of yellow paper to decorate the bags we'd fill with sand and electric tea lights.

I could feel a tug like an anxious tide, back to my phone in my black canvas bag. I let ten minutes go by, then fifteen. I knew I was being compulsive, pathetic even. And that made it worse. It hadn't even been twenty-four hours since I'd hung out with Adam. Why was I starting to hyperventilate at the idea that he might not get in touch? Yesterday afternoon I hadn't even known him. What was going on with me?

I looked over at the kids and realized how much was riding on Adam being a good guy. I was still sore from the night before. I'd spent the afternoon wondering if I should try to get in to see my ob-gyn for a suite of STI tests. But I was embarrassed because I'd just gotten tested a few months earlier.

"Don't you work at a medical school?" my nurse practitioner had asked after I told her I'd had unprotected sex with someone I most likely wasn't going to see again.

"Aren't you supposed to keep from shaming me?" I said, grimace-laughing.

Of course I knew better. She knew I knew better. Instead, I'd looked at the big engagement ring on her hand and then up at her face, hovering over my open legs.

"It's hard out there," I said. "I try my best. Sometimes my best is unprotected." And then I laid my head back down.

"Well, I think you should try harder," she said.

I left the kids with their bright plastic scissors and slunk back to my bag, slipping my phone in my pocket and excusing myself to the bathroom. Still nothing. Some part of me knew there wouldn't be and now the sudden wave of disappointment was in direct proportion to the feeling of hopefulness I'd woken up with. That is, I was in a full-on panic because this man I'd met twenty-four hours ago, who'd forced himself on me with no condom, was not responding to my texts. I went back to the kids and helped a boy whose mom had died last year of stomach cancer pour sand into the bottom of his bag.

I approached Pat. "I'm so sorry but I'm not feeling well," I said, hating myself. "And I have to drive down to the ranch tomorrow. I'm a little worried that if I don't go home now, I'm going to be too tired on the road." It was technically true. And my apartment was a good forty-five-minute drive from Josie's Place.

Pat looked at me with so much sweetness, my throat caught. "Of course, Laurel!"

"Happy solstice," I said, my voice cracking. I hoped she thought it was just the dry air of the basement as she ushered me to the door.

I got in the car and sat there for a moment before turning on the headlights.

Maybe he's dead?

He's not dead.

Maybe his phone was stolen?

His phone was not stolen.

Maybe he's playing hard to get.

Maybe he just doesn't like me.

Maybe he just wanted to have sex last night and knew what I needed to hear.

Maybe I'm a sucker.
Maybe I have a disease now.
Maybe he's an asshole.
Maybe he's an asshole who I still want to like me. Badly.
Bad.

Seven

Central Coast, California, December 2016

The next day I was on the freeway with Cedar, looking out at the rolling gold hills just south of San Luis Obispo and trying not to check my phone, when Connie called.

"How was the professor date?" she asked. After my mom, Connie was my number one cheerleader. She was also a spiritual companion through my anxiety. It had been years now since we'd dated and we were the kind of friends we were probably always meant to be. I loved her as much as ever. More even.

"I haven't heard from him."

"Wasn't the date only, like, two days ago?"

"Yes."

"Laurrrrrrel," she said, drawing my name out in exasperation.

"I know you think I should be chill but, listen, when someone likes you, it's obvious," I said. "Or at least more obvious than this. I've texted him twice, no response."

I did not tell her we'd had unprotected sex, and that I hadn't wanted to. I was too embarrassed. I still thought he might exonerate himself, and more importantly, me.

Dammit, Adam, I thought. Please, please be a good guy so I don't have to hate myself for having sex with you.

I looked at the sharp blue line of the Pacific. A few pelicans were flying evenly with the car. I could see in the rearview mirror that Cedar was watching them, nose against the window.

"I think you do this to yourself," Connie said. "You get all excited and the person you're excited about may be excited too, but you don't give them time to express it, because you're, like, right there. Ready." She paused. "But they're not going to die."

"I'm not worried about them dying," I said.

"I know you think that," said Connie, "but not texting back, or deciding they don't like you, is the equivalent of dying for you. You're very vigilant for signs. You check people's temperatures too much."

We hung up and soon I was watching the sky turn purple over the Channel Islands. It was nearly dark. I felt stupid. And sad. Was Connie right? Did I respond to every blank space, every short silence, like a death?

Maybe. The panicky feeling was so familiar. And it seemed to be getting more intense as I got older. The insecurity of early dating made it worse. Or maybe it was just worse now because of cell phones. When I'd met my ex-husband, texting was still a few years off. We actually made fun of people who had cell phones back then. How self-important they seemed because they couldn't wait till they got home to make a call. If I'd wanted to see him, I walked over to the soccer fields where he played, or his oceanography lab. Or he came over to see me. If I wasn't at home, he left a note. But now, communication with a new lover was like walking through an emotional minefield with lead boots and no sniffer dog.

Connie, I decided, was wrong. It wasn't that I went straight to thinking that a date had died on me. It was the uncertainty, the not knowing, that I hated. It was too much like the time between scans, or waiting for the pathology reports and the doctor to call with results. The infernal waiting room of the gods.

Eight

Santa Paula, California, December 2016

The next morning, I woke up to Cedar staring at me from the foot of the bed, hoping his unbroken eye contact would inspire me to let him out to chase the peacocks. Instead, I dug my sheepskin slippers out of the closet and pulled on an old flannel and a pair of jeans. I thought about my phone. The pang was less insistent but I looked anyway. Nothing.

I could hear the growling sound of the juicer in the kitchen. Mom and Sam were up.

Sam was my good friend Nancy's dad. She and I had been close since our first few days together at Thacher. Back then, whenever I was having a hard day, I'd beg her to sing me songs from the *Les Misérables* soundtrack and she'd almost always oblige. I loved her mischievous laugh, and how she was always the first person to suggest skinny dipping. Most people were so overwhelmed by her kindness that they failed to notice her searing observations.

Back in 2005, Nancy and I had been up at the cabin. I was about to get married and a group of my friends surprised me with a bachelorette fishing trip. We'd spent the weekend laughing out on the river, drinking palomas with fresh grapefruit juice, and lying around in the sun reading gossip magazines. On the last afternoon everyone else had gone in to shower but Nancy and me. We were floating by ourselves in the dark water. She flipped onto her chest and grabbed on to the metal ladder on the side of our neighbor's dock.

"I think my parents are definitely getting divorced," she said. "I'm not ready to tell everyone yet."

"Oh, I'm so sorry, Nance," I said.

If Nancy's parents could get divorced, no one's marriage was safe. They'd been together thirty-two years. Whenever I remembered Dad's memorial service, I pictured Nancy's parents and her two younger sisters, whom I loved. When Dad died, Nancy's family drove six hours, each way, from Sacramento to be at the service in support of their daughter and their daughter's friend (Nancy and Dad had had their own friendship, he thought she was razor sharp and could do anything she wanted). I'd seen Sam a lot since then—at games, at Nancy's plays, at graduation. He was an excellent farmer (pears and blueberries) and one of the few men I knew who looked at his kids the same way Dad and Mom looked at Jake and me. Once, Nancy told me that whenever she and her sisters were home visiting, her dad would pick gardenias from the yard and put them in the cup holders in their cars, the cut stems wrapped in wet paper towels, so that when they left, the air inside smelled like flowers.

We floated, listening to the water lap against the dock, not talking for a while. "Wouldn't it be amazing," I said, "if somehow our parents could be with each other?" She agreed. But it felt impossible. Mom was in a relationship. For a year or two after Dad died she'd sworn she'd never love someone again—the fear of losing anyone else was just too much. But then she'd fallen in love with a lawyer based in Washington, D.C., who liked scuba diving and scalloping in Nantucket. They'd gotten married. When Nancy and I had our conversation in the river, she was still married. But then, a couple years later, everything changed. Mom's new husband saw blood in his urine and was diagnosed with small cell bladder cancer. Eleven months later the cancer metastasized to his brain. His decline was fast, tragic, and when he died, I felt terrible for his two sons. I also felt for Mom, who was swearing off loving anyone again with new ferocity. In the meantime, Nancy's parents split up for good.

What she and I didn't know was that before Mom's husband had died, Sam's good friends met Mom, and called Sam to say, "We've met the perfect woman for you, only she's married to someone else." They didn't tell him her name and so he had no idea it was the same Lynn Braitman he'd known back when Nancy was in high school, the same woman his daughter loved. Jake, me, Nancy, and her two sisters, Kate and Sarah, liked the idea of setting our parents up. So that spring, when Sam had his annual blueberry party—everyone picking as many berries to take home as they could carry from his acres of fields, we told Mom she was invited too. She says she didn't know it was a setup. But Sam did. He practiced cooking potential dishes all week and asked Kate to help him pick out a shirt.

After that weekend, they were together. They loved doing the same things, from pruning roses and planting olive trees to researching new fertilizers and roasting macadamia nuts. Eventually Sam sold his house in Sacramento and moved down to the ranch. Our trees looked better than they ever had. His dog, Sophie, made herself at home, learning to go down to the mailbox and pick up the paper, bringing it, slimy with saliva, back to the house and into the kitchen for Mom. Sam became one of the best parts of our family and in 2015, they got married, surrounded by all of us kids and our partners, plus Cedar, Sophie, and three of their grandchildren. I officiated. We stood in front of the old stone fireplace at the ranch that Dad had built with rocks from the creek and talked about how surprising life is. How none of us could have imagined such happiness. Then we danced in the kitchen to "Jolene," spinning around the island where I'd once found Mom crying.

Every morning now she and Sam walked up the hill, past the place where I hid in the sage so many years before. They called it their "up and over" and picked fresh oranges for juice on the way down. Sam hung a wooden swing from one of the oak trees so they could sit and watch the light spill onto the orchards in the morning. When Jake decided to propose to his girlfriend, Alice, a powerful redheaded beauty we all loved desperately, he went up there too, with carving tools and cut "Will you marry me?" deep into the wood. Jake led her to the bench, as a surprise. She said yes. Now they lived in their own house on the ranch, one they built down in the lemon orchards, with their two young sons, Bennett and Wilder. Benny looks so much like me that sometimes, when he collects dropped peacock feathers off the ground to fashion into a tail for himself or his brother, or absentmindedly eats a tangerine, tossing the rind in the air, it's as if I'm catching a glimpse of my childhood happening over again.

This year everyone was going out of town for Christmas. I'd have the ranch to myself. Which was fine with me. I was planning to write, go on hikes with Cedar, eat fresh tortillas and refried beans from Tresierras, the Mexican market in town, and see Cath and my other friends who were all coming home for the holidays. There was also the cowboy from Tinder I'd been texting with just in case Adam never turned up. This was a habit—moving men around like pots on a stovetop. In case one hurt me, or I lost interest, or they never texted back, someone else would already be there, waiting. I wasn't proud of it. It felt a little bit like being a salmon in midsummer, keeping my options open as we all moved upstream to mate and die.

The cowboy, Colt, used a flip phone but texted regularly, with creative spelling. I'd googled him and discovered that he was a vaquero, a real-deal cowboy in the tradition of Mexican and early California horsemen. We went to a bar on Main Street in Santa Paula where he pulled out my stool like a gentleman and twisted the ends of his waxed mustache while we talked. He told me about his childhood driving teams, breaking horses, and running cattle with his parents in Wyoming. From there, we went out dancing in Ventura and for more drinks at my favorite dive. He leaned in and kissed me while the DJ played "Hypnotize," "California Love," and "Nuthin' But a 'G' Thang." The kiss was so good I forgot the borders of my body. We kept kissing, his strong hands gripping my waist, the top of my ass, pulling me against him. Eventually the bartender told us that we were causing a scene. But he didn't say it admonishingly. "It's like you're from another time," he said. I'd forgotten about my outfit, the black cowboy hat I always wore, my dark red lipstick. But I suppose we did look like that. Two people nostalgic for a West that never was, making out to nineties hip-hop, rocking back and forth, toe-to-heel, in our boots.

The night ended with Colt and me in the front seat of my car, next to his parked truck. I peeled off his jacket, his sweater, opened his vest. Every time I took off one of his layers I'd find something. In his shirt he had a giant knife, a flashlight, a big old piece of Navajo silver on a cord, his wallet, flip phone.

"What's next?" I asked. "Tent stakes? A carrot?"

He laughed. "I left the pistol at home."

I raised my eyebrows.

"You should carry one," he said. "Men would hurt women less if they knew they might get hurt too."

I thought about this for a second. For a moment Adam's face appeared, hovering over me in the dark. But then I felt Colt's hands on me and the thought evaporated like steam on the windows.

The next day I woke up early and took Cedar and Sophie outside. The air was snappy cold. We walked across the bridge, sparkling with frost that melted with our footsteps. I picked up the Sunday paper at the mailbox and marveled at the matilija poppies. I had a moment of fondness for my junior high self, standing next to these same bushes, waiting for the school bus with dread.

When I got back to the house, I made some more coffee and got in the bathtub with a view up the canyon. Then I put on my favorite

Willie Nelson album, *Red Headed Stranger*, and flipped open the paper. Cedar curled up on the tile next to the tub, leaning his head over the side to watch the water flow from the tap.

"Merry Christmas," I said to him, his dark eyes quick and listening. "Happy Hanukkah! Life is grand."

My phone buzzed. I reached over for it, dripping, expecting something from Mom reminding me to open the pool cover if it rained.

"Not ghosting," the text said. "Hope your drive down was good."

Who was this? Their number wasn't in my phone. It took me a second to register.

Adam.

I felt nothing. I'd already mourned this man. In less than a week he'd both lived and died for me. I was embarrassed and slightly mystified by my own emotions. I put the phone down and sank into the water, listening to Willie sing about men crying like babies. How on earth could I go from obsessed to complete detachment in a few days? Adam had come back to life and I could neither be angry nor enjoy it. I turned the hot water back on and looked over at Cedar, whose head was resting on the edge of the tub, staring at me with equal parts love and familiarity. I wanted to learn to look at myself that way and if I could do that, maybe someday I'd be able to look at someone else like that too. By now, it had been more than six or seven years of my YMCA resistance dating. I was still curious, open, but also tired of living in a will-they/won't-they romantic comedy that never seemed to resolve itself. I wanted to get to know someone.

Nine

San Francisco, California, January 2017

A few weeks after Christmas I was back in the Bay Area, planning to go out on a boat with Connie for an artist's tour of the bay that she was leading. I had Cedar with me, and traffic was terrible, so it didn't make sense to drive all the way home after work and leave him, just to come back downtown. So when it was getting close to Connie's event, I took Cedar for a walk and then drove down to the pier. He had his dinner, and I gave him a big bowl of water and put him back in the car with the windows cracked. He didn't mind the car, it was like a mobile dog crate, and he waited for me happily, napping in a soft ball like a fox.

"Be good, Nu. Love you."

Two hours later, my friend Jess and I walked back to the car, and when we were twenty feet away, I hit the unlock button on my key chain. This was Cedar's cue to pop up. I'd see his dark bat ears appear in the rear window where his bed was, or in the back seat, where he liked to lie across the whole bench leaving fur and dog grit in the cracks of the seat.

But he didn't pop up. Maybe the key fob was broken. I hit it again. This time I saw the headlights flash. It was working. Why wasn't he popping up?

My body went cold.

Was he stolen? That was always my biggest fear leaving him in the car in the Bay Area. But he barked like a demon at strangers who came too close to the car at night, so I'd figured the car was actually less likely to be broken into with him in it.

I started running. None of the windows were broken. What was going on? I reached the driver's side in seconds, but he wasn't in the front. I looked in the back and saw him laying across the bench seat, totally still.

"Cedar?" He didn't respond to my voice. He'd never not responded to my voice.

Then I saw it. And screamed.

Cedar was lying motionless, with a plastic dog treat bag over his head. Terror flooded through me. Had he suffocated inside the bag? This was a thing that could happen? I flung open the door and tore the bag off his head. I had to use both hands it was stuck on so tight, a seal above his eyebrows. I was sobbing and talking to him. "Cedar. No, Cedar. Noooooo." The treat bag had been in the car for months. It had a ziplock top. Had I not fastened it all the way? What had I done?

I fell to my knees in the street and pulled Cedar's face to mine. He wasn't breathing. I held his muzzle, his nose closed, and breathed into his mouth. Willing him to wake up. Willing him not to die.

Now I could hear Jess sobbing. "We need a vet," I yelled. "We have to go to the hospital."

Jess offered to drive, and I gave him my keys. He found the closest twenty-four-hour veterinary hospital on his phone. I don't remember how long it took us to get there. But I know Jess drove as fast as he could, running at least one red light.

I sat in the back, Cedar pulled in my lap. He was warm still. His warmth gave me hope.

"Please don't die," I begged him. "Please, please don't die."

At the hospital, I ran through the front door and the receptionists looked up at me, sobbing in my long tweed coat, arms full of Cedar.

I didn't slow down, I just called out "My dog, we need help."

One of the receptionists stood and jogged toward me.

"Take him back," she said, now running alongside me.

I pushed through the interior doors and into a large room with a metal table at the center and two masked veterinarians standing there. Their heads jerked up in surprise. I lifted Cedar onto the table. "I just found him," I gasped out, "his head was stuck inside a treat bag. I don't know for how long. Please save him. Please." I sobbed again raggedly and then I stepped back to let them do their job. To let them save him.

One of the vets leaned over Cedar and a tech stepped in next to him, so close that I couldn't see what they were doing. I folded my arms around myself, trying to stay standing. Shaking and shaking.

The vet stepped back and pulled down his mask.

"Your dog is dead."

I screamed. Except *screaming* isn't the right word for it. The sound I made was a roar, a wail, pain itself. My dog was my heart, my partner, my family, and he was gone. And it was my fault.

Later, one of the techs told Jess that seeing me collapse like that was the saddest thing she'd ever seen. Sadder than all the animals she'd had to put down. "It was her pain," the tech said, "And how destroyed she was. The sound of it."

I don't know how long I stayed crumpled on the floor, wailing and scaring the staff and the other animals. Part of me is still there.

Eventually a tech ushered me out. Jess was there. And a bunch of my other friends, whom Jess had texted. And a few people who'd been walking down the Embarcadero and witnessed what happened and followed us to the hospital. One of whom was a nurse and wanted to know if she could be of any help. I couldn't even look at them.

"We will give you a room where you can say goodbye," one of the techs said. "Feel free to stay as long as you want."

He brought me into an empty exam room the color of Styrofoam and a few moments later he brought in Cedar's body and laid him gently on the table. I shook and cried into his fur.

"Nu," I said, "I'm so, so sorry. So sorry. I can't believe I let this happen. Please forgive me."

The guilt and shame were gathering into a tsunami, darkening the edge of my vision. I wanted to trade places. I wanted to suffocate too. Bad. Bad. Bad.

Why hadn't I dropped him off at home?

Why hadn't I hidden the treat bag better? Somewhere he never would have gotten it.

If I'd walked him more during the day, would he have been too tired to go digging around for the bag?

Why had I let him die alone?

Why hadn't I gotten there in time to pull the bag off his head?

Always late. Too late.

I couldn't stop myself from picturing it. His happy excitement at finding the bag, scarfing all the treats, and then realizing he couldn't get it off. The more he tried, the more he probably pushed it farther onto his head. Had he panicked? How long did it take before he couldn't breathe? Did he shake his head side to side? Did he wish for me? Did he whine or cry? His body was still warm when I opened the door. If only I'd gotten there faster.

I was going to throw up.

My dog died terrified and alone, gasping for breath.

This was my worst nightmare for him. For anyone.

I told Jess I wanted Connie to be able to say goodbye. "But please don't tell her yet," I begged. "She has to do another tour on that boat. She won't be able to get through it." I couldn't stop stroking Cedar's head, his ears. His body was getting colder by the minute.

When the boat docked Connie called me. I couldn't even speak. I just cried into the phone and heard her say, "I'll be there as soon as I can."

Sometime later, I don't know how long, she burst into the little room.

"Nu . . ." she said, leaning in to kiss his snout. She started to cry.

"Why? Why did this happen?" I said, again and again, while Connie just looked at me, her eyes red.

"I don't know, Laurel. I really don't know."

We stood there, shocked, petting him.

"Something weird happened on the boat I think you should know."

I listened, trying to memorize the softness of Cedar's ears.

Our friend Kim, who was dating Jess at the time, had spoken to him and knew what was going on. She was at the dock and had told Connie right before the boat pushed off.

"I welcomed everyone and then I hid . . . I actually got under a table where no one could see me so I could cry. And I was just sitting there, meditating, I guess? But I feel like Cedar came to me. I know it sounds nuts but that's what happened."

I looked up from Cedar's body at her. She was deep in the memory of the moment. Not focused on what it was doing to me.

"He said something too," she continued. "He said, 'It's okay. I'm here. I'm inside you. I'm inside Laurel. I'm grateful. I'm just grateful. And it's fine.'"

"But why?" I couldn't stop crying.

"I think we don't get to know right now. We might never know. I have no idea. Maybe you'll find a partner soon. Maybe you'll be pregnant. Maybe something else will happen that this is making room for. I have no idea. All I can tell you is that Cedar came to me and he said it was okay."

I listened, grimacing. I didn't want to think about having to trade Cedar for something or someone else. Plenty of people fell in love and their dogs were still alive. Lots of people had dads *and* partners.

I thought about one of the young girls at Josie's Place, who'd drawn a time machine during one of our sessions. She explained that it brought dead dads back to life and told me I could use it too. God, how I wanted that time machine now. To go back and become a totally different person, someone who never let down anyone she loved, someone who could never ever be late.

Ten

Oakland, California, January 2017

It was 11 a.m. and I was alone, laying on Connie's bed in West Oakland, staring at the plaster ceiling. She was at work. I hadn't stopped hating myself for more than five seconds and couldn't face the idea of going home. I kept replaying Cedar's death in my mind. Shrieking in horror at myself and what I'd let happen.

I went to the bathroom and as I was washing my hands a thought passed like a cloud. My period was late. It wasn't usually late. How long had it been?

I checked the app on my phone.

Eight days late.

My stomach lurched.

Grief. I must be grief pregnant. I'd been unable to sleep or eat. Every time I dozed off for a second I'd wake up wondering why I couldn't feel Cedar's weight on my feet at the end of the bed. That must be it. I was exhausted.

My period had stopped only that one time before, after Dad died. I didn't get it for a whole year. Back then, I'd been numbing myself with exercise and overstudying, willing myself to move on. Of course, that's what this was. I'd barely eaten or drank anything in two days. My body wasn't about to bleed, to rejoin the cycles of the living and the fertile. It was protesting.

But then I remembered that thing Connie had said over Cedar's body going cold on the table in front of us.

Maybe you'll be pregnant.

Her words knocked around in my dehydrated head.

No way.

I got back into Connie's bed and pulled the covers to my chin. I thought of the men from the last month. There was the professor who I still wasn't thinking about as someone who'd assaulted me, even though he had. And Colt the cowboy. We'd had sex once, a few days after our first date. He'd come over to the ranch and we'd slept together in front of the fire. But he hadn't made any effort to make me come and so when we'd said goodbye the next morning I knew we wouldn't go out again. Was there anyone else? My stomach sank. There was. I'd tried to block out the memory. His name was Julian and I'd met him at the dog park with Cedar. We'd slept together and I'd immediately regretted it. He'd had a girlfriend he said he was planning to leave and was so soft he reminded me of the little white seal stuffie at Josie's Place. Worse, he laughed too late at my jokes and often misspoke, saying things like *self-depreciating* when he meant *self-deprecating*. I didn't see myself with any of these men. I was thirty-eight years old. Didn't a lot of women my age have to try to get pregnant?

There was no way I was going back to sleep. I got up, put on my shoes, and looked for my car keys. Jess and Kim had cleaned it out, removed Cedar's bed and tried to vacuum the dog fur. Even through my numbness I was grateful. They'd wiped down the back seat where he died. And taken out all of his bowls and toys. They'd driven the car back from the hospital to Connie's house and left it there for me for when I was ready to drive again. I wasn't. But I needed a pregnancy test.

I drove to a Walgreens on the edge of West Oakland. The pregnancy tests were locked up and I had to ask for help. They were expensive. I bought the cheapest one.

The store had a bathroom so I went right in to pee on the plastic stick. I barely had enough urine. Then I set a timer on my phone and stood there. Looking at the dirty wall, waiting for the little plastic window to fill in. One line if you're not pregnant, two if you are. Like a fertile ghost emerging from the shadows a second pink line began to appear in the indicator window.

I panicked. I picked up the test, eyes wide, and flung it in the trash. Busting out of the bathroom and down the hair care aisle toward the parking lot. I slid behind the wheel of my car and tried to breathe.

Maybe you'll be pregnant.

This could not be happening.

"Laurel, you are an adult, whether or not it feels this way," I said aloud to myself. "You cannot throw away a pregnancy test and pretend not to know."

I breathed.

I was going to have to go back in there and get another one.

But before I could go back inside, my cell phone rang. It was my friend Wendy, who'd heard about Cedar and happened to be nearby and wondered if I needed anything. I told her I needed a reliable pregnancy test, and she called her wife, Caroline, who turned up with one that promised to spell out the verdict in clear bold letters. We went to an alley full of fancy shops in Oakland that had a nice, public bathroom. Wendy peed on one too so I wouldn't have to do it alone. "I'm the control," she said laughing.

A few minutes later the word "PREGNANT" surfaced in black on mine.

They hugged me and offered to buy me an ice cream cone from the bougie shop next door.

I thought about thirteen-year-old me hiding out in hotel bathrooms during bar mitzvah dances, or pretending to use the pay phone at Thacher when the slow songs came on, and then all those years of erotic energy diverted toward athletics and excellence, anything but being in my body, connected to another living person in an intimate way. I'd been one of those kids I'd heard about on that *This American Life* story to a T, liable to run off before someone could get close enough to cause any pain. I was the last of anyone I knew to lose my virginity and it took even longer to get into an actual relationship. Now, here I was clutching a positive pregnancy test in an alley wondering who'd knocked me up. I felt a pang of relief that Dad was dead. I wouldn't have to see the look in his eyes while I explained this mess. He'd be horrified. And then I searched myself, wondering if he'd ever talked to me about kids of my own. It was funny, I knew what he'd thought about everything from early computing to the problems with clear-cut logging in the Pacific Northwest, and I knew exactly what he'd wanted for me: a career as a writer or something else that sent me out into the world like I'd been shot from a cannon. But for the life of me I couldn't remember him talking to me about being a parent. I don't think he ever had.

After our ice cream, Wendy, Caroline, and their little black dog, Susan Sontag, left me at a pizza place on Telegraph. I assured them that Connie would be along shortly to meet me. When she pulled up, she saw the look on my face and read me like she always did.

"What is *up*?" she asked, reaching over to open the passenger door of her panel van, so I could hop in while she finished parallel parking.

"You're not going to believe this."

"You getting a dog?"

"No!"

"Well, what?"

"Remember the other night when you said I might be pregnant?"

"Yeah," she said, raising her eyebrows.

"You were right."

"No fucking way."

"Yes way."

"Who?"

I just shook my head. "Let's get pizza."

• • •

We ordered slices, sat down at a two top, and I told her about all three men. She put her head in her hands.

"Do you want a baby?"

I didn't answer. Instead I said, "I swear they didn't finish inside me. Maybe this is the messiah? I *am* Jewish." And we laughed because I was too tired to cry anymore.

Eleven

Oakland, California, January 2017

I stayed at Connie's for a few more days but eventually I needed to go back to my apartment and face my new life, no matter how confusing it had become. The silence of the place, without Cedar, was terrible. So was the nausea. Sudden, unrelenting waves of it. Not just in the morning but all day, as if my body were a dinghy in a storm. I was busy cleaning out the fridge to get rid of lingering smells when I got a text from my good friend Shoham, confirming breakfast in New York City the coming weekend. I'd made plans to fly out there months ago and I wanted to go. I still didn't know what I was going to do about the pregnancy and figured that maybe some time out of town would help. This could be my last chance to be a parent. Was it a sign that I'd gotten pregnant at the same time I'd lost Cedar? Maybe I needed to say yes, not no, to this terrifying question in front of me. But if I kept this baby, what was I going to do about money? I didn't have maternity leave at Stanford. Was I going to have to move back home, into the room over the garage, and ask Mom and Sam for help? What would I do for a living if I couldn't write or teach? I definitely couldn't afford childcare, at least not in the Bay Area. I looked up Stanford subsidized daycare and it was more than I made in a month. Not just for teaching but with writing too. I thought about the men I'd slept with. I would not be asking them for help. And why exactly was I sleeping with men whom I'd never ask for help? Probably because it was safe. If I didn't love them, it wouldn't hurt as much if they disappeared or I left.

I finished scrubbing the fridge, drank some water, ate a cracker, and was feeling better when my friend Lauren called. I'd told her about Cedar and finding out I was pregnant, and she'd gotten me an appointment with a woman named Jessica Lanyadoo, an astrologer and psychic medium with a yearlong waiting list and a $325-an-hour price tag. I'd never gone to a psychic before, let alone spent so much on something that felt so ridiculous, but I'd heard about Jessica for years. She was queer with wild curly hair and great red glasses, swore a lot, and dispensed really sound advice. When I googled her I saw she described herself as someone who helped people help themselves and I followed a link to an article she'd written for *Vice*.

"I can hear, see, and feel the dead," she wrote. "From my perspective, our soul doesn't reside in the body; it's the body that lives in the soul. So when the body is done doing what it came here to do, our soul keeps on trucking,"

I liked this but wasn't sure I believed it. I kept picturing Cedar's soft body on the table at the vet hospital. Where was his soul now? "Please God," I muttered, "tell me it's not inside my uterus."

Twelve

Oakland, California, January 2017

Jessica's office was full of plants hanging from macramé cords, crystals of many shapes and sizes, and delicious incense smoking on a windowsill. She asked if I'd found a more exact birth time. Mom had told me her best guess was between two and three forty-five in the morning. When I said this to Jessica she made a clicking sound with her tongue and told me that was actually a pretty big window.

"Not to worry, though," she said, shuffling cards across from me, and then consulting a few different charts. "We'll narrow it down."

"One of your parents is a professional and put a lot of pressure on you and whatever siblings you have to do something, be something?" she asked, peering at me over her glasses.

Was it that obvious? I nodded.

"Okay, that puts us closer to four a.m. Wait. Three, three thirty a.m. . . . Fuck . . . ," she said, looking down at the charts. "Motherfucker." She wasn't angry, just talking to herself.

"I cuss a lot. Does that offend you?"

"Definitely not," I said. Already this was the most fun I'd had in days.

"You grew up in the same house your whole life?" she asked.

"Yes." The ranch. I knew it tree by tree, rock by rock. After Mom and Jake, it was the steadiest thing in my life. Home as long as I'd been conscious. The drawers in my childhood bedroom were still full of my drawings and photos and old sweatpants that were too comfortable to get rid of but too embarrassing to wear anywhere else.

"There was a break-in?"

"No," I said. We'd always left the doors unlocked. It was the safest place I knew. In fact, I brought anything I cared about there for safekeeping—art, jewelry, my favorite books—because the odds of someone breaking into my place in the Bay Area were so much higher.

"Or a fire?"

"Fires," I said. "Plural. But the house never burned down or anything."

"But there were some scary fires?"

"Yeah." But they always veered away. And firefighters showed up to protect us.

She made another clicking sound and looked at me, her eyes a question mark, waiting for me to talk.

I wasn't sure how much to say. If I told her too many details, how would I know she was having any extra insight? Then again, what did I have to lose? I took a deep breath and began.

"Oh God, I'm so sorrrry," Jessica said when I got to the part about Cedar suffocating in the car.

"Then I found out I was pregnant."

Jessica laughed in a shocked way and said, "OH MY GOD."

I told her I didn't know who the father was.

She asked me to say each man's first name aloud.

"Adam. Colt. Julian."

As I spoke, she leaned away from me, and her eyes rolled slightly back and moved from side to side. If she weren't a medium I would've wondered if she was having a seizure.

"The third one," she said quietly, almost to herself, "he doesn't want kids. He is a very serious problem. Julian is some man," she snorted sarcastically. "I've definitely dated butch girls a lot more masculine than this guy."

"Me too," I said.

We both cracked up. It felt good to laugh like this.

"Do you intend to keep the child?"

"That's why I'm here," I whispered.

"Okay. Very big."

Then she changed course.

"What I will say is that Cedar's death, it was an accident. Which he feels very embarrassed by."

I made a sad gulp-laugh sound.

"That was not how he meant to go—

"Hold on," she interrupted herself, and her eyes went side to side again.

Five or ten seconds passed.

"He's going to stay with you. As your companion. But you're not going to always trust that because you're who you are, this is what he's saying."

My nose was snotting up and I sniffled through my tears. I was so skeptical of all of this, but still, it was comforting to imagine him with me. And I really could picture him embarrassed by his death. It was just so shocking and ridiculous. A treat bag. Jessica changed course again.

"Do you want to parent?"

"I don't know," I said softly. "Not babies. I like kids though. Like, if I gave birth to a seven-year-old or a teenager, I'd be thrilled. I figured that maybe I'd adopt someday or fall in love with someone who already had kids. But I'm taking pregnancy vitamins because I don't want to be an irresponsible mom. Even if I don't want to be a mom at all."

It was true. Even if I decided not to keep this pregnancy, I sure as hell wasn't going to be a bad parent while I was one, even in this deeply abstract way, so I'd gone to the drugstore to buy folate, avoiding eye contact with the cashier because if he asked me when I was due I thought I might start wailing.

I've been pro-choice since I was old enough to know what it meant, and I also believe abortions can be a small, quiet snuffing out, not of a person but of possibility. I'd wondered, while choking down the horse-pill vitamins that only made me more nauseous, if taking good care of a fetus only to destroy it weeks later was at all like fattening lambs in springtime. Sitting here now though with Jessica I realized abortion is not a death at all but instead the birth of something else: a chance, shiny and new.

She looked at me. "You don't have to have a baby to be whole."

We sat in silence for a few moments. And then I told her about Connie's vision on the boat, how Cedar came to her, and said he was inside me, inside us. And that Connie had wondered if it meant I'd be pregnant soon. But that no matter what, he was okay.

"That feels one hundred percent accurate," Jessica said.

"Here's the thing, though," I croaked, "I only took the pregnancy test because Connie mentioned it over his body. I'm worried they're connected."

"Well, they ARE connected. Of course they're connected. But that doesn't mean you have to have a baby." She paused.

"This is something you do a lot to yourself, Laurel. You're like, 'Okay, when I crashed my car, I looked up, and there was this person and therefore I should date them for the rest of my life.' NO, no. There is something powerful there, but sometimes the powerful thing is to make a choice. And that choice is sometimes 'no.' "

She continued. "That feeling you have—about finding out you're pregnant right after Cedar dying, about what Connie said to you—that's what I call a rainy day in Portland. This is a stupid metaphor of mine, but you know how in a scary movie it's dark and raining and you're like 'Don't go in the house!' but if the movie takes place in Portland, it's not a sign that something scary is going to happen because it rains there all the time?"

I nodded.

"Evidence! Evidence! Evidence!" she said emphatically. "And that doesn't mean ignore your feelings. It's just that feelings are not definitive data."

"I will say too that you're no good with endings."

I nodded again, tears streaming.

"So, this is going to make you feel terribly depressed. And it's going to change your life one way or another. And that's not a bad thing. But I do not encourage you to evade the loss. Dig a hole. Sit in it. Let yourself be there. You're not going to lose yourself. You will feel like you're losing yourself but you won't. You are resilient. It's just that your depths are really deep, and solo, and scary. So, you feel like you're never going to see light again but then fifteen minutes later you see so much light. You have to remember that about yourself and not rush toward the light. Because there's wisdom in the dark. Stay with the dark. The dark is a huge part of you. I would say some of your best parts are in the dark. And I will say, if you're going to be partnered, you need to tolerate your darkness more. Because you need to stop protecting people from it. It's one of your best parts. Don't fucking hide it. And Julian, this little bitch who I believe got you pregnant, he can't take your darkness. He can't take any woman's darkness."

A half hour later I was back in my car, crossing the Dumbarton Bridge on the way to my office in Palo Alto, when I realized I'd just paid a medium to tell me to pay attention to hard evidence. I laughed.

And then I understood. When I wanted something I went after it. And not halfway. Feeling so ambivalent about having a kid was, for me, actually the feeling of not wanting to have one at all. At least not now. This was my decision and I'd already made it.

In my hopeful scanning for signs, I'd convinced myself, with zero evidence, that having a child would somehow undo the loss of Cedar. And if I was being honest, Dad too. That in some crazy way the kid would bring them back to me. But no. This child would only bring a man I didn't know and couldn't trust into my life, forever. And saddle me with a responsibility so great it took my breath away. Mothering would not prove I was a good person, that I wasn't bad or bound to disappoint the people I loved. I was going to have to figure out how to prove this to myself on my own.

Part III

Inside the word "emergency" is "emerge"; from an emergency new things come forth.

Rebecca Solnit, *Hope in the Dark*

One

Aleutian Islands, Alaska, 2017

One month later, it was February in Dutch Harbor, a time of year when many of the most hard-core residents often prefer to be out of state. It took me four flights to reach the tiny town in the outer reaches of the Aleutian Island chain, roughly nine hundred miles from Anchorage, at the edge of the Bering Sea. I'd flown a lot in the Alaskan bush—doing research on grizzly bear behavior back in college, reporting stories, or on fishing trips with Mom and Jake. But flying into Dutch is special, especially in winter. And by "special" I mean dangerous. Pilots are forced to land in a narrow slot between two large mountains, on a short runway bookended by frigid bodies of water. High winds can knock a plane into a mountain sideways, and if a pilot overshoots or undershoots the tarmac, they're landing in the Bering Sea, where without dry suits, people die of hypothermia in minutes. There are no flights in or out at night and only experienced pilots are cleared to fly there. It took my friend Corey, the *National Geographic* photographer I was on assignment with, three tries to get to Dutch earlier that week. Every day the plane made it all the way to the island and then couldn't land because of high winds and low visibility. So they flew back to Anchorage, six hours round trip. Once I'd had to fly in with a medevac team when commercial flights were grounded, and the pilot had looked over at me and said "Put your spurs on" right before all the terrain alarms started going off and we bucked and jerked close enough to the surrounding mountainsides that I could make out game trails.

I got into town on a freezing February afternoon; Corey was out on a crab boat taking photos, but I wanted to start interviewing. We were doing a story about the town's surprisingly large population of bald eagles, who flocked like seagulls, especially in winter, and took people's groceries in the Safeway parking lot. Once, one flew off with a hiker's cell phone.

My first morning in town I went on KUCB, the local public TV and radio station, to ask folks to reach out to me with their eagle stories. We'd barely signed off before I started getting texts. One man drove over in his snowplow to catch me before I left the parking lot, to tell me about an eagle that liked to sit on his porch railing and watch him eat dinner. Other people called and left me messages about eagles slamming into their windshields or swooping down on their dogs. One woman was attacked at the post office, and then came to the clinic to be stitched up, but before she could get inside, she was attacked again after parking her car.

More than one person told me to speak to a woman named Suzi Golodoff, who knew a lot about local birds. I drove out to her place in the late morning, as a big storm was kicking up out on the bay. Her house was red and wooden, nestled in a line of other charming houses, in the part of town folks often call "Unalaska." The town of Dutch Harbor is split across two islands—the Dutch side of town is on Amaknak Island and has the big commercial port, the hotel, the airport, and most businesses. Unalaska Island has the cemetery, a pizza place, more churches than you'd expect for a town of a few hundred people, the high school, and a few more things, but most of the giant island is wilderness. The two islands are connected by a short bridge. Suzi's place is a few houses from the old Russian Orthodox church, where a bald eagle often sits on the white cross at the top of the tallest cupola like a living weather vane. On windy days like the day I first met her, the Bering Sea spray blows right up against her windows.

Suzi met me at the front door and ushered me into her house full of bird drawings and paintings, pelts, bird books, prayer flags, and what looked like a Buddhist altar. She explained that she'd lived in Dutch for forty years, working to protect and advocate for all birds, not just eagles. "Ben, my husband, and I loved watching them.

"He passed away," she said, noticing me looking around. "A lot of the art and artifacts were from his family. He was Aleut."

Every summer they took a boat out to their fish camp, a half-day's ride around the perimeter of the island. There, they caught and collected all their food. Suzi had kept going after he died, even though everyone told her it was too dangerous. One summer her boat engine broke down and her radio didn't work. She had to hike back to town overland, nine miles through trailless, roadless wilderness, over multiple mountain passes, all by herself.

"Wow." This soft-spoken bird-advocating Buddhist was a badass.

"You've had so many incredible experiences," I said, immediately regretting that I'd used the past tense.

"Nah," she said, laughing. "You just think I'm wise because I'm older than you."

But this wasn't true. I thought about all the kids at Josie's Place, some wise as wizards even though they could barely tie their own shoelaces. Age had nothing to do with it.

"I've made plenty of bad decisions," Suzi said. "In fact, I heard something on a podcast recently about this. It was something like, 'How do you gain wisdom?' "

"How?" I asked.

"With good judgment," she said. "And how do you get good judgment?"

I waited.

"Through bad judgment," she said.

We both cracked up.

"I've heard a similar thing about guilt," she said. "It's that guilt is only really helpful once, in the exact moment where it tells you, 'Oh, I really shouldn't have done that.' As soon as you've had that thought, the guilt should go away because it's not useful anymore. But for some reason, we keep carrying it around with us anyway."

And then my mind was gone from Suzi's house. I was back on the street in San Francisco, opening the car door to Cedar's body. And then I went back further still, kneeling beside my parents' bed while Dad breathed slowly in and out. I was inside the phone booth in my Thacher dorm, slamming the receiver down on the hook as hard as I could.

Guilt was always right there in my peripheral vision waiting for me. And to make sure it stayed there, I set myself up from time to time to let down the people I cared about—all to confirm that what I believed about myself was true. That I deserved to feel bad. Mostly this involved dropping out of text conversations with friends for months and sometimes years, or not calling people back when I knew they needed me. The longer it went, the guiltier I felt and the harder it was to reach out. It was an ouroboros of shame.

"What was it like after Ben died?" I asked. We'd strayed so far away from the interview I'd thought I'd be doing about eagles.

"Well, I told people I was taking a year off and to not expect anything from me. When you lose something big—a person, a job, a place—you have to honor it."

During our Josie's Place training Pat had introduced a concept called the Three Tasks of Grief (based on something called the Four Tasks of Mourning developed by the psychologist J. William Worden). These tasks are, in a way, a reaction to Elisabeth Kübler-Ross's famed stages of grief. Giving people tasks can give them more agency over an experience that feels defined by powerlessness. As Pat explained it to us, the first task is to "Acknowledge the death," the second is to "Feel the feelings (and think the thoughts)," and the third is to "Move the relationship from presence to memory." I was pretty sure Suzi hadn't heard of these theories but here she was, telling me something similar. All the tasks were just different ways of saying honor the death, honor the place this person filled in your life, and figure out how to go forward in this new world without them even though you don't want to. Even though you don't know how.

She poured me a cup of tea, while I stroked a dark brown pelt lying over the arm of her couch. It was the softest thing I'd ever touched.

"Otter," Suzi said. "Aleut hunters have always made the most beautiful things out of those pelts.

"Life gives you stuff that you can handle. You don't think you can. But you can."

This was the kind of thing that other people posted on Instagram over a photo of hikers gazing down from a mountain summit. But when Suzi said it, I didn't want to roll my eyes. It felt helpful, not cringey. Sometimes clichés are cliché for a reason. The best wisdom is basic. So damn obvious that it's easy to glide right on past and miss the timelessness and the truth.

Eventually we said goodbye and I walked back out into the blowing Bering winter, but not before Suzi pressed a few different books into my hands. One was a dictionary of Aleut, or Unangam, words. "'Eagle' in Unangam," Suzi said, "literally means 'to grab.' Isn't that great?"

I smiled at her, nodding, and thanked her for the books and the tea and letting me interview her about much more than birds. When she turned and closed her front door, I walked across the gravel road to the edge of the bay, close enough to get the tips of my boots wet. I wanted to let go of all the useless stuff I'd been carrying around to bludgeon myself with, the guilt and the fear and the regret. There was a brief pause in the howling wind. I took a quick look around to see if I was alone, pulled my arm back as far as I could, and cast a wish like a line into the waves. Please, please, I said silently into the spray, let me eagle on to something new.

Two

Dutch Harbor, Alaska, February 2017

Corey made it back to port on the morning of my thirty-ninth birthday. I drove to the top of the hill on the Unalaska side of town, not far from where Suzi's husband was buried, and watched his ship come in. The ice was so thick on the deck it looked like a sculpture. After he unloaded his gear, we spent the rest of the day doing exactly what I wanted to be doing on my birthday: driving around town in our borrowed red Jeep, interviewing boat captains and crew members, and stalking eagles perched on the edge of dumpsters behind the Grand Aleutian Hotel tearing through trash bags looking for meat.

There's a common saying in town that there's a woman behind every tree. In this part of the Aleutian Islands, there are no trees. Just being in Dutch as a female can feel like being famous. Sometimes you walk into a room and conversation pauses, all eyes swinging toward you. It can be disconcerting and makes me self-conscious, but I'd be lying if I said I didn't enjoy it sometimes. All that week, though, at the Rat, the most popular bar (out of two in town—three if you count the sushi bar next to the liquor store), I avoided talking to anyone. Men wanting me still felt like something I needed to protect myself from. I was back in high school again, scared of my body and what it wanted, while simultaneously wanting to be wanted really badly. I wrapped myself up in invisible bubble wrap and duct tape and avoided making eye contact.

Valentine's Day was three days after Corey and I started reporting. I wouldn't have noticed if I hadn't woken up to him trying to shoot a video for his Norwegian girlfriend, featuring the obese tiger-striped cat named Lillard who lived in the house where we were staying. He was shooting selfie style with a paper heart in his hand.

"Morning, Corey," I said. "Morning, Carpet Walrus," which is what I called Lillard.

"Want some coffee?"

"When I'm done here," he said, looking up from the floor where he was now rubbing Lillard's belly, "I'd love to get some shots of the *Arctic Lady*, unloading crab."

I had a few files to upload for the editors of my story, who wanted to talk. But my phone wasn't working, so I told Corey I'd be at the Grand Aleutian where there may be better satellite signal, and he could meet me there. I dressed for our day outside, my plaid hat with the wool earflaps, long underwear, my brown rubber Xtratuf boots, old jeans, and a dark green plaid flannel, all underneath my puffy down coat. My hair was bent at odd angles and dry from the heat that blasted indoors, but looking at myself in the mirror, I figured it didn't matter. The Grand Aleutian had a fancy name but the fanciest thing about it were the eagles in the parking lot and the price tag. The hotel cost over three hundred dollars a night as it was the only joint in town, full of folks coming in from crabbing trips or heading out to sea, plus a few *Deadliest Catch* camera crews drinking overpriced Alaskan Ambers in the bar and ordering nineteen-dollar halibut sandwiches.

That morning, though, I was the only one in the hotel café. I chose a table where I could look out the window. It was almost 11 a.m. and finally getting light. I could see a dozen sea otters bobbing in the water. Overhead, at least as many eagles circled. I ordered an omelet and began transferring audio files onto an external hard drive.

While I worked, I chatted with the kind Filipina waitress and asked if there was any news about the F/V *Destination*. Everyone was talking about it. The boat went down on my birthday. The crew was six men, ranging in age from twenty-nine to sixty. The skipper was one of the most experienced working out of Dutch that year. But experience didn't always protect you up here.

The *Destination*'s distress signal had never gone out, which meant the boat had probably rolled. There's no way to survive something like that. The pressure of the water on the windows and doors makes them impossible to open from the inside. The men most likely hung there, upside down, in the dark, before the water eventually rushed in. Now they were presumed dead. The boat hadn't been found.

I caught movement out of the corner of my eye and looked up.

A tall man, six foot five or six, walked in, wearing the Bering Sea uniform: Xtratufs, navy blue hoodie from Alaska Ship Supply, beanie, except instead of gray sweatpants tucked into his boots, which is what most of the fishermen wore, he wore jeans. And instead of the standard-issue overstuffed JanSport, he was carrying a giant backpacking backpack that he set down with a thud next to a table by the window. He looked like a combination of crabber and college student heading out on a Eurail Pass.

He glanced at me and I noticed his dark scruff and long eyelashes. He didn't have the sallow look of many of the men in town who worked in the fish-processing plants all day, or the hungry, wolfy gaze of the cod-fishing or crabbing crews returning after weeks at sea, the men who catcalled me from the boats but got too nervous to speak when I approached them to ask questions about birds.

I gave a slight nod and went back to what I was doing.

The man went to the lunch buffet, which they'd just opened, filled his plate, and walked back to his table. He was sitting in my direct eyeline. It seemed awkward not to say anything since we were the only people in the place. Also, now that he was sitting in the brightening light from the window, I could see he was beautiful.

Talktohimtalktohim, I urged myself. Momentarily forgetting the bubble wrap.

"How's the buffet?" I asked. "Worth it?" It was wildly expensive for what would be a basic, budget breakfast anywhere less remote. But that was Dutch.

I was glad the waitress had already cleared my plate. I didn't want this man to think I was making up questions just to talk to him, even though I apparently was.

He looked relieved I'd said something. His eyes were blue as glacier water.

"It could be worse," he said, smiling. "It *has* been worse."

I laughed.

"My name is Josh," he said, putting down his fork.

We talked for less than twenty minutes but I learned that he'd grown up in a family of fishermen who fished out of Kodiak, and that he'd spent more than a decade after 9/11 learning Arabic and living in the Middle East. He'd done a Fulbright in Jordan, run an English-language magazine in Yemen, and been in Egypt during the Arab Spring. Josh came back to the US not long after and now he worked for a large seafood company that owned one of those giant fish-processing boats out by the spit where Corey and I had been hanging out. A floating factory festooned with eagles.

He said he was based in Seattle. I said that he should come to the live show I'd be doing there. I'd be sharing the eagle story, part of a live *Pop-Up Magazine* tour. Soon Corey walked in and he and Josh talked about people they had in common. Corey scarfed down his breakfast, Josh finished his lunch and told us he was shipping out with a female cod fisherman on a boat called *The Progress*, but if they couldn't get out because of weather, we should all grab a drink. I wondered, briefly, if he thought Corey and I were dating.

We all stood up to say goodbye. Josh gave me his card and I gave him mine.

"Email me," he urged.

I smiled and nodded politely but honestly didn't consider it. Striking up a conversation was one thing, but reaching out over email was something else. I could barely hear him from inside the bubble wrap anyway, which had closed back over me like a shroud.

Three

Dutch Harbor, Alaska, February 2017

A week later, I was booked on the last flight of the day out of Dutch. It was nearly dark even though it was barely 4 p.m. The cloud cover was thick, and a light snow fell on the eagles perched on the lampposts in the airport parking lot. Miraculously, my flight was going out anyway. Corey was staying a few more days and I hugged him goodbye. As I walked to the plane, I looked at the half dozen more eagles sitting on the roofline of the terminal and flashed them a peace sign.

The pilot gunned it up past Mount Ballyhoo and then arced around another set of craggy snowcapped peaks rising straight out of the ocean. Rain and snow streamed past my window, and I felt the acceleration in my stomach. Suddenly, we broke through a final bank of clouds and a blaze of light shot through the cabin, startling all of us. It was so bright my eyes watered. Dutch Harbor had vanished beneath the soft gray carpet beneath us, and every direction was sparkly crystalline. Deep, deep blue as far as I could see.

I was bleeding still. Almost as much as a period, even though the abortion was nearly three weeks ago now. I still got occasional gut-wrenching twinges of pain too. But they were getting less frequent. Blessedly the nausea was also totally gone. I felt a wave of gratitude to not be pregnant, to not have had to handle the smells of fish and garbage the last two weeks on a seasick stomach. I shuddered at the thought and blinked in the sudden sunlight, remembering something I'd heard in New Zealand on a trip with my family, nearly ten years earlier.

Mom, Sam, Jake, and I went there for my friend Auriga's wedding. She'd fallen in love with a sweet, rugged Kiwi on a beach in Greece and they were getting married at his family's sheep station. Afterward, my family traveled around the South Island. I tried to pay attention to the beauty of the place—so affrontingly lovely with its waterfalls and fern trees and parrots that liked to break into cars. But my marriage was falling apart. I was also in my second year of graduate school, studying for my general exams, which meant reading at least a book a day for an entire year, and then a week of grueling daylong tests on the material, plus a three- to six-hour oral exam with my committee. I woke up at night, gasping, trying to outrun myself. "Nothing lasts, Laurel," the voice in my head shouted over and over. "Not love, not life. You are going to fail."

The divorce had been my decision, but I was still terrified that no one would ever love me like my husband had. And the less I slept, the more I worried. It felt like a nervous breakdown or an early midlife crisis. Just before the trip, I'd gotten myself into therapy for the first time, with a kind woman who had a practice a few T stops away from my basement office in Cambridge.

"Sometimes when you speak," she'd said, "I feel like I'm with an eighty-year-old woman, not someone who's barely out of her twenties. You talk as if death is right around the corner."

We were halfway through the New Zealand trip, filing onto a bus that would take my family to see yet another gorgeous waterfall that I would barely notice through my anxiety goggles. Mom was ahead of me and she paused, turning to the driver who was standing at the base of the stairs leading onto the bus, offering her his hand. It had just begun to rain.

"Too bad about the weather," she said, looking up at the low gray ceiling.

The man grinned.

"It's actually quite nice out, ma'am. It's just that sometimes clouds get between us and the sun."

Mom and I both laughed then. And sat down on the bus reminiscing about all those times we flew as a family in the old Cessna, breaking through a cloud ceiling into something epic and sunny. Ever since, I'd thought about what the bus driver said. Remembering the sun is shining on the other side of the clouds is a lot like remembering that you're going to die but haven't yet. And now, sitting in this cabin so suddenly flooded with light, I leaned back against my seat and thought about it again. Maybe once in a while I could just enjoy the warmth.

Four

Seattle, Washington, March 2017

Our live *Pop-Up Magazine* tour made it to Seattle a month after I got back from Dutch. The sore throat and conjunctivitis I'd picked up sometime between the D.C. and Austin shows had dried up, my sinuses stopped making weird noises, and I finally wasn't bleeding from the abortion. I'd also had two email exchanges with Josh, the guy from the lunch buffet. He'd offered to lead me to some bourbon when I was in town and so we made plans to meet up the night before the show. He still hadn't mentioned a wife or girlfriend, but I knew better than to assume he was single.

I'd told my friends that I didn't care whether it was a date, but I wasn't fooling anyone. Least of all myself. My ill-fated sexual rumspringa felt like a long time ago now. I wanted a date and I wanted it to be with someone I liked, maybe even someone I could see myself with for more than a night or a handful of months.

It was raining hard in Seattle, so I wore a dress with a pair of rubber boots. I figured since we'd met in the Aleutian Islands, Josh probably wasn't expecting me to show up in heels. I was doing a final check in the mirror before heading out when I realized the dress was see-through. I grabbed a slip, nude-colored and matronly, that fell past my knees. Just as well, I thought. An incentive to keep my clothes on.

When my Uber pulled onto Ballard Avenue, Josh was already

waiting on the wet sidewalk, his hands in his coat pockets. He was even taller than I remembered. And more handsome than I remembered too. He seemed nervous. This was sweet. He sort of didn't know where to put his hands as we walked. I could also hear it in his voice—which was deep but also a little quavery. He suggested we cross the street to a bar that a friend of a friend managed. We threaded through clutches of people in dark rain jackets waiting for tables and went to a back room with flickering votives and ordered old fashioneds. His favorite drink too.

He lit up telling me about his life in the Middle East—there was the magazine he'd edited but also a rock climbing and backpacking club he'd founded. He told me stories about being recruited to play professional basketball on a Yemeni team and about the time he'd taken a delegation of Yemeni Special Olympians to Boise, Idaho, to participate in the winter games. In the Arab Spring, a few weeks after protestors took to the streets in Yemen, Josh was kicked out during a governmental purge of foreign journalists. From there, he went to Egypt and then eventually came home to work in Alaska but spent the winters in Nicaragua. Now, though, he was tired of always being on the move. He wanted to set roots down in the US again and stop working seasonally. He said he wasn't entirely sure what he saw for himself in the future, but it probably didn't involve what many other people considered a normal life for a grown-up: marriage, 2.5 kids, a house.

"You sound like a wild horse," I said. "That's what I am too."

But I felt a small twinge. Here was another man I wouldn't be building a life with.

"To wild horses," he said, lifting his bourbon.

"To wild horses," I said, clinking my glass against his.

The truth was that I wasn't sure I still wanted to be one. I wanted to be independent and wild and in a herd at the same time. I had a feeling we disagreed about this, but I tamped down my thoughts. I was on a date with a gorgeous, enchanting man whom I'd met at the edge of the

Bering Sea and I just wanted to enjoy myself. He didn't have to be my husband. We ordered another round.

Our conversation was breathless and easy, and we forgot we were supposed to sit down for dinner. When we finally did, the food could have been anything. It was the kind of night where everything else becomes two-dimensional, like the backdrop in old hand-drawn cartoons. Later we walked to another bar with exposed brick and poorly taxidermied animals. We played Skee-Ball and sat down at a rickety wooden table, watching a bachelorette party across from us that was oddly silent. At some point, he moved to sit next to me and I put my hand on his thigh. I didn't think much of it. I had my slip on, like beige-colored chain mail.

We talked some more, and then he invited me back to his apartment, a few blocks away. I could tell it was still new, a lot of his shelves were empty. But not his bookshelves. I scanned the titles while he dug in his cabinets for wineglasses. There were at least a dozen books about fish and writing. I had my own copies of nearly every one. His couch was what impressed me most, though. It was a tweedy sectional, the kind he must have measured the room for and special ordered, or at least gone into a furniture store to look at. I quickly tapped out a text to my friend Samin. She's a famous chef and author now, but we became friends ten years before all that, when we shared a drafty writing space in the Marin Headlands, dreaming about writing books someday. Now we are basically family. Of course she knew I was out on this date.

Omg he has a couch with THROW PILLOWS.

Laurrrrreeeeel, she wrote back immediately, *you need a higher bar.*

I wanted to tell her that I didn't care about the couch, not really. It was that the couch was proof that this man knew what he wanted, at least when it came to upholstery. But before I could explain myself, Josh walked over with wine, set the glasses down on the floor next to us, and kissed my neck, holding the back of my head with one hand and my lower back with the other, pulling me against him.

Soon I was straddling his lap and we were kissing like I'd never kissed anyone before. I let him envelop me with a hunger I recognized. It was just like mine. His hands on my back, his mouth on my neck, my nipples between his teeth. It was so good it made me dizzy. After a while he asked me if I wanted to get into bed with him and I said I would but that I wouldn't have sex. I thought of my granny slip, my plan to protect myself from myself. From him. From anyone leaving, including me. From disappointment. He just nodded.

Then we were in his bed. On our knees looking at each other. And before I could push his hands away, he lifted my dress over my head.

"What is *that*?" he said, looking at the wide expanse of nude polyester in wonder.

"Self-control," I said, laughing. "Or it used to be."

He pushed me gently onto my back and pulled it slowly off of me.

We made out for what felt like hours and eventually we were both naked. The feeling of his skin on mine made me drunker than I already was. His mouth on my neck. I wanted him so badly it felt like an earthquake, like the plates of my body were grinding against each other in pleasure.

Forget your rules, I told myself. You may regret this. But you may regret not doing this more.

So I whispered, "Yes, please, yes," and he reached into his bedside drawer for a condom.

It was incredible. He was confident and strong and knew just how to touch me. Like he was holding on to me for a reason. Like he didn't want to let go. Focused.

Afterward we lay next to each other in the dark, breathing, and I felt a small wave of panic. Why had I slept with him? It felt so good but was I going to regret this? Josh got up to go to the bathroom. While he was gone, I put my clothes back on and opened Uber on my phone.

He appeared again as I was tapping in his address. Pausing in the doorway to the bedroom, in his underwear, he looked at me. "What are you doing?"

"Calling a car. I know you have to get up early. And I have to perform tomorrow."

He raised an eyebrow, walked toward me, and gently took the phone from my hand, setting it facedown on the edge of his bedside table.

"It's two a.m. Get back in bed. I want to do this again in the morning." Then he kissed my forehead and pulled my dress off over my head.

I let him tumble me into his light blue sheets. It felt good, but confusing. I could still feel my heart racing. Would it be weird in the morning? I thought you were supposed to leave a one-night stand.

I barely slept, electrified by his presence. Half-drunk and curious. He continued to wake up during the night and every time he did, he kissed my forehead before rolling over and falling back asleep. I couldn't remember the last time a man had kissed my forehead.

All throughout the next day he sent me texts about how much he wanted to slip off my slip, and then he came to the *Pop-Up* show. It was a packed house, and while I waited backstage, I thought about him out there in the dark. It felt good even though it was also a little embarrassing because so many of my friends were there too, watching us on our date. We went to the afterparty for five minutes and then decided to go back to my room and order room service.

The tray of tuna sashimi, a salmon burger, and hummus sat on the carpeted floor between us like a picnic. Our backs to the big windows that overlooked the bright lights of the Seattle skyline.

I asked him when his last relationship was and he told me about the Nicaraguan woman he'd dated for the last couple of years, in between Alaska summers. They'd broken up in June.

"It's rare that I get into relationships." Then he turned away from the view to look at me directly and asked, "Do you date often?"

This made me laugh. "I guess so?"

But inside I felt a small balloon pop. I'd gotten my hopes up despite telling myself not to. I guess it will just be this, I thought, and hugged my knees to my chest, still in the black two-piece suit I'd worn to the show.

Josh shrugged. "It's just hard with my lifestyle going back and forth to Alaska, being gone every summer. I haven't had much stability."

"But wouldn't two wild horses together be amazing?" I said. "Provided they could make it work."

He looked skeptical. I shrugged off the conversation and tried to tell myself I could be someone who enjoyed one-off weekends with attractive men without having to make it into anything more.

He slid the room service tray across the floor, out of our way, and leaned over to kiss me. "Come to bed," he said.

We were wrapped up in each other, my breath against his ear, his mouth on my neck, when I said, against my better judgment, "I'd be excited to get to know you better, Josh."

I cringed.

"Is that what you want?" he said, pulling back a little bit to look at me. "I think there's a place for you in my life in some way."

I immediately stiffened, picturing myself like a secondhand ottoman he moved around his living room, trying to find a spot for.

My heart cooled ten degrees.

He must have sensed something because he pressed his lips to my ear and said, "I am a big Laurel Braitman fan."

"In some way?" I said, trying not to sound defensive. I didn't want a fan. I wanted a partner.

"You misheard me." But before he could try to take anything back, we were having sex again and whatever we said or didn't say just hung there till it faded away entirely.

• • •

The next morning Josh took a quick shower and I gave him a granola bar for the road.

"You're here for the weekend?" he said, unwrapping the bar and pulling his leather messenger bag over his shoulder.

"Yep. Going to go to Bainbridge Island to visit my friend Jon and his family."

"Will you be back in the city?"

"It depends," I said hesitantly. I felt like this should be it. I liked Josh but didn't want to keep liking him if this was a two-night stand. I was anxious to seal off our time together, to contain it in a way that its inevitable ending would be as painless as possible.

"I'd love to see you . . . get dinner, anything," he said.

"How about Saturday night? That gives me some time with my friends, but we could still see each other before I fly out the next day."

"Sounds good. Let me know when you know what ferry you're on. I'd really like to see you again, Laurel."

"Me too," I said. And I meant it, but I was doubtful. Maybe this was a charade we'd both done before. Trying to be the people we weren't. Making plans to see each other even though we knew it wouldn't happen. Even though our hearts could have galloped somewhere new and different. Even though it would probably end before it began.

Five

Seattle, Washington, March 2017

Saturday afternoon I walked off the ferry from Bainbridge and Josh was waiting for me at the end of the dock. He'd texted multiple times to confirm. Every time he did, I told myself to check my expectations like I was tugging a steel bit across my heart.

I spotted him before he saw me and paused to watch him scan the crowd. The only other person who looked for me like that was Mom. I felt a nervous bolt of pleasure. And then immediately checked myself. Don't have any expectations. Do NOT.

I waved. It was awkward for a moment. The intimacy of people who are more than strangers but the more is still a question with no floor and no ceiling. He said he wanted to take me to Elliott's Oyster House and scooped up my rolling green suitcase as we headed down the stairs from the terminal. We got seats at the bar and looked at the long oyster list. His favorite were from Hump Island and we ordered them to try. We also got cold glasses of white wine and before I knew it I was telling him about Dad. Then he told me about his mom. She'd been diagnosed with breast cancer when he was thirteen. His parents had tried to shelter Josh and his four siblings from the pain of her illness, sharing very little about what was going on. But they still watched her feel sick, get chemo, radiation, and surgery. As the oldest kids, Josh and his sister stepped up to take care of the rest, packing their siblings' lunches and babysitting while their mom was in treatment and their dad was fishing in Alaska, for months at a time. Then one day his mom told them she was in remission. He still didn't know when or how it had happened exactly.

When I'd talked to Donna Schuurman at the Dougy Center, she'd said that it's important not to keep kids in the dark or they start to fear it. I wondered what living with this kind of uncertainty had done to Josh. Our parents had taken opposite approaches. Dad said goodbye to us again and again and I'd learned details about targeted radiation therapy and chemotherapeutics when I was barely old enough to read. It was a lot, too much maybe, but I was glad I'd known. Even if what I'd known was hard. I'll always be someone who wants to know. But there was and is no right way to do any of this. Not sharing information isn't always the same as hiding it.

By our second glass of wine Josh and I were talking about our own deaths. Like me, he had a feeling he'd die young too, but wasn't sure why. If he did get old, Josh said he wanted to say his goodbyes and then go to the island of Socotra off the coast of Yemen, get in a rowboat, and just push himself out to sea.

"I don't want to go too quickly. I want to really experience what it's like to die, to feel it."

I headed to the bathroom to put on more lipstick and decided that this was the best date conversation I'd had in years.

Josh paid the check and we headed to Elliott Bay Books where we walked up and down the aisles, pulling out our favorite things to show each other. It felt just like taking our clothes off had, piece by piece, exposing ourselves. He bought me *The Fault in Our Stars* because when I'd told him about Josie's Place he said the kids in the book, Hazel Grace and Augustus Waters, were dealing with mortality and death too.

Back at his apartment we had sex in the big blue ocean of his bed. Afterward, we lay there naked while he read aloud to me from the book. I felt as if I'd fallen through a trapdoor into another dimension, listening to his deep baritone, feeling his strong arm under my head. *Wild horse, wild horse, wild horse*, I tried to remind myself. *He said he's not looking for a relationship. Just be in the moment. Enjoy this for what it is*. It felt exquisitely painful and also exquisitely good.

I was supposed to fly back to California the next day. When I started packing first thing in the morning, I was already late. "I've got to leave soon or I'm going to miss my flight," I said, looking over at Josh who was still in bed.

"What flight?" he said in fake puzzlement. "You mean the one you're changing so you can stay another day?"

I laughed.

"I have to go to something today you might like," he said. "It's called the Blessing of the Fleet. Be my date?"

Laurel, I hissed at myself, *say no. You know this is just for fun. Let him break someone else's heart*. But my mouth betrayed me.

"Sure," I said, putting my bag back down. "Why not?"

Six

Seattle, Washington, March 2017

At Fishermen's Terminal, a commercial boat harbor in Josh's neighborhood, a forest of masts bobbed above the calm water of the marina. We joined a small crowd leaning into the wind and the light rain in front of a tall bronze monument. At the base, salmon, halibut, and flounder were frozen mid-swim. At the top, a fisherman lifted a large halibut toward the sky. Josh explained that this was a memorial to the members of Seattle's commercial fishing community who'd been lost at sea. There was a pile of flower bouquets on the ground, still in their grocery store cellophane, unopened cans of Jolly Roger beer, and greeting cards going soft in the rain.

A pastor walked up to a makeshift podium in front of us, wearing a cassock embroidered with a ship on a bright blue ocean. He motioned to the pile of flowers. Today's ceremony, he said, was especially for the men of the F/V *Destination* and their families. This was the boat that had gone down on my birthday out of Dutch Harbor. I had no idea those men had been from here. I heard someone start crying softly behind me.

The boat had eventually been found. An investigation would show that they'd hit terrible weather and the boat flipped and sank. The crew's families would never have bodies to bury.

"A lot of these folks are commercial fishermen," Josh whispered, motioning to the people around us. "Every year this blessing happens before the start of the spring season. A lot of these boats are headed up to Dutch. Or other places in Alaska."

The sound of his voice went straight to my center where it vibrated. If I concentrated, I could still feel him inside me. I felt used up, in a good way. We'd tried to leave his apartment for coffee, the farmers' market, and Bloody Marys that morning, but we couldn't . . . not before having sex again. My skin felt new. My body felt purposeful. I'd experienced that feeling before playing sports—blocking shots as a goalie, or muscling through the end of a 2k crew race in college, but all of it paled in comparison to how it felt to be in my body with Josh.

Another man walked up to the podium, from the Ballard First Lutheran Church, and started the invocation. "Holy Creator, whose way is in the sea . . . say to the waves, 'Peace. Be still.' You hold the human heart in the hollow of your hand . . ."

I pictured Dad holding people's hearts in his hands and knew how much he'd appreciate talking to the fishermen here. And then I said a silent prayer of my own, for the person crying behind me, for the son- or brother- or partner- or friend-shaped hole inside them they'd be living with forever now. The big sneaker waves of grief I knew would follow them on and off the water till the end of their days.

A chorus sang a few hymns, trying to be heard over the sound of the keyboard that was amplified to stadium levels, even though we were standing in a small circle. Eventually, the pastor welcomed a state senator, Reuven Carlyle, to say a few words. "It is our community's sacred obligation to protect our ships and crews," he said. "And to do so with the unimpeachable power of love . . . We pray that you may have more days of wonder than hardship . . ."

Someone else spoke afterward, but I was stuck on what the senator said. The unimpeachable power of love. More days of wonder than hardship. I so badly wanted this to be possible. To know love like a life preserver instead of a storm.

I couldn't imagine it for myself but I knew it could happen because

I'd watched Mom fall in love again after Dad died. And then after her second husband died too. She'd sworn up and down to Jake and me that she'd never marry again. That everyone she loved got sick and she didn't want to doom any more men. But she was only sixty. So alive—her goofy lit-up self—and so beautiful still that people approached us in restaurants and at Home Depot just to tell her that she was a knockout. She had so much life ahead of her. Then, despite herself, she'd fallen in love with Sam.

I looked over at Josh. He had his camera out, waiting for the light to shift, illuminating the pastor and the ships behind him.

Letting myself fall for someone after knowing the truth—that they can be taken away for no good reason at all—felt dangerous. Sometimes there *weren't* more days of wonder than hardship. Sometimes things sucked and then stayed that way. Sure, Mom's experience was an example to the contrary, or so I thought back then, but who knew if she was the exception or the rule. I might never know for sure if the path was safe and I was supposed to forge ahead regardless. Where was the blessing for this kind of hazard?

I wiggled my toes in my rain-drenched shoes and tried to stop myself from reaching for Josh's hand.

Seven

Oakland, California, April 2017

I'd been back home for a few days when I went to a therapy appointment. I'd found Judy after Cedar died, realizing that I needed professional help to get through that and the pregnancy. She was kind and motherly, like a warm and insightful Jewish aunt. I told her all about Josh. How even after I'd gotten home, he kept calling. Every night he read aloud to me, over the phone. We were almost done with *The Fault in Our Stars*, and he wanted me to come back to Seattle the next weekend, so we could finish the book in person. I was letting myself get excited but also trying desperately not to. It was too early to have any sort of talk about what we were doing but the uncertainty was killing me.

"There's a Yiddish word that's pretty perfect for this," Judy said. "Mishegoss!"

"I'm very familiar with mishegoss," I said, thinking of Mom, my aunts, my grandparents. *Craziness*. Especially in the face of loss. We all had it. Like a blood type.

"You can just tell him, 'This is my mishegoss, but I start to get scared about people disappearing. And it makes me anxious.' You don't need to ask him for anything or ask him to fix it. You are just telling him where you're coming from."

My first and only therapist till then, the one I'd seen in Boston during my divorce, had said that I needed to be "more me" not "less me."

I'd had no idea what she meant at the time. But now maybe I was starting to get it.

"Well, I'm not fully opening my heart yet," I said.

Judy raised her eyebrows.

"I think it's too late for that. You can't control it, Laurel. And that's okay."

I groaned. "It's not okay. This is terrible."

I slumped down, farther into her leather couch, but I was smiling.

Our session ended and I wrote out my check. I was standing up to leave when she said, "I want you to know that what you're doing is really brave."

"Really?"

"Yes. A lot of people would have retreated after what you've been through, and this is very much NOT retreating."

"Yeah, this is more like diving in," I said, laughing. "I am really scared of getting my heart broken, though."

"That's why I think it's brave. If you're not scared then you can't have courage."

I wanted to tell Judy something else but we were out of time. A few weeks earlier I'd been tagging along on rounds in the cardiac ICU at Stanford. We'd just left the room of a woman recovering from an angioplasty when the attending physician said the phrase "cardiac memory" in passing, to one of the residents.

"Wait," I said, as we hurried down the corridor, "you mean the heart muscle actually remembers things? Not as a metaphor but literally?"

"Yes," he said.

Later, the resident explained to me that cardiac memory refers to a time after a period of arrhythmia, when your heartbeats stay weird and jumpy, even though there's no longer any reason for them to be abnormal. I looked it up myself and realized it's an old idea. Medieval

Christians believed that our hearts had memories too and not only that, but inside each one was a book. They called it the book of the heart. Our deeds, bad and good, were recorded there. Ancient Egyptians believed something similar—that our hearts kept their own records and could testify against us. A heart was weighed at death, and if it was light with goodness one could go on to the afterlife. If it was heavy with misdeeds, then you were doomed to the underworld. This is where the idea of heavy- and lightheartedness comes from.

Bravery is tied up in this too. Cor/cordis is Latin for "heart." It's baked into the word "courage." Recordari has a heart root as well. The word is Latin for "remembering," the mother of our word *record*. If the English language had taken just a slightly different turn we might say "I heart" instead of "I remember." Instead, we say "take heart" when we want someone to feel a little bit braver.

Eight

Lake Como, Italy, April 2017

The spring before I met Josh I'd been offered a residency by the Rockefeller Foundation at their villa in Bellagio, Italy, on the shores of Lake Como. It was an honor like I'd never had before. An entire month to write, with all my meals cooked for me, and my own private writing studio with a view of the lake. We were told to bring formal clothing for dinner every evening. And spouses or domestic partners were welcome. I'd been looking forward to it for a year.

Josh was going to be in Norway on business while I was in Italy and had some vacation time saved up. I knew I wasn't supposed to bring someone I'd only been dating for a few weeks. The application made that clear but I invited him anyway, hoping it wouldn't jinx us. He said yes and planned to come for two of the four weeks of my residency.

And so, in early May, I limped out of a taxi in front of the Villa Serbelloni, hunched and rumpled. I'd packed all my journals and notebooks from childhood and high school to write from. I'd been too paranoid to check them in my baggage in case they got lost, so I'd filled my carry-on and was lifting it into the overhead bin when I felt my lower back give way. By the time we were halfway across the Atlantic it was spasming so badly I couldn't stand up from my seat. The pain was so intense it made me nauseous and sweaty. A flight attendant saw me grimacing and trying to rearrange myself and bent down to ask if I was okay.

"I know it sounds silly," I said, "but I can't really sit down and I can't stand up."

"Oh, the back," she said, in a clipped but warm British accent. "Happens to me too. Follow me."

I gingerly lifted myself out of my seat and made my way down the aisle. She drew a curtain across a small alcove between the bathroom and the emergency exit and spread an airline blanket down on the floor. "Lay here and try to do some stretches. My husband is crew up in first class. He has something that will help. I'll be right back."

I was too grateful to speak. I didn't care that people coming and going from the bathroom could see me below the hem of the curtain, or that the floor peeking out from under the blanket was sticky with pieces of stray toilet paper. I looked up at the plasticky ceiling of the cabin and thought about how ironic it was that I'd hurt myself trying to lift the literal weight of my childhood.

When the attendant came back she pressed a slim red plastic package into my right hand. "It's a heat patch from Boots," she said. "Stick it on your lower back and stay here as long as you need. I can also give you some anti-inflammatories, if you like."

My eyes filled with tears.

"I was scared to check what's in my carry-on," I said, trying to explain, "but I made it too heavy. I shouldn't have lifted it by myself. It was so stupid."

"Oh honey," she said, "everyone does that. Carrying more than they know what to do with."

At the villa, a smiling man in a cream uniform with shiny gold buttons opened my taxi door and didn't blink when he saw me inch out, bent at the waist like a fairy-tale crone. "Buona notte. Signorina Braitman?"

"Yes," I said. "Grazie."

He called to another dark-haired man in the same uniform, who whisked my luggage away.

"Follow me. You have missed dinner but we saved you a tray. I will let you settle in and then bring it to your room. Vino?"

I followed the man up a wide staircase, past a series of antique Chinese vases almost as tall as me. Embroidered tapestries hung floor to ceiling alongside twinkling sconces. Thick carpet muffled our steps. On the walls were engravings of the lake and people sailing small boats along the shoreline. There were paintings that looked like they belonged in the Uffizi or somewhere else fancy and well guarded, certainly not in the same house as me.

"This is your room," the man said, pointing to a name tag slid into a slot on the thick wooden door. DR. LAUREL BRAITMAN.

I followed him inside and stopped breathing.

The sun was setting, and golden light angled through the tall French doors into my bedroom and adjoining writing studio, each with its own balcony. There was a simple white-clothed bed, a wide wooden desk, and empty bookshelves waiting for me to fill.

The man in the uniform smiled at my shock and said he'd be back soon with my dinner.

I opened both sets of doors and walked out onto the balcony off the studio, too overwhelmed to do anything but gape. The sky was pink and purple over the mountains. I stood right where the fingers of Lake Como met and spread out on either side of a promontory dotted with more villas, blooming gardens, deep-green forest, and narrow roads. I could see the winding driveway my taxi had just climbed, lined with cypress trees. I saw red-roofed villas and houses in tiny pockets all around the lake, the nearly hidden churches tucked in at the tops of the mountains, and in the distance, the snow-capped peaks of the Alps. The gardens down below were full of blooming roses and twisting purple wisteria. As I listened to the chugging boat motors out on the lake, the clanging of the church bells carrying over the water, I thought about how Ernest Hemingway and Mark Twain had written here. The air smelled like night-blooming jasmine and water. This was heaven. Of course it came with a writing studio.

• • •

A few days later I was taking a shower in the black-and-white-tiled bathroom when I heard a text come in. I hoped it was Josh, and felt a kind of slow spreading delight and I thought about my therapist, Judy.

I'd gone to see her before I'd left and told her about how amazing my time with Josh had been. We'd seen each other a few times now, in Seattle and in the Bay Area too. But I'd also been feeling some anxiety because he invited me to visit him on his work trip in Norway. I'd bought a ticket to Oslo, but this would mean I would have to leave my residency for four days and that didn't feel right. I'd been looking forward to this for ages and knew it would be over in a flash. I didn't want to leave, and I regretted telling Josh I would. As soon as I'd bought the ticket, I realized that I'd done it not because I was excited to go but because I was scared about what would happen if I didn't. I'd been midsentence explaining all of this to Judy when she stopped me.

"Hold on right there."

"What?"

"Your face. When you told me about your guilt and worry it was like you morphed into a tiny child. Even your body language. Can you tell me what was going on with you just then? What is that feeling like and does it remind you of anything?"

No one had asked me this before.

"Sure," I said. "I'm super familiar with that feeling. It feels bad. And shameful. Guilty, really."

"And when have you felt that way before?"

"With my family." I paused. "With my mom."

"Why?"

"I just don't want to disappoint her. I didn't want to disappoint my dad either. I feel a lot of shame. Because I know I *did* disappoint him."

"Josh is not your mom or dad," Judy said slowly. "This relationship is very different from your relationship with your parents, and here's a chance for you to learn that you can say to Josh, 'You know I am so excited to be with you and I want to do this but I feel like I really need to focus on my work,' and then see what he does. Let him teach you that it's safe to do that."

I sat there, trying to take this in.

"It's not real intimacy," she said, "if you are trying to take care of his feelings. Real intimacy is you saying how you feel, even if it's something you think he's not going to like hearing. Not doing so isn't fair to him. You can then listen to him say that he doesn't like your decision, or that he's upset or sad, but that doesn't mean you've done something wrong. Does that make sense?"

During our appointment I'd said it did. But it hadn't. Not really. Now, though, standing in this Italian bathroom under the hot water, the phrase "the Big Guilt" floated into my mind. The Big Guilt may have been lots of little guilts as a kid and adolescent but had congealed into a giant soul-crushing boulder the day Dad died.

At one of our Josie's Place training sessions Pat had announced offhandedly that we'd be covering "guilt" that afternoon and we'd all laughed, but then Pat and Andrea had gotten serious.

"Kids often feel responsible for a death," Andrea said, "even when they know intellectually it's not their responsibility."

This, I'd figured, explained a lot of kids' magical thinking. Coming up with things like my repeated listing of hazards in order to ward them off.

Andrea said that children often think that something they did or didn't do might have caused whatever bad thing is happening in their lives.

"This makes the loss rational," she said. "Even though it hurts, thinking about painful things as having a straightforward cause is protective. At least against the senselessness that is loss. It gives you a reason why."

I'd asked if there was a downside to thinking this way.

"Taking unrealistic responsibility for a death gives children a false reassurance that they can prevent unwanted events if they only try harder," said Pat. "A child might just need to feel the guilt until she's ready to feel what's even harder than that: the awareness that we don't control the world around us and we can lose the people we love."

I turned off the water in the shower, grabbed a towel, and wandered out of the bathroom, leaving small puddles on the beautiful floor.

I finally understood. Ever since Dad died, I'd felt a guilt so deep and wide I couldn't find my way across it so I'd just sat down in the middle. For more than twenty years. Not ready to admit the truth.

The people we love will die and there is nothing we can do to stop it from happening. But keeping the guilt with us, shoving it deep down into the electric muscle of the heart where it beats twice a second, a billion times, till it stops when we do—that makes a part of us die too.

This was just another way of saying what Suzi Golodoff had told me in the Aleutians. Guilt is only helpful once. I flopped across the bed and put on a meditation I liked to listen to whenever things feel slightly unmanageable. It's from the meditation teacher Tara Brach.

"Who would you be," she asked through my iPhone speaker, "if you didn't think anything was wrong with you?"

Nine

Lake Como, Italy, May 2017

Mom and Sam decided to visit Italy while I was there. They planned to overlap with Josh and me for a day in Bellagio, and then Mom and I were going to travel for a week after my residency was over. Josh and I waited for them at a small coffee shop at the base of the stairs up to the villa and I explained to him how Mom had visited me everywhere I'd ever gone for more than a few weeks, no matter how far away. She'd come to rural Venezuela, Colombia, Northern Thailand, Boston, upstate New York, and now Italy. I said it calmly but inside I felt a spike of fear. I know it's natural for parents to die before their children but even though I was almost forty, I never let myself think about losing Mom. Certainly not before I was ready, or sooner than any of us might imagine.

Mom and Sam showed up early and I introduced everyone. We walked through the gardens to the villa—stopping to take photos of the rosebushes winding up palm trees, the hedges of rosemary and the ancient pomegranates, the olive orchard with its carpet of flowering purple clover and tiny daisies, the trimmed cypress trees like sentinels looking out over the towns tucked along the lake. Mom and Sam could barely talk except to say "My God" over and over again. Finally, we got to the ruins of a castle beyond the villa and saw the Alps dusted with snow. We took turns posing for photos on a bench, with the north arm of the lake and the Alps at our backs.

Josh and I explained our plan for the day: We'd decided to surprise them by renting a speedboat and had made lunch reservations at a little place across the lake with its own dock.

We picked up our boat at the lido, Mom wrapped in a scarf like Greta Garbo, and set off with Josh at the wheel. He guided the boat past Villa del Balbianello with its elaborate pruned plants, the little villages of Lenno and Tremezzo, and then to Sala Comacina, where we tied up. It looked like Italy out of central casting—the ancient sycamores, the docks with blue-and-white-swirl-painted poles, the old green public fountain, and the restaurant tables laid out under a tent on the tiny piazza down to the water.

At our table, bottle after bottle of Lugana Prestige wine appeared, the crispest, most delicious white I've ever tasted. The scallops were so fresh they glistened in the sunlight. And then there was the starter of pickled trout, the pâté of lake fish, and molten Alpine cheese crusted with pistachio. Next came the pillowy lemon ravioli stuffed with mascarpone cheese, and fried calamari, soft and delicious, with the sweetest carrots on the side.

The sun shone bright on Josh and me. Mom and Sam sat in the shade, asking Josh about his family and his time in the Middle East. Mom had prepared by reading up on the war in Yemen and asked Josh to tell her more about the Houthis. He thanked her, as most Americans didn't ask follow-up questions, if they asked questions at all.

After dessert we got back on our boat and Mom put on her dark glasses and laid back in the bow next to Sam, who was wearing a wool cap like the Italian men in town. She let her silk scarf trail in the wind and pretended to wave to passersby even though we were alone on the water, laughing the whole time. Sam put his arm around her and smiled into the wind. Big puffy clouds passed over us and we sped in and out of their giant shadows.

At some point, Josh asked if I wanted to drive. The speedboat roared along beneath us. I hugged the shore, and we went around the point at Bellagio and into the arm of the lake that goes to Lecco. Mom said, "Look, it's your little house!" pointing at the grand Rockefeller villa. We laughed and then raced on past the overgrown olive orchards and all the shuttered mansions with their elaborate paint jobs, some crumbling and some pristine, till I turned us around.

Josh moved to the prow of the boat next to Mom, while Sam faced back toward me, looking up at Varenna with its tall steeple and the Fiumelatte river running like frothy milk down the mountainside. He caught my eye at the wheel and smiled. Then, over the engine, I heard a snippet of Mom and Josh's conversation. "We called it Breakfasts of the World," she said, miming a Viking hat.

There are times that are perfect. When everything, down to the tiniest detail, is right and beautiful and you are not scared of anything and no one is dying. Or rather, everyone is dying, but not quickly. And if you're lucky, you notice how good it is while it's still happening. Usually though, you don't. Usually it's like Hazel Grace says in *The Fault in Our Stars*, a part Josh read to me while we were both naked in his bed in his apartment: "There's no way of knowing that your last good day is Your Last Good Day. At the time, it is just another good day."

Ten

Montefollonico, Italy, May 2017

A few days into my trip with Mom we ate dinner in a tiny hilltop town in Tuscany. We drove there through vineyards and forest patches, the setting sun casting Montepulciano across the valley in blazing yellow and then thick pink light.

I don't remember how it came up—maybe I was a little drunk on prosecco. But I know we were sitting at our table in a cozy trattoria talking about how Dad had a problem with authority. Mom said that in hindsight, he wished he'd let himself be closer to his mentors. She said they had tried. There was the famous surgeon from Hopkins who'd brought Dad to UCLA for his residency. He'd tried to befriend Dad but Dad was standoffish. Mom said he would have had an easier time if he'd allowed himself to be close to the people he admired.

I took a bite of my ravioli, hoping she'd continue.

"You know what he loved most?" she asked. "Being a mentor himself. He wanted to do more of it. He loved teaching."

"He taught at a medical school?"

She looked at me skeptically. "UCLA. You didn't know that?"

I shook my head.

"We'd fly ourselves down for his classes from Santa Paula or the Oxnard Airport. He'd teach and I'd go see my mom or tool around LA. And then we'd fly back at the end of the day."

Dad was a fly-in professor? Even at Stanford this seemed unheard of. I imagined him getting out of the Cessna and changing from his pearl snap button shirt and cowboy hat into a sport coat. I pictured him looking out at a class full of curious medical students as shiny and bright as mine.

I ached to tell him about my job. How I'd come to love the students with my whole heart and how the first ones were already practicing doctors now, some of them doing the same surgeries he'd done, albeit with many new tools.

Jake was at a barbecue in Ventura not long ago, when he met a new heart surgeon in town. The surgeon told Jake that the patients Dad had operated on thirty, even forty-five years ago were coming back in to have new procedures done. It happened enough that he could tell without looking at their charts if they'd been Dad's patients. It was the neat line where Dad's stitches had closed up the thoracic cavity. "It's how he opened and closed," the surgeon said. "It's unmistakably your dad." I loved thinking about these people, all of them still walking around with Dad's signatures on their hearts.

Cor. Cordis. Recordari.

The book of the heart is immortal. Or at least it's longer than we think.

Eleven

San Francisco, California, Fall 2017

The September after I came back from Bellagio I went to see Andrea Bass, the co-leader at Josie's Place. It had now been a couple of years since I'd started my training there and it had been a while since I'd volunteered with the kids. I'd moved away from the houseboat to the East Bay and was an hour and a half drive from the church basement. I missed the kids and facilitators, but I was teaching a writing class for medical students on the nights Josie's Place met and was also going back and forth to Seattle to see Josh.

I kept in touch with Andrea and had done a series of sand tray sessions with her too. This was a modality that we used with the kids. It's pretty much exactly what it sounds like. Children (or adults) choose figures to arrange, or play with, in a plastic or wooden tray of sand. Sometimes they narrate what they're doing to a therapist nearby and sometimes they don't. In Andrea's office she had her own tray she used with clients, and she had cabinets bursting with tiny figures—people, animals, fruit, houses, ghosts, cars, trucks, ambulances, fairies, fireplaces, wishing wells, mythical creatures, and monsters. Pretty much any object or being you could imagine, she had. Andrea explained that watching the things someone chooses and the way they place these things in the sand can be like an X-ray of the psyche. And one of the most common things she sees with grieving kids is how often they hide, and seek, things in the sand—burying and unburying things as a way of grappling with death.

It wasn't just in the sand. "Kids who have had a loss can also have a harder time with subtraction than addition," she'd told me. "Because it's about taking away numbers. It's a sense of losing something. Adding things is easier."

My eyes drifted over to her cabinets and fell on a small Pegasus with white, spreading wings. And a peacock.

Andrea looked at me looking at the figures.

"With sand tray therapy we say that the first tray contains the problem and its solution. But as with dreams, the person doing the tray may not see it themselves. That's why when we work with the sand tray we do successive trays. It gives your subconscious room to figure something out, or explore."

Now, nearly a year later, I was doing my last session, in which we were using black sand instead of white, to represent the subconscious. I went through Andrea's cabinets, pulling out objects: the white Pegasus, a bright yellow dreidel, the peacock, a studious-looking grizzly bear, a frog wearing a crown, a skeleton typing at a desk, a cup, a sword, a watermelon, an angel of death figurine riding a horse, a small skunk, and a man on a stretcher, among other things. I arranged each of them in the tray and then I walked her through my choices.

Andrea waited to make sure I was done talking, then put down her pen.

I sighed, suddenly, inexplicably tired.

"How do you do this?" I asked.

"What do you mean?"

"Help kids die, help adults grieve, sit here and hold all the hardest things that happen in people's lives."

"Oh, Laurel, it's a lot of things," she said. "Meditation, making art, tapping into the personal and collective unconscious to see the things we all have in common, ceremony."

"What kind of ceremony?" I sounded more desperate than I wanted to. She closed her eyes halfway and thought for a second.

"Have you ever done a vision fast?"

I cringed before I could stop myself.

"No offense but are we talking white shamans here?"

She shook her head patiently.

"You go out into the wilderness," she said, "without food for a few days. And you see what happens. What you learn about yourself, what you learn from following your intuition in nature with no one else around and no distractions."

"Not even any books?"

"No. I took some art supplies and lots of water, but that was it."

"And you were totally on your own?"

"You do the fast alone. But I went with a group who organized it and made sure that someone knew where I was, but I doubt it's still around. This was thirty-plus years ago."

"What was it called?" I asked, curious now. This didn't sound like the spiritual LARPing (or live-action role-playing) the Bay Area was so full of these days.

"The School of Lost Borders."

I felt a tug deep in my chest, a good kind. It was a feeling I was trying to pay more attention to.

As soon as I got to the car, I googled it. The first link that came up was to their website and it was blessedly straightforward. "Teaching Rites of Passage for 35 Years" read a black banner at the top of the screen. Below there were links to programs for young people and adults and something called "The Practice of Living and Dying," led jointly by a wilderness guide and a palliative care physician. "As our modern culture has grown ever more sophisticated . . . ," I read, "we have pushed Death away from Life, the dying away from the living—all in order to impose the illusion of control on the uncertainty of change. We have lost touch with the natural world and with our place in it as mortal animals. We have forgotten 'how to die.' "

According to the website, the school's rites of passage programs for adults were two weeks long, with a four- or five-day fast alone in the wilderness sandwiched in the middle. There was one for women in the spring. Location TBD.

Throughout my facilitator training I'd read about how common it is for children to get stuck developmentally at whatever age they are when a trauma happens. I'd been wondering if this had happened to me. Maybe a rite of passage would be the perfect fortieth-birthday present to myself. But who knew if I could do it. The longest I'd ever gone without eating was maybe half a day. The idea of camping all by myself without a tent didn't bother me, but doing it without any food? And without books or a phone or anything else that might be considered a distraction? That was terrifying, which is exactly why I wanted to do it. I couldn't have known, at least not consciously, but I was training for something more.

Twelve

Richmond, California, December 2017

I was watching *The Marvelous Mrs. Maisel* on my laptop when my phone buzzed. It was my friend Maria, who lived in Ojai, messaging our Thacher group chat, six women I'd gone to high school with whom I loved as much as ever. Maria wanted to know if we'd heard about a small wildfire off Highway 150, the curvy two-lane road from Santa Paula to Ojai.

I felt a twist of fear. I'd been having fire dreams. They'd started in late summer, gotten more frequent in the fall, and were always the same. I was at the ranch by myself and knew there was a wildfire heading for the house. I rushed to get the old F-250 ranch truck and then backed it up to the garage, throwing down the heavy liftgate. Then I ran through the house, tearing all the paintings I loved off the walls—the desert landscapes, the ones of mules hauling loads through the snow—and filled my arms with all the things my parents had bought on our travels. I tried to grab the Navajo rugs too, my old stethoscope from Dad, the boxes of family photos, the notes and letters from my friends, but it was just me and it was all so heavy. I knew I wasn't going to get everything in time. I threw what I could, haphazardly, into the bed of the truck and ran back in, again and again and again. I always woke up knowing that the fire got to the house before I could save what we loved. I'd lie in bed, panting and exhausted, as if I'd really run through every room.

That October the Tubbs Fire killed twenty-two people, burning right through the town of Santa Rosa. I started driving around the Bay Area with extra N95 masks in my car to hand out to people to protect them from the smoke. It took weeks but eventually the air cleared. My dreams didn't stop, though. I wrote them down in a little leather notebook and told Josh they were anxiety dreams. But they were disturbing enough that I looked up my renters insurance policy and realized that I hadn't increased my coverage in a decade. I tripled it and tried to put the nightmares out of my mind.

Now, looking down at Maria's text, an eerie sense of déjà vu settled in my chest. I opened a new search window and tried to find out what I could online. The fire had started less than two hours before and was still small. Still, though, fires moved fast in our area and there was nothing but fuel in the wild parts of the ranch. Twice in my life wildfires had gotten close to the house, but each time a fire truck showed up and the firefighters watered down the roof and nothing had burned.

I called Mom. She and Sam were in the living room eating dinner and watching the news. She told me they'd just found out about the fire and that they'd keep an eye out.

I got on Twitter to follow the local fire scanner and a few firefighting accounts.

A half hour later I could see that it was growing. Fast.

I called Mom back. "It's moving really quickly. Just promise me if it gets bigger, you'll pack up and leave."

She agreed but I could tell she didn't think I was serious so when I hung up I texted again.

I'm sure you guys are on top of this already, but requests from house (in addition to your important documents) if it comes to this: jewelry, paintings from the walls, whatever photo albums you can grab.

Jake had a few days off and that morning he'd left at first light to drive to the cabin in Oregon with his friend Dave, another Santa Barbara County firefighter. He'd just finished the fourteen-hour drive and sat down on our old blue couch when Alice called to let him know.

On the scanner I saw the fire had now reached the end of Adams Canyon. Happy Talk Ranch. My friend Cath's place, where we'd played under nearly every tree. I made a silent plea for it to go right past. The blaze had swelled from fifty to twenty-five hundred acres just since I'd been watching.

I called Mom back and begged. "I know this is going to sound insane," I said, nearly choking with fear, "but I've dreamed this. I need you to get our photos, the art, anything you can carry."

"Don't worry, Lar," she said. "It's going to be fine."

Her voice sounded slightly muffled.

"Are you eating something right now?"

She giggled. "Yep. Sam and I are having ice cream and I'm heating up brown gravy." (This is what she called her homemade fudge sauce.) "I just licked the spoon."

Fury rose in me and tightened my jaw. Why was I the one needing to be responsible here?

"Mom," I said, trying to sound as calm and authoritative as I could, "it's not the time for ice cream. I need you to pack what you can. Please, please, grab anything you have time to get. Put it in the cars and drive the cars well down the canyon. I know it's a pain in the ass. But I swear to you if I turn out to be wrong I will come down tomorrow and help you put everything back where it was. Please."

I fought back hot tears. Crying, I figured, would only make me sound more hysterical and less trustworthy. I was a kid again and I couldn't understand why.

"Okay, Lar," she said. "I will."

But I knew her voice as well as my own, probably better, and could tell she was just humoring me. For some reason I'd become the family alarmist, the one who worried about our pesticide exposure and forwarded articles about carcinogens and agriculture. Now I wished I'd never said anything, bided my time to wait to ask for something when I really needed it. When we all did.

I called Jake.

"Please," I said, trying not to cry, "tell Mom to grab what she can and get out of the house. I'm following this thing on the scanner and it's going so fast. I've told her but she's not listening to me. We know she listens more to you. Please."

"I'll tell her, but honestly it's such long odds it'll get to the house. This has happened before. Don't worry."

My heart sank. He didn't believe me either. My dreams had been real. And the more I tried to make everyone feel as much urgency as I did, the less it seemed to be working.

I hung up and realized my shoulders were shaking.

I was alone.

I waited twenty minutes and texted Mom and Sam again. I couldn't give up. I called. No answer. My friend Maria texted that her parents, who lived a few miles from the ranch, closer to town, were evacuating. Then my friend Leyla called. The fire looked like it was heading toward her parents' house too, even though they were in Ventura.

Mom and Sam didn't pick up.

Tell me you're packed and heading down the road. At least to watch and see.

Sam finally responded, said the fire was still a long way off.

Except it wasn't. I could see the live map and hear what the Ventura County fire scanner was streaming. They were talking about sending strike teams to our canyon and were evacuating people from Upper Ojai. I heard an announcement of lost structures in a canyon not far from us to the east. My heart was a racehorse sprinting toward the place I loved most. Only it wasn't fast enough.

Late. Bad. Late.

Sam texted that the sky was red, the power was out.

Flanking fires moving into our canyon, I typed.

Get out. A car accident has trapped cars on Wheeler Canyon Road. I don't want that to happen to you guys.

I called Jake again and he told me a firefighter buddy of his drove by and it looked like there were engines heading up our road. We'd have fire crews after all. I hoped they'd get there quick enough to keep Mom and Sam from doing anything reckless on their own. But a few minutes later I heard the name of our canyon over the scanner and turned the volume up. They were calling off the fire crews they'd just sent our way. There would be no one coming to help us. No engines. No crews. Mom and Sam were going to face it alone.

I looked at Google Maps. If I left now I could be there in five and a half hours. I'd never make it in time to help. We had minutes, not hours. I started getting ready anyway.

Mom and Sam weren't answering their phones. Sam's daughters were calling me now, scared. I told Nancy what I could and then I called Cath. She was sitting in her living room in Minneapolis in the dark while the rest of her family slept, watching snow fall outside, trying to picture a storm of fire cresting the hilltop at Happy Talk.

"They were eating ice cream!" I wailed into the phone. "What on earth are they thinking? It's like they can't see how serious it is. My mom isn't listening to me. I'm begging her to get stuff out of the house. I'd have packed the shit out of everything by now."

"My parents too," Cath said. "They were drinking tea and watching the fire move over the hill from Steckel Park. I was like, 'Get the hell out of there!' But they were like, 'It's fine, Catherine. It's far away.' "

"Our parents are nuts."

Finally I got hold of Mom.

"Have you packed?" I asked, trying to keep from screaming at her.

"We will," she said. "We went up and looked at the top of the hill and it's heading this way."

As she said this I could see on my feed that the fire was already upon them. It was too late for her to pack. I knew it and she didn't, and this filled me with hatred, not of her but of the feeling itself. I didn't want to know more than she did. I never had.

"There's no time now. You and Sam need to get out of there."

"We're fine, Laurel," she said, exasperated. "If we need to we'll go into the lemons." This was their plan, I realized. There was less to burn in the lemons, unlike in the avocado orchards where surely the fire was now raging through all the dry, crunchy leaves on the ground, the high winds whipping them into tornados of sparks, which would spread the main fire farther and faster. I closed my eyes against the images of flames.

"Mom, the lemons won't save you. There is only one road in and out of the canyon. You could get trapped. You need to get out of there."

The line went dead.

Thirteen

Santa Paula, California, December 2017

Two hours later, at 10 p.m., Mom finally texted me that she and Sam were leaving. That it was not safe to stay. But just before midnight Nancy called to tell me that the little blue dots that showed our parents' location in her Find My Friends app hadn't evacuated after all. She and her sisters were scared. And so was I. Angry too. I knew if our roles were reversed that Mom and Sam would be livid with us. No place, even one we loved as much as ours, was worth them being injured, or worse. I tried not to think of a family I'd read about in Northern California who tried to flee the Redwood Fire. Their son was burned alive when they'd been forced to leave their cars and outrun the flames on foot.

I tried calling Mom's cell again but she didn't answer.

I texted. *You guys left but went back?*

No response.

I'm on my way down.

No response.

What do you see?

For seven minutes I just stared at my phone, my heart beating so hard I could feel it in my teeth. Hoping, hoping, hoping. Then I saw the gray dots, Mom was typing.

Our house is gone.

I heard a single anguished cry, like an animal being dragged across gravel, her skin tearing free. With some other part of my brain, I realized the sound was me and I'd made it before. Once.

"Our house is dead," I said, alone to the room.

How did I miss this? I thought about my prayers as a kid. How I named car trouble and sometimes murder, coyotes killing our barn cats, and, after reading *The Hot Zone*, I'd added Ebola to the list. But I never named our house burning down.

I called Mom. She picked up on the first ring but all I could hear was her crying.

"Mom?" I felt hot but still untethered from my body. On my laptop next to me, balanced on the couch cushions, I could see *The Marvelous Mrs. Maisel* paused, mid-scene, next to the window where I'd been streaming the fire scanner. The plate of green bean salad I'd been eating when the first texts came in was still sitting on the coffee table. Everything now completely, terribly new.

Mom tried to catch her breath.

"I'm sorry, Lar. I'm so sorry," she said through tears.

"I'm just glad you're okay," I said.

"We couldn't save it. We tried. No one came," she was sobbing again.

"I know, Mom."

"I didn't believe you. I didn't get anything out."

Ghost hands tightened around my lungs, my chest ached.

"I have to call Jake," she said. "Their house is okay. But we need to go get more water."

"Of course. I'm on my way."

Fourteen

Santa Paula, California, December 2017

An hour later, my stepsister Sarah came over to get me, insisting that I shouldn't drive myself. At dawn we were a few miles from the ranch and Josh texted that he'd bought a ticket from Seattle and would be there by nightfall. I was grateful but I was having a hard time knowing that he'd be seeing the place I loved most in the world this way, in crisis, a smoldering heap of debris. We'd been planning his first visit for months—it was supposed to happen two weeks from now, for Christmas. He was so excited, and so were Mom and Sam. They'd already wrapped everyone's presents and stocked up on bourbon. I couldn't wait to bring Josh up to the oak trees at the top of the hill, where he could carve his name into the picnic table, and swing with me on the wooden swing. He was going to meet Jake, Alice, my nephews, and Antonio, the man who worked with us on the ranch and took care of the trees with such immense pride. We were planning to eat guacamole and collect eggs from the chickens and walk back and forth through the orchards so I could show him every tree. Now, Josh would never know it like it was. He wouldn't know me.

Mom and Sam met us at the mouth of the canyon in one of the cars they'd saved from the flames. We followed them back to the ranch and up the driveway past small, still-smoking fires under the avocado trees. I leaned forward against my seat belt, struggling to understand what I was looking at. Not a blade of grass was left on the ridgeline. Blackened tree trunks were all that remained of the oak forest. The hill was naked, as if it had been shaved bare.

Sarah pulled over where the driveway split between Jake and Alice's place and the main house. I opened the door and the smell was overpowering. The smell here was always overpowering: avocado and lemon blossoms and sage, and if it was hot, the asphalt driveway baking in the sun. But this was totally different. It was dark and toxic, like a chemical explosion.

During the fire, Mom and Sam had tried to fill water hoses in the pool and stretched them across the driveway to try and protect Jake and Alice's small house. It was a miracle they'd done it. The flames stopped feet from the bank of pomegranate trees near Jake and Alice's front door.

If only our house, the house I'd grown up in, had been spared too.

We walked through the spot where the backyard gate had been. Smoke billowed from what was left of the persimmon trees. On our right a huge fire still burned hot in the woodpile. We could hear the flames spitting. A few steps farther, I started to see the scale of the loss. A great yawning debris field stood in the exact footprint of our house. It was smoking still, and burning from within, making the air shimmer and dance. Great gusts of noxious fumes and ash lifted in the wind. Twisted hunks of metal were only partly recognizable as the stove, the refrigerator, the washer and dryer. Pools of melted window glass sat on the ground around the edges. All the tile my parents had brought back from Mexico was still there, shattered into pieces by the roof's collapse. The only thing still standing was the river rock fireplace Dad had built with stones from the creek. It looked like an air control tower now, alone and looming over rubble.

I looked around, trying to shake the feeling that I was hallucinating. It felt like I was somewhere else and soon we'd all be able to go home. A gust of wind lifted a plume of ash from where the living room used to be into a small tornado. I watched it feeling hollow and numb, still too shocked to be anything but disoriented. It was as if my internal compass had been wiped clean, the needle spinning for home but finding nothing.

Once, Jake gave me a book about surviving disasters. How hard it is for people to react decisively in the moment, because what's happening doesn't match anything that's ever happened to them before. They mill around or act weirdly normal when they should be running for their lives. During 9/11 one woman walked in circles around her office in the second tower, trying to decide which of her paperback novels to bring with her down the stairs. Or in so many plane crashes, people see smoke and fire but instead of racing for the exits, they stop to get their suitcases out of the overhead bins because that's what they've always done. The authors called it normalcy bias.

I looked at the smoking rubble in front of us, knowing that every object I cared about was now turned to ash and wondered if this was why Mom hadn't gotten anything but her jewelry from the house, why she couldn't hear me begging and pleading with her to take more. A parade of all the things Dad built or made for us marched behind my eyes—my walnut jewelry box, a wooden chair, the jars and buckets of honey. The napkin in Mom's top dresser drawer of the stick figure family Dad drew for her like a contract before his leg was amputated. The rug I wove in Rock Point, the turquoise pin, all my books and photo albums, twenty-plus years of notes and letters from Cath and Leyla and my other high school friends, Mom's wedding dress.

The house was like a person she couldn't believe might die. And by the time she saw that it could, there wasn't time. Maybe instead of normalcy bias, it should be normalcy hope. The process of trying to make the comprehensible world match up with one that exists in our minds and then refusing to acknowledge that it never will.

The weirdest thing, or one of them anyway, was that less than twenty feet from the house our wooden patio chairs and table sat in a circle beside the swimming pool, totally untouched, as if ready for a luncheon.

Nearby, my blue nylon camping hammock hung between two burnt avocado trees, swinging back and forth in the breeze, totally unharmed.

"We have a camping hammock but no house?" I asked, incredulous.

"Yes," Mom said. "We also have a stack of firewood." She nodded at another woodpile near the chimney that was also untouched even though it was feet from where a bank of windows had melted.

I laughed my darkest laugh and thought of Dad. He'd think this was funny too.

Thankfully, the fire also spared the chicken coop. I wondered what it had been like for the ladies, which is what we called them. But when we walked past we saw them pecking and cooing as if it were a normal morning. Mom lifted one of the latches on their nesting boxes.

"My lord," she said. And held up a light brown egg.

We all laughed again and then started coughing because our throats were raw from the smoke and fumes.

"And it's not cooked!" Mom said, shaking it lightly by her ear.

At sunset we went to her good friend Myrna's house in East Ventura. She'd evacuated but she told Mom where she had hidden a key in case we needed somewhere to go. I went into the guest bathroom to take a shower and looked at myself in the mirror. My face was smudged with ash and my hair was so heavy with soot it felt like rope. I didn't want to shower because now my outsides matched my insides. Once I washed and changed they never would again.

I'd just put my dirty clothes back on, I didn't have any others, when Josh walked in. He strode through the door in two steps, wrapping me in his arms and kissing my forehead and my ear. "I'm so sorry, Laurel."

I cried and hugged him. It was the first bit of comfort I'd felt since getting Maria's text twenty-four hours earlier. It seemed preposterous that it had only been a day.

Next, he hugged Mom and Sam. He offered to bring in water from the car. Mom asked if he'd like some pizza. When had we gotten pizza?

I couldn't remember but now I saw it, sitting out on the counter in a cardboard box.

"Don't get comfortable," Mom said. "We're going back to the ranch. There's no water or power but we can sleep at Jake and Alice's house. He's not home yet and she is still evacuated with the boys."

Once we pulled up to their dark house I turned on the camping lanterns I'd brought, and by the time I turned around, Mom and Sam had each taken a small section of couch in the living room and passed out. Josh and I climbed the stairs to a room above Jake and Alice's garage and looked across the canyon. The fire was still burning. The flames spit tall columns of sparks we could see clearly in the darkness.

"I'm so tired," I said, "but we can't go to sleep. I know there's no fuel for the fire anymore over here, but what if it comes down the other side of the canyon, into the creek bed full of brush, and gets here that way?"

"We'll be able to see it coming," Josh said. "How about I set an alarm for an hour from now and we'll see if it gets any closer?"

Hour after hour, all night, our alarms went off and we got up to make sure it was still safe to stay. At one point there were huge orange shadows flickering on the ceiling and we got in the car to drive down the road and make sure we could still escape if we needed to. Eventually, though, the light from the flames got less bright and we could hear airplanes start making water drops somewhere nearby. We went back to the house and Josh took off all his clothes and got into bed. "Come here," he said, an order, but not an unkind one. I was still standing at the window facing south, toward the fire, which was shrinking. But I was scared to stop watching. When the flames went out, it would all be over and this would be real.

"Come here," Josh said again, more insistently now.

I went over to the bed and stripped my clothes off. I knew that even though I'd showered I must smell like the chemical fumes from the house site where I'd stood for too long. But Josh pulled me against him and I cried into his chest, snot and tears pooling in his armpit. He let me cry, and with his free hand he held my lower back like he was keeping me up even though we were laying down. When I finally stopped, he moved his hand to my face.

"Dame un beso," he said, his favorite phrase from the winters he spent in Nicaragua, and lifted my chin to his lips. I gave in to kissing him. Deep and long.

"I love you, Laurel."

I smiled so big that my cheeks hurt, tight with dried tears.

"I know," I said, cracking up. I'd told him first, by accident, as I hung up the phone a few months before. I'd been hoping he'd say it back. But also figured he'd get there in his own time.

"Did we have to lose the house for you to say that?"

"Maybe, but when I say it, you can be sure it's true."

Fifteen

Santa Paula, California, December 2017

When the house site finally stopped smoldering, I waded in to look for anything that might have survived. I was hoping for my favorite book, an old copy of *Brighty of the Grand Canyon*, about a pack burro who helps solve a murder. It seemed irrational to hope that any of the books could have made it but from a distance I could see a pile of them where our shelves had collapsed.

It was slow going, picking my way through the broken floor tile and the ash like snow drifts up to my knees. I wore an N95, but I could smell the chemical fumes through it and tried not to think about the carcinogens swirling around us like doom. It took me a full fifteen minutes to wade my way to the book pile. The spine of one on top was burned and flames had destroyed everything but a hunk of pages, char marks covering most of the text. I could only make out a few sentence fragments.

. . . pressures in their patient's average . . . 60 mm Hg lower than brachial . . . although they did not report . . . without arterial obstruction.

One of Dad's cardiology books. There'd been at least a hundred of them. Their dark-colored spines embossed with impenetrable language that I loved to try to pronounce. I reached out to touch it and as soon as I made contact the page dissolved under my fingers.

I sank down on my heels, too tired now to wade out. Of course the paper hadn't survived. Not even the windows made it. But I hadn't realized that ash could look exactly like what was no longer there.

Sixteen

Santa Paula, California, December 2017

Alice and the kids came back home a few days later and almost immediately, my three-year-old nephew, Benny, started asking to go to "Grammy's house." Because of how they're situated, it's impossible to see one house from the other even though they're not far away. Benny was insistent. He'd been having nightmares since Alice and the boys evacuated and occasionally disagreed with us when we talked about losing the house. "Grammy's house didn't burn down," he'd say, and then we'd calmly correct him and explain that it had but that everyone was safe. Now, though, Alice looked at me with questions in her eyes. I'd learned at Josie's Place that it was good practice to let a child, if they were ready and asking, see the hard thing up close. Seeing with their own eyes can help them understand and say goodbye. Pat and Andrea had meant a dead or dying loved one, but I figured it extended to a dead or dying place. I told Alice that Josh and I would take Benny to check it out.

We walked up the driveway to the spot that had been the wooden porch off of the kitchen. This was where the peacocks liked to perch and snip leaves and flowers from Mom's potted lemon verbena and pink geraniums. The porch was gone now but the birds were still here, standing on blackened, twisted frames of what looked like a metal patio chair and a freezer. Benny looked up at me.

"Sophie died," he said, his voice somber.

"Yeah," I agreed. Sam's sixteen-year-old little Labrador had died the past spring. "But Sophie wasn't killed in the fire. She died of old age."

As I spoke, I realized I'd misunderstood. Benny wasn't saying Sophie died in the fire. He was just listing the other biggest saddest thing he knew. That a soft white dog wasn't here anymore.

I looked out across the field of rubble. He was right. Every loss is all the losses. All at once. They're never separate. Or at least that's how it feels.

Yet again, here was a kid reminding me of something, everything, worth remembering.

Later that week I scheduled a call with Judy. We talked from the parking lot of a small motel in Santa Paula where Josh and I were staying through Christmas.

I told her how every night I lay awake walking through the house in my mind, and then when I finally did sleep, it was only to wake up and remind myself it was gone.

"This sounds like a death," she said.

"We lost all the things my dad left for us," I gulped. "Every photo, all of it. Everything he tried so hard to . . ."

"Just remember, Laurel," she said, "those things, they were vessels. For love. And it's only the vessels that are gone."

I knew she was right but that didn't make it easier. Instead, I kept repeating an old joke to myself I hadn't heard in years: What happens when you play a country song backward? The cowboy gets his girl, his truck, and his dog back.

That's what I wanted. To play this whole thing in reverse and get back all the things we loved and lost. I wanted a do-over, another chance.

For weeks, Mom, Sam, Josh, and I made phone calls and wrote emails to insurance companies, attended county meetings for fire victims, filed claims and googled "insurance law," tried to replace birth certificates and deeds, and bought pajamas. Buying anything else felt overwhelming and made Mom cry. We also watched the surviving trees. We'd gotten them water as soon as we could but still the avocados were papery and sad. What looked like red tears ran down many of their pale trunks. Ben, our ag extension agent, visited and told Alice and me that if the trees started to leak sap like that it meant they were dead. Some would start now, he said, and some wouldn't start for a few weeks.

"So we just have to wait for them to die?" I asked. "Not knowing how long it will be or if any will survive?"

This felt familiar. Too familiar.

"Do you have a choice?" Ben said.

In early January it was time for me to go back north to teach. The county had deemed the debris toxic waste and was going to remove it as soon as they could. Who knew how long that would be, but I wanted one last minute at the house site before everything was scraped away.

It was raining lightly as I took a few steps into the wreckage. One of the peacocks perched near the chimney turned to look at me. The tips of his tail feathers were gray with wet ash.

"Hey, bird," I said. That's how I always addressed them. For some reason we never named them—except for one. Raymond was a male we had forever. The rest were just "bird."

Disconcertingly, our flock had turned mostly white over the years—an unintentional eugenics experiment—so now the birds perched among the rubble looked even more startling, bright against the charred remains. Haggard and a little soggy, but still regal. I was impressed they'd survived the fire and doubted the wedding doves would have made it. Thankfully those birds had been released thirteen years ago.

I'd married my first husband at the top of the driveway, while the donkeys had looked on from their corral. Before the ceremony, Jake went up to the dove coop to choose a few presentable birds to set free. This wasn't easy. Over the years they had gotten incestuous, their babies warty and gray instead of white. A few had only one eye and waddled around like cooing pirates. Jake chose the least disturbing of the lot and put them in an old wicker picnic basket till the part of the ceremony when Dad's best friend, Phil, whom we'd asked to officiate, told everyone the story of how Dad wanted to be present for my wedding and was doing it, now, with these birds. Then Jake opened the picnic basket. I felt my heart swell and waited for the doves to shoot up and out to freedom like arrows of love.

Only nothing happened. We waited a few seconds more. Then a minute.

Jake looked down, confused. The birds were cowering at the bottom of the basket, unsure of what was being asked of them. Cath and Leyla, who were standing with me as bridesmaids, smiled supportively.

Jake lifted the basket again, this time giving it a hard shake.

No doves.

He shook it.

I started to laugh. Mom did too.

Jake brought the basket back behind him to get some more momentum and then let it go. Three doves came tumbling out. One flapped unevenly to a low branch of an avocado tree about ten feet away. Another flew awkwardly into the branches of the pepper tree above us, and the third, fat and gray as a pigeon, landed with a thud next to one of my cream satin heels and stayed there, looking dazed.

Everyone else was laughing now too. And then I was laughing so hard, I was crying.

In all those years it never occurred to us that the birds might not want to go anywhere. That doves who'd never flown free in their lives wouldn't have the slightest idea what to do at a wedding they'd spent years unwittingly preparing for.

I looked down at my feet covered in wet ash and saw I was standing on a pile of terra-cotta tile from what had been our guest bathroom. I bent down and picked one up. It was brown and white, hand painted in Mexico with a little brown dove angling toward the sun. I brushed off the ash and stuck the tile in the waistband of my jeans. I was turning around to wade out when I heard a truck pull in to what had been the driveway.

"You Lynn Braitman?" a man said, leaning out the driver's window.

"Her daughter," I said.

"We're the debris removal team from the county. We just wanted to tell you we're okaying the property for removal, should start in eight weeks or possibly sooner."

"Okay, thanks."

He looked past me, to the birds sitting on the river rock fireplace mantel, like sentinels. Behind it, the orchards spread out in the mist, clear across the canyon.

"Must have been a beautiful place," he said.

"You can tell just by looking at this mess?" I asked, skeptical.

"Of course, you can tell a lot from what's left."

For a little while in my early twenties, I worked as an outdoor guide, leading backpacking trips in the Adirondacks and the White Mountains. Besides teaching folks how to dig holes to poop in, one of the most important lessons was about false summits. When you're hiking up a mountain pass there are times when you think you've reached the top, only to realize you couldn't see the real summit from where you were standing and you are not, in fact, done yet. The best thing to do is drink some water, eat a handful of trail mix, and keep going. I had no idea this was what was happening, even though it definitely was.

Seventeen

Northern New Mexico, May 2018

Five months later, I was driving too fast down the I-25 West from Santa Fe. I was late to the School of Lost Borders campsite at Cochiti Lake, the spot where we'd spend a few days before heading out to do our solo vision fasts. Everyone was already circled up in the shade of a metal pergola. It turned out that the women's fast I'd signed up for was taking place at Ghost Ranch in northern New Mexico. I was excited but worried too that we'd be a bunch of hungry white people wandering around the high desert looking desperately for signs on someone else's ancestral ground. For centuries, newcomers to the American West have approached the landscape as, at best, a mirror reflecting their own aspirational identities, or at worst, something to steal. Too often, it's been both. But rural places and people are more than a vehicle for personal awakening and every spot of ground already has meaning to someone. Knowing all this didn't make me different, but it did make me second-guess myself.

Emerald, one of our two leaders, asked me to find a spot to sit down. She had a throaty voice, chin-length gray hair, and seemed to be in her late fifties or early sixties. "The point of life isn't to heal your broken heart," she said, leaning forward in her camp chair. "It's to have your heart broken so many times, letting it be so shattered, that you can't possibly put it back together again. That's how you get an open heart."

She looked around the circle at us. I felt like she was sensing my hesitancy, my skepticism toward the rest of the group sitting in camp chairs or on yoga bolsters. So many of the women smelled like natural deodorant or patchouli and were slathering on organic sunscreen from a co-op that probably required everyone to bring their own containers. They seemed nice enough, smiling at me in welcome, but I wondered if I'd found one of the few spaces on earth in which I'd be the most corporate. Next to me, a white lady was idly handling a rattle she'd made out of a gourd and crying softly. I tried to fight the impulse to bolt.

I'd read something in the Lost Borders student manual that I really liked: "You can be a legal adult and be an emotional basket case and take no responsibility whatsoever for yourself and others." All you had to do was stay alive. The authors also wrote that teenagers and young adults naturally hunger for trials that test their limits. Some do it by driving too fast, taking too many drugs, or making risky decisions—but the impulse to test ourselves is natural. I understood this, even if my way of testing myself had been extreme goody-two-shoeing and having sex with people bound to disappoint me.

If I left now, before we got to talking about all this, it would be my own fault.

Our other leader was Petra; she was tall and thin with short blond hair and mischievous blue eyes. While poking around the Lost Borders website I'd learned that she'd been diagnosed with breast cancer and had undergone a few grueling rounds of chemo and surgery. When she spoke she seemed wise, centered, and sounded a lot like Dad, if Dad were a tan German woman who lived in the Sierras and liked to wear statement necklaces.

Pretty quickly we got to talking about the transition into adulthood. "In most cultures there were initiation rites," Emerald said. "And they were dangerous, and that's where the meaning came from. If you are not scared then you are not able to be brave."

This sounded just like what Judy had said when I told her I

was scared to love Josh. You can't have courage if something doesn't scare you.

"The classic rite of passage," said Petra, "is a process that allows you to take your rightful seat alongside your mother and father."

"But separating from the mother and father inside us," said Emerald, "is not separating from your actual mom and dad. It's not murder." She laughed. "It may just set you free to show up for the real versions of them once this is over.

"We take away food, company, and shelter," she went on.

"And you will learn to help yourself," Petra said, finishing Emerald's sentence. "You will be the person who rescues you."

We spent the next few days in camp learning about what Petra and Emerald called "self-directed ceremony" so that we might be able to do it for ourselves out in the wilderness. This sounded exciting. I was a secular person but I didn't want a secular life.

"All ceremony was once self-directed," Petra told us. "People alone in nature, or in small groups, doing things to help them make sense of their lives and the natural world, to mark turning points and transitions."

"Organized religion," Emerald added, "is just a few of these self-directed ceremony traditions that got really, really popular. But in the beginning it was just someone out in nature, talking to the water, the earth, the trees. Asking for help, for guidance. Realizing they were a part of the whole. The cycle of birth and death. Don't be embarrassed to talk to the trees. To tell them about your grief. Ask them to listen."

I wondered about the first person to decorate a tree at the winter solstice, the first kid to think it might be fun to hide eggs in springtime, or the first Hebrew to build a candelabra that looked like branches. And I thought about my bat mitzvah. Till now, that had been the only official rite of passage I'd ever taken part in. I could barely remember most of it, only that we'd done the Electric Slide under the big sycamore behind the house, that the theme of my party was "donkeys" (Mom told me that my first choice, "infectious diseases," was not appropriate), and that Mac the miniature donkey had been able to attend until he tried to bite my great-aunt Becky.

After the fire Alice had been going through things in her office and found a recording I hadn't known existed. Together, we watched my thirteen-year-old self read her Torah portion in broken Hebrew at our temple's wooden podium and listened to Dad and Mom say how proud they were of me. The most surprising part of the tape, though, was the rabbi's speech. "The oldest Jewish symbol, more authentic perhaps than the Jewish star," he said, looking over at me in my bubble-skirted teal and black velvet dress and matching headband, "is the menorah, patterned after the tree of life. And you, Laurel, were named after a tree. You told me you'd like to be a writer and also care for animals. Like the tree of life itself, both things bring light. The light of healing, the light of knowledge. No matter what path your life takes, Laurel, you will bring light wherever you are."

"May it always be!" said the crowd in unison.

And then everyone popped up to hug each other and share their congrats. I came down from the bimah and hugged Dad, Mom, Jake, and everyone else.

Watching the video with Alice, while Benny sat eating guacamole at the kitchen counter, felt like looking through a window, not into the past but into a continually unfolding present. It was shocking to me that this rabbi had given me such kindness, a generosity of vision that I'd held on to, consciously or not, that I still wanted desperately to be true.

Eighteen

Chama River Canyon Wilderness, New Mexico, May 2018

The hardest part of the fast wasn't being hungry. It was the endless expanses of time. Every morning I woke up just after sunrise and moved my water jugs into the shade. Then I brushed my teeth, changed out of my warmest clothes, and put on sunscreen. If it was warm enough, I didn't bother putting on pants because, why? All of this took about five minutes and then I was done with my tasks for the day. I had another fifteen hours before I could reasonably go to bed.

The first and second days I slept a lot. I wrote in my journal. I painted a watercolor picture of my tits, and then a splintered tree stump. One afternoon, for hours, I sat in my little Crazy Creek camping chair watching insects crawl around on a prickly pear flower. I watched a few cows eat grass on a distant mountainside. I took off all my clothes and walked down to the river in my hiking boots. I didn't know how near the nearest person was, but it was far enough away that I didn't worry about running into anybody. The spot where I picked to camp was at the base of a juniper tree, with enough open space to lay out my sleeping pad and have some shade. It had the view I wanted: a huge mountainous plateau with sloping shoulders and yellow, red, orange, and white cliffs that softened into rolling foothills dotted with juniper, cholla, and sagebrush. The green-blue Rio Chama snaked along the base of more sandstone cliffs, with narrow sandy beaches and stands of willow. If I turned my head just a tiny bit to the left, I could also see Georgia O'Keeffe's mountain. Pedernal. Flat-topped and dark against the horizon. She'd painted it so many times. In every kind of light. She didn't own it, but she made it hers by looking at it closely for so long.

By the time we'd all set off alone into the wilderness, I'd done a complete one-eighty on my fellow fasters. I may have been one of the few people who'd never skipped a meal in the name of enlightenment, but I'd come to respect and admire these women who were willing to do this wild thing. We were artists and handywomen, university administrators and recent college graduates, writers and long-distance hikers, mothers and sisters and daughters and wives and girlfriends. So many of us were grieving people we'd lost, or divorces we'd scrabbled through, watched grown kids move out into the world, survived menopause, heartbreak, breakdowns, disappointment, or our own lost childhoods. We were white, Black, and brown. We ranged in age from twenty-three to seventy. We were queer and we were straight. Yes, we smelled like patchouli. But now, after a few days camping, also like dirt and sweat. And yes, some of us had made our own rattles. Some of us cried a lot. But I'd stopped worrying about it.

I shook out my sleeping bag, thinking about a Dolly Parton quote that I love. "A peacock who sits on its tail feathers is just another turkey." I imagined our white peacocks back home, perched on the rubble of the old house, their tails spreading in the light, and wished a version of this for us too.

The sun felt great on my skin. I felt beautiful and strong without a mirror. I skipped stones. I watched ants. I collected rocks that I liked. Then, at some point, a few days in, because I'd run out of other things to do, I started talking to the trees, the rocks, the water, just like Emerald and Petra said we might. The self-conscious silliness of it went away after a while and it felt good to hear a voice, even if it was only mine.

• • •

In the beginning, not eating made me feel weak and a little dizzy but by the end of the second day I had lots of energy and only a rare, quick wave of nausea. Whenever I got hungry, I drank water. And eventually it was almost as if my body stopped caring about food. Hunger turned into a state of being, with only an occasional cramp in my stomach. Once in a while I'd think about eating, but I tamped the thoughts down and got up to do something else. Even if that was walking in a circle around my juniper tree. It mostly worked.

Unfortunately it was harder to keep certain thoughts at bay. Lines of songs, parts of old conversations I wished had gone differently, angry monologues or to-do lists would appear and then play on repeat for hours at a time inside my head. Without someone to talk to, a feed to scroll through, a snack to grab, a place to go, a podcast to turn on . . . without anything to switch my train of thought—the most annoying snippets stayed there and kept chattering at me.

I know that watching your monkey mind and noticing your thoughts is supposed to be a normal part of meditation, maybe even the whole point—but I wasn't meditating. I was just alone with no distractions. I had no idea my brain was so noisy.

Petra had told us that "No feeling is final. Keep going." Emerald said that we shouldn't worry if we felt a little nuts the first two days, that eventually the space between our thoughts would lengthen.

I knew not eating for days would be hard. As would going without a tent and being all alone for days—but my brain? I hadn't known that it would be so tough to just listen to my stupid self talking. Also, when was everything going to get spiritual? I was dirtier and hungrier than normal, but otherwise I was still the same secular me. I looked over, accusingly, at the small circle of objects I'd brought with me. There was my Auryn necklace I'd bought on Etsy during the worst of my fire dreams, a replica of the ouroboros medallion in *The NeverEnding Story*. This was my favorite movie growing up. The main character is a lonely half-orphan kid named Bastian. He finds a book with the Auryn on the cover and reading it, crosses into the story for real. Eventually, using the power of only his imagination and a magical grain of sand, he saves the realm of Fantasia from total destruction. My dream had always been to go inside books too. Maybe becoming a writer is the ultimate version of this. You get to cross into the story and see the people you love again, and if you're lucky, maybe you get to use your imagination to make them real for other people too. This wasn't so different from what the kids were doing at Josie's Place and the Dougy Center in their play, it's just that I was doing it on purpose.

I'd also brought a small length of vertebrae that I'd found while pretending to be dragons with my nephews in the lemon orchards back home. It looked like it was from a wild pig but I wasn't sure. It made me think of my own spine and I wanted to be tough as those wild boars that travel in noisy herds through the ranch at night. And I brought some of Cedar's ashes. I hadn't opened the box since picking it up at the veterinary clinic, but the night before I left for New Mexico I'd unscrewed the lid and poured a few handfuls into a ziplock.

So far I hadn't been inspired to do any kind of ceremony and was feeling stupid for hiking all these things out into the wild. Emerald said we couldn't fail the fast, but what if all I did out here was walk around with no pants on and write in my journal?

The third day I woke up feeling a little different. I was halfway through. Nothing earth-shattering had happened but also, now I knew I could go days without food, shelter, and company and be fine. Bored maybe, but fine. This was comforting. Since the fire I'd obsessed over reviews of water purifiers, space blankets, axes, and first-aid kits on survivalist message boards. My wildfire PTSD took the form of lecturing my friends about making sure they were sufficiently insured and assembling emergency kits. I'd started sleeping with a crowbar under my bed just in case I needed to pry Josh or myself out from under rubble during a nighttime earthquake.

I'd signed up for the fast before the fire, but over the last few months

I started to think about it as yet another way to prepare for what scared me most. The inner cataclysm and the outer cataclysm.

Just before sunset I dragged my chair down to the edge of the cliff over the river and every night, at the same time, the swallows came out to hunt insects in the gathering dusk. A big swerving ballet company of birds. The first night I'd noticed someone else too. A few hundred feet below me, a beaver slid down the bank and into the deep green river water, headed upstream to gnaw off willow branches, and then swam them back to a lodge. I watched the beaver for a long time before I noticed a second one, working the other side of the river. It was a pair. They took turns swimming branches, working in tandem, calmly and steadily, but I could swear it seemed like they were enjoying it too. My eyes started to water. I missed Josh. Was I crying about the beavers? Lord, Laurel.

On the afternoon of the third day I'd had enough of writing in my journal and sketching in my notepad. I kept hearing what I thought was a generator or boat engine in the distance, a low droning hum. But it never got closer and then I noticed the sound went away whenever I breathed in. At some point when the wind died down, I realized with some horror that the droning sound was me. The sound of my own body. My own mind? If I stayed really still, I could hear my heartbeat too, or rather my pulse against my clothes. Concentrating on it made me feel worse—lonelier. And I started to think about food. The blue corn taco I'd eaten at the Shed in Santa Fe right before the fast. The can of smoked wild salmon from our friend Dexter in the trunk of my rental car back at the group campsite. Songs were the only thing that worked to distract me from thoughts of eating now. The two songs that alternated in my head were "Down to the River to Pray" and "Amazing Grace." I didn't know the words to either one very well but that didn't stop me.

I sang about the river to the river, as I picked my way through the spiny cholla, over the rocky cliffs and down to the narrow sandy shore. It was a perfectly sunny day, big white cumulus sailed past in the wind.

I imagined the beavers' thick, furry bodies heaving up and down this bank, dragging away purple blooming branches in their teeth, and I looked at the gnawed stumps around me. Every single one had new growth, green leaves and shoots, just beneath the beaver tooth marks.

"They're farming!" I said out loud.

They cut down to grow more.

I slid onto my hands and knees to look closer. Sure enough, lots of new growth sprouted at the base of every beaver cut. Next to a few particularly big stumps I noticed piles of shavings. They were about four inches long and a half-inch wide, strips of bark and branch and trunk. The trees had been big but the bites were small. The beavers felled trees dozens of times their size, bite by bite by bite.

I sat back on my heels. I'd taken a lot of stream ecology courses and even done a research study on beaver behavior back in college. I knew that their dams flooded streams that turned into lakes. Those lakes eventually collected enough silt to fill in and become meadows. Eventually those meadows would grow trees that became forests. But I'd never been taught that beavers pruned just like we did at home, cutting the avocado, lemon, and orange trees back in order to let in more light and help them grow bigger, stronger, and produce more fruit.

The new growth comes from the gnawed-off places.

"That's you," said a voice that sounded like my voice. "You can do this too."

I started gathering the beaver bits in my hands. I found one shaped like a heart that I slid into my pocket for Josh. The rest I tied up with a thin willow stem and put in my backpack. This is what I needed to do with my life. Bite by bite by bite—we can do all of the biggest things, like letting ourselves love people, knowing they can be yanked away at any minute for no good reason at all. Or we can become the parents we wish we'd had, or had for longer. Even if it's just for ourselves.

Joy rose like champagne in my veins, bubbling up from my feet out to the tips of my fingers. I sat with it, enjoying myself for a while, and then decided to head back to camp. I was running low on water. The sun was high and it was hot. I was climbing onto the top of a bluff when I heard a voice.

"Psst," it said. "Dig a hole. Bury your parents' guilt and shame in it."

Up until now I'd heard this voice a few times during the fast. But so far it had only told me about the beaver sticks, to get more iron in my diet, and to consider getting off the pill because it might be messing with my hormones. Now, though, the voice was more insistent. It sounded like me, but it was coming from behind or above me.

I looked down and saw a big, smooth black stone. "Mom," said the voice. I picked up the rock and kept walking. Eventually I came to a small sage bush. It was dead but stunning. Like a sculpture, twisting in air. "This is perfect," said the voice. Ravens flapped past talking to each other as the river slid softly by below, marked with the bull's-eyes of rising fish. I could hear the *rat-tat-tat* of kingfishers down by the water, see Pedernal off to my left in the distance. To my right were the red mesas and the white-and-yellow-banded cliffs that Georgia had painted.

I bent down and dug with my hands, till I had a hole deep enough and the undersides of my fingernails were tight with dirt.

"Say something," said the voice.

"To all that is and ever was and ever will be," I said, nearly choking on my embarrassment to be talking like this. "Please take my mom's biggest fears, heal her. Take her into this earth and make her whole. And me too. By releasing what isn't mine to carry. I love her so much."

It didn't feel ridiculous anymore. I put the rock in the hole and filled it with dirt, red and dark as dried blood, and then made a ring of small stones on top.

"Dig another hole," said the voice. "One for your dad."

I dug and dug till I had another good-sized hole and my hands hurt from scraping the ground. I paused for a few moments appreciating the breeze from the river, and then I pushed up from my knees and started to look for a rock for Dad. Something caught my eye about ten feet away. It was a tan hunk of sandstone, shot through with red. Big and maybe too heavy to lift. I walked over and bent down to look at it.

The rock was shaped like an enormous heart, not the symbol but the organ. And it was cracked. Right between the right and left atria. I heaved the pieces into my arms and walked over to the twisted bush, where I set it carefully into the hole. Then I placed my hand on top of the heart, hot from the sun.

"All that is, has ever been, and ever will be, please take my dad's pain, the body stuff that he put on me, the shame he had about being unable to heal himself. The fear he had in anyone seeing him as ill or suffering or one-legged. Even though I thought his stump was always great. Anyway, please take him in and heal him."

I felt the heat in my hand radiating from the stone and started to cry. Big snotty tears, the first trickles of a great flood. And then I realized that it wasn't just his shame and guilt I was burying. It was him too.

I was burying his heart.

To set myself free.

"Dad," I said, through a rush of tears, "I know you never wanted me to get stuck. I know you want me to be an adult. I was just scared that if I changed, you wouldn't know me anymore. That you wouldn't be able to find me if you came looking. And I really, really wanted you to find me."

I wiped my nose on the back of my hand. One of the ravens cawed. I looked out at the river.

"I know you did everything you could. I wish, though, that you'd been a little less controlling. I wish you'd let me say goodbye. I really hope Elisabeth Kübler-Ross and the doctors at Stanford are right, that hearing is the last sense to go. That you heard me read the poem I wrote and say how much I loved you. That you heard me promise to make you proud.

"I'm sorry I was scared to touch or hug you.

"I am sorry I was late. And that I didn't say goodbye.

"I love you so much.

"And I need to let you go.

"May the earth heal you. And set you free. May it heal and free both of us."

I pushed the soft piles of red dirt over the broken heart till the hole was filled in and then grabbed one last handful to spread across the top. I thought of the beaver bites in my backpack, the new growth at the base of their cuts. Everything a cycle. Every beginning an ending. Every ending a beginning. Every part, no matter how small, a never-ending story. Dad had done the best he could as my compass, but now I needed to be my own.

I tamped the dirt down and then, as soon as I lifted my hand, a giant clap of thunder boomed right over my head. I jumped and looked up at the sky. It was bright blue and sunny. Only now there was a single dramatic Snoopy cloud almost directly above me.

"Are you KIDDING?" I said to the cloud. "Isn't this a little on the nose?"

Back at my tree, I laid on my sleeping bag, watching the light filter through the branches, hoping it wouldn't rain. I stuck my hands in the sandy ground on either side of my sleeping pad and let it slip through my fingers. God's sand tray. That's exactly what I was doing out here. Making and finding meaning in everything just like the kids did in Andrea's office. Sometimes we need to use our hands, our bodies, to do what our words can't.

When the sun got low over the mountain, I sat up again. The voice that was my voice told me I wasn't done. I grabbed the ziplock of Cedar's ashes. And another one of dried sage I'd picked at the ranch before the fire.

The sky was turning pink, orange, and purple and I had just set down my things by my parents' stone graves when the voice said: "Build a house. A house of the heart."

It sounded cheesy but I knew it was from an essay I'd printed out about ancient Egyptian death practices and tacked above my desk. The house of the heart is what ancient Egyptians called the human body. Sacred architecture.

I collected a handful of long stones and built a little structure out of the yellow rocks. I folded up the sage and placed it inside. Humming, I opened the ziplock of Cedar's ashes. The wind was blowing and as I dropped them—the gritty bits of bone, the soft white chalk of him—they made a white circle that covered the front of me too. By the time I was done, the moon was up. Venus, the only other light in the sky, was just visible over the mountain.

I noticed wet tears on my cheeks and sighed, thinking about all the years I hadn't cried. All the years I'd shoved those feelings into busyness, distraction, the chasing of yet more prizes, anything to help me not feel. How worried I'd been that if I dipped my toe in the lake of sadness I'd drown in it. That if I started crying, I'd just never stop.

I'd been right, in a way. But what I hadn't realized was how good it would feel. I'd headed into the Amazon by myself at nineteen, followed grizzly bears alone into the Alaskan bush, gone to MIT to do a PhD that scared me to death, broken up my marriage, thrown myself into dating strangers like it was an Olympic trial—but all along it was feeling my feelings that scared me the most. And now here I was, alone with my greatest fear of all, in my little nylon chair at the edge of a vast wilderness. Nowhere to escape to. And I felt okay. I wiped my cheeks on the dirty sleeves of my down jacket and pulled my sleeping bag around me. A pack of coyotes yipped together across the river and then a second pack howled from somewhere behind me. I sucked in a breath so deep my chest hurt, leaned forward in my chair, and howled back, as loud as I could.

Nineteen

Chama River Canyon Wilderness, New Mexico, May 2018

On the last day of the fast I woke up before sunrise. I was almost done. Thank God. I was fantasizing about buttered toast, coffee with heavy cream, and churros. The sky was purpling in the east. Without turning my head I could see the west was still velvety blue-black. There were so many stars out, thousands, even though the sun was coming up soon. I was right up against something so infinite and beautiful and daunting, a quilt of forevers.

Then I saw him.

"Hey, beebs," Dad said. Looking straight at me. He was in front of the stars in the southeast, superimposed over the lightening sky near Pedernal but also inside it. He was wearing his Stetson and jeans and a blue and white pearl-buttoned short-sleeved shirt. I know this sounds impossible or like some sort of hunger dream. But I could see Dad like I could see my sleeping bag and the stars above me and the junipers. I was totally sober. It was not like being on mushrooms or having a high fever, or even a lucid dream. I was looking at him and he was real and not only that—he was standing in the den at the ranch. He picked his pipe up from the silver ashtray next to his brown leather chair. And smiled.

"Oh my God," I said aloud, still in my sleeping bag. "He has the house."

Just then Cedar ran into the den through the old wooden doors to the kitchen. Levi and Oliver and all the other dead dogs were behind him. They swirled around Dad's feet, a happy darting pack.

The dogs!

Before I knew it, I was crying horizontally. Big tears sliding down the sides of my face, pooling at my temples. I wasn't sad, though. I was happy. I shook my head side to side to dislodge the image of them all. But it didn't go anywhere. Dad just kept smiling at me. I noticed he had both legs.

What the hell was happening here? I knew if I ever told anyone about this that I'd sound unstable—or worse, too woo-woo to be trusted. But I was looking at something as real as anything else I'd ever known. I could see the dark outline of my water bottle, the last gallon jugs of water, and my straw hat hanging from a low branch of the tree next to me. I could feel a sharp stone pressing through my sleeping pad and into my right hip. This was nothing like vivid memories I'd had before, memories that felt real. No, this WAS real.

Dad turned away from me and I felt my stomach drop. Was he leaving? But no, I recognized a sound, a sharp *tap-tap-tap* on the tile. And then young me, maybe five or six years old, wearing my favorite brown leather cowboy boots, red cowboy hat with the white chin strap, and a flower-print cotton dress, came barreling through the door after the dogs and ran straight for him in front of the fireplace, the basket of *Wall Street Journal*s we used as kindling on the floor beside his boots. Dad broke into a grin so wide he had to take the pipe out of his mouth.

"I'm there too?!" I said to the air.

That's when I heard the voice again. The one that was mine.

"He's not at the ranch," the voice said. "The ranch that burned down, anyway. He's at the ranch that didn't burn and he's there with Levi and Sophie and Oliver and Cedar. He's healthy. They're healthy. And Mom is there too. And you."

I caught a flash of her in the kitchen, behind the wooden doors, humming her surprise song, the one she hummed whenever she was planning something good. She was wearing a blue wraparound skirt printed with strawberries she used to have, and her hair was pushed back from her forehead. She looked to be about my age now.

"Why me?" I asked. "Why Mom?" But the voice was silent.

Then, like any other realization I've ever had—that I should talk to that guy at the buffet in the Grand Aleutian, that I'd like to write books one day, that I should probably, always, add more hot sauce to the guacamole—the voice answered.

There is a world in which we are whole. And it runs parallel to ours.

The people that we love exist there, and we can almost reach out and touch them if we just get quiet enough. They never leave us. We are together always. There, too, are the selves of ours that need healing. And all the things that we love and have lost.

I thought of the stones, the little house I'd built the night before. Of course! I'd sent the ranch off to the afterlife without realizing and now it was there. Only it wasn't an afterlife. Not really. It was more like a parallel life. One we don't have to wait for in order to believe in. It is already here.

My tears had begun to make my ears itch. I sat up in my sleeping bag and the image of Mom and Dad and the ranch and the dogs faded. But just like when you close the door to a room and walk into another, the one you leave doesn't stop existing. It's just that now you're somewhere else.

Twenty

Cochiti Lake, New Mexico, May 2018

After the fast, back at our group campsite, we all brought our chairs down into a rock-strewn wash and talked about what had happened out there. We'd ended up facing our biggest fears, and while a lot of people had eaten their emergency granola bars, especially on the last night, when we'd been drenched by a surprise thunderstorm that lasted hours, no one had left the fast early or wound up injured or hurt. We'd made it. I was a little concerned, though, because I didn't hear anyone else describe parallel worlds or seeing their dead parents.

When it was my turn, I dug the Auryn out of my pocket and passed it around. Then I told them everything. Not just about the last five days but also about how Dad died and how I'd been late. My shame and guilt. And Dad's shame too. How in my family we were expected to be excellent, not pitiable. I told them about Cedar. And the fire. And Josh. And all the men before him. And the kids at Josie's Place. The pregnancy. And how I thought I might have gotten stuck emotionally at seventeen and why. I told them about burying my parents out there and spreading Cedar's ashes. About the sage I'd brought from the ranch and put in the little house of stones. And then waking up, the next morning, to see Dad and Mom. And the ranch. And young me. The dogs. How real it was. It is. The parallel world.

When I got to the end I looked around the circle, expecting them to be looking at me like I was nuts. Or worse, self-indulgent. But they were crying. For their own people and dead pets, the ones they wished they could see again too. And they were smiling at me.

"I'm so embarrassed," I said, laughing. "Now I'm going to be one of those people wandering around the Bay Area telling others they have to go into the desert. I really was a skeptic."

Petra smiled. She was holding the Auryn. Turning it over in her hands.

"You're cutting down to grow more," she said. "That is your medicine. Love takes time. It takes dedication. It's not all going to happen in one day. Don't forget, too, that there were two beavers. And part of why they don't burn out is because they work together.

"You ARE your father's daughter," she said. "But this needed to be done. The severance. And it didn't just need to be done for you, it also needed to be done for him. This father loved you so much that he couldn't say goodbye. And I think you've now forgiven him for that."

Petra handed the Auryn to Emerald, who closed her eyes and started speaking, rocking back and forth in her camp chair.

"You know beavers, they don't just cut down trees. They build dams. They dam up rivers, they create floods, they create ponds, they create communities. Sometimes they create nuisances for the farmers and those who wish to keep them small. So when you found the beaver that's you, in you, you set something free. The dammed-up shame, the dammed-up guilt, the dammed . . . the dammed-up, damming, damning, 'Damn you for fucking dying without me!' That dam broke."

She was right. I started laughing and then so did the other women. I could feel the circle buoy with relief and hope for their own rivers of shame to crest the banks and break the dams that needed breaking. We could be, would be, free. Even if life wasn't quite done with us yet. Even if it never was.

Twenty-One

Santa Paula, California, November 2018

After the vision fast there was one last thing I knew I needed to do in order to complete whatever strange journey I'd been on. It took me six and a half months to screw up the courage. Actually, it had taken me the better part of twenty-three years. I needed to ask Mom what had really happened the day Dad died.

I saw her a dozen times between May, when I'd done the fast, and the following fall. She even came up to Alaska to visit me and Josh where we were living for the summer, and then I saw her again in Berkeley, where Josh and I had moved in together in a small apartment off Live Oak Park, but it never felt like the right moment. I told myself that I didn't want to upset her, even though it was me I was worried about.

Eventually it was Thanksgiving. I was staying with Mom and Sam at their rental house in Ventura that the insurance company was paying for. On my last day Mom was headed to the ranch to check on some new irrigation lines and we made a plan to meet at the top of the driveway. That's what we said now, instead of "at the house." The top of the driveway was just dirt, scraped clean now by the county debris removal teams. As soon as Jake and Alice's permits got approved, they would be building a big new house where our beloved old one had been. They'd had another baby in August, Toby, who'd come out smiling just like

Jake had. In their current house, the boys all slept in a small bedroom. Toby in his crib and Benny and Wilder in a bunk bed. When Jake and Alice finished building the new place, the plan was for Mom and Sam to move into their old house and make it their own. I was happy for everyone, but gutted too. Not only was the house I loved dead and gone, but what was replacing it would be unrecognizable. I'd need to ask permission to go in, knocking on the front door like a visitor.

When Mom showed up, we decided to walk to the top of the hill. At the wooden picnic table, next to a big charred oak, Mom sat down and cracked open a beer.

"I'm ready," she said, looking a little pained.

And then we heard an owl. And another. And another. All coming from different directions.

"I need to know about the day Dad died," I said.

She blanched a little, under her tan.

"I need you to explain to me why you didn't tell me what was happening, so I could be there in time to say goodbye."

She looked surprised, or maybe just relieved.

"Because he didn't want you there, Lar," she said.

"Really?" I asked, but I could tell she was telling the truth.

"You know he never wanted you to see him in the hospital. It was the same with his death. He said that he wanted you and Jake to remember him the way you'd seen him last."

"But our last conversation was a fight," I said, my voice faltering. I could feel the tears coming.

"It was?"

Did she really not know? Dad hadn't hung up the phone upset and then told her all about it? How ungrateful I was? How stubborn and rude?

"So I wasn't late?"

"To what?"

"'To what'?! His death! My whole life I've worried I was late. That he wanted to say goodbye to me and I missed it."

I started to cry now, sob really. I hoped I wasn't scaring the owls.

"But he'd already said goodbye to you, sweetie. He loved you so much. He was probably glad you'd had that conversation the night before."

"But I hung up on him, I didn't say I loved him."

"Oh, Laurel. You know he was in so much pain. I tried to get him to wait. I told him that you were about to hear about college early decision. And didn't he want to wait and find out where? You know what he said?"

I rubbed my nose on the sleeve of my jacket. "What?"

"He said, 'I know she's going to get in. And if she doesn't, she's going to be just fine, Lynn.'"

I sucked in my breath. This was NOT what I was expecting to hear. In my mind, he was worried that I wouldn't be okay and that's why he'd pushed me so hard, so relentlessly, for so long. And then, after he was gone, it was why I'd pushed myself.

"He said that it was a good time to die. That you and Jake would be off from school."

"How far ahead of time had he planned it?"

"I don't know."

"You didn't know?"

"Not in advance. He told me that morning." She shook her head side to side. "What would I have done if I'd known?"

"Wow," I said. "He was protecting you too. In his own way."

The sun was all the way down now and the stars were coming out in the east. The crickets were loud between the hooting of the owls.

"Maybe he thought if you were there that he wouldn't be able to do it," she said. "But I know he didn't want you to watch him die. I'm so sorry. I didn't know you felt this way. I always thought you were dealing with the loss just fine."

"Well, that's what I wanted you to think," I said. "I buried it. I had to wait till I was forty to find out the truth." And then I asked her to tell me what it had been like, his death.

She said they sent Jake over to a friend's house in the morning. And then it was just the two of them there, in their bedroom. She got into bed next to him. He told her the medication was bitter and asked for a glass of cranberry juice. She didn't really want to tell me more. Or maybe it was that she had never explained this experience to someone else. Had never had to put it into words. Or maybe it was just theirs. But I pressed her.

"We talked. He said, 'I'm going to miss my memories so much. I have so many good memories of us all.' And he kept reassuring me, saying, 'It's going to be all right. You're going to be all right. The kids are going to be all right.' And we talked about your future."

I pictured him listing college and graduate schools for us, maybe marriages and kids of our own, his ideas for the ranch.

But Mom shook her head. "He said, 'Laurel and Jake know how much I love them. They know how much they mean to me.' That's how he knew you'd be okay. He believed it with all his heart and soul. I think that's how he lived. To make sure it would be true."

I let her words sink in, feeling the night air on my hands. He *had* lived that way.

"I think the greatest gift of my life is knowing what it's like to be loved like that," I said.

It was true. No matter what came my way, love was a spring I trusted never to run dry. It was why I was so scared of loss. I knew the stakes. He and Mom had given me that. And then Mom had proven it again after he died. We'd gotten Sam.

Dad's goodbye to me wasn't our last fight, it had been my whole damn life. The lesson he'd fought so hard to teach Jake and me wasn't that we needed to be perfect, it was that we were loved. I'd just misunderstood.

Like so many of the grieving kids I'd met, I believed in some irrational but emotionally true place, that if I'd only gotten there in time to say goodbye, then losing him would have been less terrible. But shame and guilt are just different forms of grief.

I'd diverged from Dad's plan, not by being late, but by blaming myself for his death. Because I'd needed someone to blame. The alternative was admitting I was powerless, and that was worse.

There it was. Evidence. All I'd ever needed. And I was about to get a chance to prove it.

Part IV

If you want a happy ending, that depends, of course, on where you stop your story.

Orson Welles

One

Oakland, California, January 2020

I was standing at my desk in downtown Oakland, the one that Jake made for me using Dad's woodworking tools, reading my clinical chaplaincy materials when the phone rang. I had no idea what a clinical chaplain was when I'd started working at the medical school. But I saw the Christian, Jewish, and Muslim chaplains at the hospital's monthly Ethics Committee meetings. They were scattered among the physicians, administrators, and ethicists wearing name tags that read SPIRITUAL CARE. They understood medicine, spoke thoughtfully about complex cases, and helped patients and their families articulate what they needed and wanted. Over the years I'd realized that teaching writing was sometimes indistinguishable from spirituality. On my best days, I was a channel not a font. I decided to apply to the part-time chaplaincy training program convinced I'd never be accepted. The application had questions like "describe your congregation" and "religious affiliation" and "spiritual practice." Most of these I marked "N/A." There was no option for "secular skeptic who believes in parallel realities" or "wanders wilderness in search of meaning while watching beavers." I wrote that I was Jewish by blood but not by practice. I hoped to be a safe harbor for patients and families who might be a little like me—raised in a certain faith tradition but not a member of an organized religion. I wanted to be a bridge to a kind of solace they couldn't access on their own, or maybe I would just help them feel less alone for a few minutes. When the Stanford Office of Spiritual Care emailed, offering me a spot, I was shocked. My first training session was in three days.

Now, though, my phone was ringing. It was Mom. I picked up, a little nervous.

I'd seen her two weeks before. She, Sam, Josh, and I went to Santa Fe for Christmas. We'd spent a week eating green chile and drinking thick Mexican hot chocolate. We went to a concert at the Loretto Chapel, where Mom cried at the beauty of the chamber music. We'd bundled up against the cold and walked around the east side of town, marveling at the warm glow of farolitos in the snow—the hundreds of paper lanterns lining streets and rooflines. We got drunk on Albariño and laughed till we cried over tapas at a small café off the plaza. On Christmas Day we went to Jemez Pueblo to watch the deer and buffalo dances and then drove up to Ghost Ranch. I wanted Mom, Sam, and Josh to see where I'd done my vision fast.

We bounced down the long dirt road to the spot where I'd headed out between the juniper trees, the three of them marveling at the purple silhouette of Pedernal and the bright smell of snow on the wind. When we got out of the car Josh took me by the hand and led me to a rocky outcropping over the Chama, running brown now with silt. It was a little strange to see him in the landscape where I'd spent so much time thinking about him. I wondered what the beavers were doing down in their lodge or if they were out gnawing on something.

"I know this place is special to you," Josh said. "I hope it's okay if we make it special for both of us." He tipped the brim of my hat back and put his arms around me.

"Will you marry me?"

Yes. Yes, of course Yes.

We kissed and he pulled me against him in his puffy coat. Then we walked back to the car holding hands and told Sam and Mom, who were standing nearby admiring the view. She cried. I think we all did. And then Mom told us how happy she was. Josh said their relationship gave him hope. We looked at the red, white, and yellow cliffs and I said silent thanks for the waves of joy that kept coming and coming and then we drove back to town to toast our happiness with prickly pear margaritas, hot fresh chips, and guacamole at Maria's. I was so completely in my joy I'd stopped scanning the horizon for danger.

Now, the trip felt like a year, not a month, ago. In the last week Mom had two brief episodes of double vision and then one very scary half hour during which her right arm rose on its own and she couldn't control it. Sam took her to the emergency room where they'd done some imaging and discovered she'd had a TIA—a transient ischemic attack—or minor stroke. Her primary care doctor, an old friend of Dad's, ordered more tests. At first I was terrified about a brain tumor but her scan in the ER had been clear, thank God. We expected heart disease, which, while not great, wasn't cancer. She had to be okay. She was the healthiest person I knew. She hiked long distances with friends, carried heavy pruning shears for hours, walked faster than me, and had never had a real injury or illness. My greatest fear was that something would happen to her, but I talked myself out of it. She wasn't going to die younger than her own mom had—a woman who smoked, drank scotch like water, and still lived to ninety-eight. Her father had lived even longer and read nearly a book a day till the very end. I figured we had twenty more years together.

"Lar," Mom said. And suddenly I was five years old again, or eleven, or seventeen. She was scared. Something was wrong, really wrong. Her voice was cracking. Every muscle in my body contracted.

"I have pancreatic cancer," she choked out. "And it's in my liver." She started sobbing. I think I said "what" probably ten times. I wasn't calm but I'm guessing I sounded that way because that's what I do. Become a prey animal that freezes.

"It's the worst one, Lar. The very worst one. I can't believe it. I'm going to die."

Fear, like light, travels faster than sound, and when it hit me it was a cleaver.

"I just don't get it," she was saying. "Me?!"

We were both in shock, time felt suspended.

"I'm coming down," I said. After hanging up, I typed "pancreatic cancer stage four" into Google.

"Stage IV pancreatic cancer has a five-year survival rate of 1 percent," I read. "The average patient diagnosed with late-stage pancreatic cancer will live for about 1 year after diagnosis."

One year.

One percent survival.

Whatever potential avalanche of terror was inside me suddenly broke free. I heard wailing. And then I was choking. It was dread. Thick in my throat. I couldn't feel my hands. Still, somehow, I shut down my computer and picked up my keys. Walked out to my car. Sat in the driver's seat and tried to turn on the windshield wipers so I could see. Only it was my eyes. I called Josh and tried to explain what was happening.

"Oh no. No," he said. I remember wondering in my confusion why we do this. Say no when we hear truths we hate. As if we could refuse what's already been handed to us. As if we could argue with what's already happened.

I thought of Dad's promise to Mom, back when he was first diagnosed, that everything would be okay, that he would make sure that it was. Somehow I'd inherited their contract without realizing it. It was a part of me now. I didn't know whether or not "okay" was even possible, but I knew we had to try.

Two

Santa Paula, California, January 2020

By the time Josh and I pulled in to the driveway in front of Jake and Alice's house at the ranch it was just shy of midnight. As Josh drove, I'd spoken to half a dozen colleagues at the medical school and UCSF and was working on getting phone numbers for oncologists at Cedars-Sinai, UCLA, and MD Anderson in Texas. I was bludgeoning my terror with information, marshaling all I'd ever learned for this.

There was still a chance Mom had the "good kind" of pancreatic cancer. The kind Steve Jobs had, slower growing and potentially operable. He'd lived for eight years! I clung to this like a soggy Kate Winslet on a piece of the *Titanic*.

Adenocarcinoma, though, was the most likely possibility. And it was lethal. Especially since Mom's scan had turned up a few metastases in her liver.

A day or two later, Mom, Sam, Josh, and I gathered in the driveway before heading to City of Hope, a cancer center in Los Angeles whose name made me gag with prescriptive optimism. Sam handed each of us a white three-ring binder with all the research I'd turned up in it, along with Mom's initial scan and test results. He'd labeled them "The Silverfox Playbook." We laughed. "Silverfox" was our nickname for Mom ever since she'd gone gray in her midthirties. Dad started it and it stuck. It was what we called her whenever we weren't using her other nickname, "the Hammer," for her ability to get the best deal without pissing off whoever she was negotiating with.

At the hospital, we sat in a tiny exam room while the surgical oncologist, Dr. Susanne Warner, explained with precise and encompassing kindness that the biopsy would confirm it for sure, but looking at Mom's scans she believed this was adenocarcinoma.

I could feel my grip on the bobbing hunk of shipwreck slipping. This was not the good kind of cancer. But was it operable?

No, she said. And no, there were no good chemotherapies. If effective, the top two drugs extended life by a few weeks. There was a chance Mom would qualify for one of the new immunotherapies, but in Dr. Warner's experience, rarely did adenocarcinomas turn up the right genetic markers for treatment. We would be doing genetic sequencing of Mom's tumors immediately just in case. What about trials? We could look into it, Dr. Warner explained, and she would be happy to advise, but she believed those too were a bit of a long shot with pancreatic cancer.

"What exactly is my prognosis, then?" Mom asked.

Dr. Warner looked at us with heartbreak in her eyes.

"A year, maybe less, maybe more. We can't really say, but this is a terrible disease."

In my memory the floor of the room fell out and we started tumbling, like in a bad dream, through darkness. Nothing to hold on to. In reality, though, we said our goodbyes and wandered, dazed, into the sunshine before driving to a Jewish deli in the valley for a lunch of cold cuts on rye. We ate them while crying.

On the way home I called around for second opinions and wondered if I could be even a tiny bit hopeful. Dr. Warner had said that there were outliers to the statistics and not only that but any stats we saw about life expectancy were five years old now or more. They didn't account for recent advances because those wouldn't have been factored into any models yet. I'd wanted to lean over and kiss her. Somehow she'd given us obliterating news but also just enough room to reach for something else instead.

That night, back at the ranch, Josh was sleeping next to me. But whenever I closed my eyes I saw myself jumping off the wooden bridge over the creek where I used to catch pollywogs, the bed dry now and littered with sandy boulders. It scared me. I'd never had thoughts like this. Eventually I got out of bed and walked up the driveway to the old house site in the dark. Jake and Alice had started construction on their new place and the foundation was an unrecognizable footprint. Nearly all the old trees were gone. Heavy machinery threw long shadows in the moonlight. The new house was months from being done, maybe a year. The insurance money for Mom and Sam's rental house had run out so the two of them now lived in a freestanding room near Jake and Alice's place without a kitchen, an unsustainable living situation. If Mom needed treatment she was going to have to stay in this room till Jake and Alice finished building and moved. Josh and I would need to stay where we were too, in Jake and Alice's guest room over Jake's workshop. But I couldn't think about this now.

"Dad," I said into the darkness. "I need you."

I wanted him to appear in front of the stars like he had in New Mexico and tell me who else I should call. I wanted to send a message like a bat signal that he would answer with a clear plan for us and advice on treatment options. I wanted him to tell me how to save Mom like he'd saved himself, for all those years, again and again against all odds.

But he didn't appear. It was just me there in the moonlight, alone and talking to myself. I wished I believed in prayer, or at least had the kind of faith that would let me find God in this somewhere.

On the drive down to the ranch, when it became too late for me to call cancer centers and doctor friends, I'd turned on an audiobook that touched on this—*Here If You Need Me* by Kate Braestrup, a chaplain with the Maine Warden Service. Josh and I had been driving through a rainstorm on the Grapevine—a pass on I-5—when we got to a part that made me turn up the volume. A little girl had fallen through the ice of a frozen pond and drowned. One of the Maine wardens, a fellow named Frank, pulled her out, cradling the small dead girl in his arms. Now Frank was asking Braestrup, the chaplain, how it could be possible that this tragedy was part of God's plan.

Braestrup was a widow herself, her husband killed in a car crash leaving her with their four young kids. She considered Frank's question and then said that when her kids asked her why their dad had died, she told them it was an accident.

It made me think of the well-meaning teachers at Thacher who'd told me to trust in God when Dad got sick, that He had a plan. Other people sometimes suggested that God just wanted Dad back. That one made me laugh. The last person I figured God wanted close by was someone who'd storm around swearing at him.

But Kate Braestrup had a different idea. She told the warden he shouldn't look for God in the girl's death. That it was an accident. God, she said, was somewhere else.

Frank had taken the girl out from under the ice with his own hands. He'd tried to resuscitate her even when it was futile and then he'd gone home to his own young daughters, to hug them tighter, his heart broken for the mother whose daughter would never come home again. Frank, Braestrup said, was where God was in this.

Sitting in the dark, looking at the foundation of the new house, I thought about Jake racing to put out fires at other people's homes, loading other people's loved ones into ambulances while he worried about his own mom. I thought about my Thacher pals bringing over stacks of meals, and my best friends in the Bay Area who'd started having regular conference calls to figure out how best to support us. Other friends spent days combing through research to identify potentially useful Phase III trials and made custom playlists for us to listen to on our long drives to medical appointments. Mom's girlfriends were mailing prayer flags and delivering croissants and deli platters. Dad's best friend Phil and his wife Jill sent matzah ball soup and black-and-white cookies, the comforting shorthand of our people. Sam's daughters, who were as devastated as us, were writing heartfelt letters, and Nancy, my good friend and Sam's eldest, flew out to visit as soon as she could, just to sit quietly with her dad, drinking beers and watching the sunset. My student Pablo, whose own mom and dad had died when he was in high school and college, went to Nordstrom to buy Mom a silk scarf and pillowcase. She wrapped the gauzy fabric around her neck, clucking in amazement at the thoughtfulness of this young man she'd never met, and twirled, saying, "Tell me again how old Pablo was when he lost his parents?"

God was, apparently, in the Accessories department. In my pinging text streams and the Tupperware containers stacking up in the fridge. God was in the clinicians who were taking my calls and the receptionists I was badgering for appointments. In Susanne Warner and Audrey Shafer, my mentor at Stanford who was calling in favors to get Mom seen quickly. Maybe, too, God was in me.

We found Mom a world-class oncologist at UCLA who advised she start Folfirinox, a cocktail of chemo drugs that sounded like something we'd use to kill aphids on the ranch and turned out to be just as brutal. It made her skin mottled, her food taste like metal, and sent her to bed miserable and nauseated for a week. Her infusions were a full thirty-six hours long, thirty-two of which she spent carrying around a pump connected to the port in her chest. She hated it. She had no practice being sick. She'd throw up for hours, sweat through her sheets, feel foggy and exhausted but unable to rest.

Sometime in late February, Mom woke up unable to control her arm again and this time she couldn't speak. She was terrified and dazed. Sam and Jake rushed her to the emergency room. It turned out that she'd developed a syndrome related to pancreatic cancer that stimulated the formation of blood clots that could travel to her brain and cause strokes. She'd had another mini stroke. Thankfully her ability to speak came back, along with her ability to control her arm, but the full use of her right hand never did. This enraged and scared her. She was terrified of strokes. She knew how she wanted to die and if she had a stroke that incapacitated her, then she wouldn't be able to do it.

We'd started talking about death right after her diagnosis. I was lying next to her in their wooden four-poster bed, looking at the bright green orchards through the glass doors across the room. You couldn't tell from here but the trees that survived the fire had been doing all right, coming back to life, slowly but steadily.

"I promise, Mom, you will not suffer a minute more than you want to. You will not die in pain. I swear it." This was something I could commit to. She wanted to die like Dad had, on her own terms. And now, almost twenty-five years later, it was legal.

At Stanford, I was part of the Center for Biomedical Ethics and I'd sat in on plenty of meetings about California's new right-to-die legislation. Considering that hers was not a curable disease, talking about Mom's inevitable death seemed reasonable but I knew that many oncologists saw stopping treatment and/or a patient's assertion of their right-to-die as a professional failure. I did not want Mom to have that kind of oncologist. We needed a partner on speaking terms with mortality. When, a few minutes into our first appointment, I asked her doctor if he'd support Mom's choice to die if and when her treatments stopped working, he shifted a little uncomfortably on his rolling stool, but agreed that he would.

And then her tumor marker, a sign of aggressiveness of her disease, went way down. Mom's six-week scan showed no tumor growth at all. Her twelve-week scan was even better. Her back pain lessened. A good sign, her team said. So she kept going with the chemo. She wanted to see Jake and Alice move into their new house and do renovations on their old one so it would feel like hers. She wanted to see the end of the Trump presidency. She wanted to finish reading this book, the one you're reading right now. "Just give me two years," she said over and over to the sky, an incantation, a prayer.

In the meantime, school district by school district, state by state, country by country, Covid was forcing the planet to shut down. I made a final trip to the Bay Area to teach but I didn't spend the night. Josh and I decided we were moving to the ranch. A few of my friends worried. "What about your own life?" they asked. "Maybe you should sublet, not give up your lease?" But this *was* my life. There was nothing more important than spending time with Mom right now and I was lucky enough to be able to do it. I'd been hearing the ticking of the mortality timer since I was old enough to tie my shoelaces. There would be no convincing me otherwise.

On Saturdays, out of fear and a frantic desire to be doing something other than worry about Mom's tumors and our Covid risk, I started offering free reflective writing workshops for healthcare workers and their loved ones. Till this point, the workshops were something I'd only done at Stanford but considering what was happening now, that felt wrong. I called it Writing Medicine and hundreds of people showed up every week via Zoom from around the world, a kind of ad-hoc support family that transcended time zone and medical specialty, a fellowship of folks seeing the same terrifying things day in and day out. I showed Mom how to join on her iPad and she and Josh would listen from her room while geriatric nurses read essays about the patients they loved vanishing one after another and ICU physicians and respiratory therapists in NYC talked about triaging care in the Covid wards.

After the sessions wrapped up, I'd go over to Mom's room and sit in the upholstered chair at the foot of her bed and we'd talk over what we'd heard. In our family, the most popular dinner conversation was always medical. The more disturbing, the better. So this felt weirdly normal. I would have done anything for normal.

"No one suspects the days to be gods," Ralph Waldo Emerson wrote, but they are. Especially when they're numbered.

• • •

A few years ago I read a book, *Death and the Creative Life*, by Lisl Marburg Goodman. It included an idea I love. Goodman proposed that we count our age not from birth forward but from our death backward, based on how much life we realistically had left. This would make an American woman in her seventies ten or so years old, and my nephew Toby closer to eighty. Of course, there are no guarantees and life expectancies are tied to so many factors outside our control. But still, if we counted our ages backward instead of forward, I think it would be harder to take the time we do have left for granted. I wondered if Mom was a year old now and what age I was too.

On her good days—or during her good hours on mediocre days—Mom walked around the ranch with all of us. She supervised as Josh, Sam, and I did a big prune of the olive orchard. She sat on a chaise lounge we brought up to the garden and directed as we cleaned out the previous year's overgrowth and patched the fence where rabbits were getting in. She bought me a gardening bag, a good pair of gloves, and a sharp pair of shears. She was proud of the seedlings I'd started in the greenhouse and my improvements to her cutting garden. And a lot of the time she brought with her the device she called "furry man."

My friends Pat and Annie, radio journalists and podcast producers, had sent me a brand-new audio recorder to use to interview her. I put a furry black windscreen over the mic that made it look like a little troll (hence "furry man") so Mom could use it outside. I recorded her a bit, but I also taught her how to use it herself and gave her a list of questions to answer whenever she felt like it. When she had the energy, I'd find her outside standing in her new butterfly garden talking into the thing as if she were directing us. "Please make sure the water doesn't dry up in the birdbath. They [meaning the birds] will expect it to be full."

Seeing her like this, up and moving around, full of energy like her old self, I felt such exquisite and painful happiness that it was like a balloon in my chest, nearly lifting me off my feet. I knew I was losing her, and I knew how much, every single day for the rest of my life, I would want her back. It made my whole body ache. Anticipatory grief this is called, but it's also anticipatory longing. I knew that one day I'd trade anything and everything for one more moment just like this, coming across her in the garden talking into the recorder about how she didn't want us to drive the UTV too fast down the avocado rows because their shallow roots wouldn't like it, or the way she called out "Larrr" from whatever room I wasn't in, her donkey hee-haw laugh that's just like mine, the way she looked over my shoulder in the kitchen and constantly asked if I was sure I wanted to "do it that way."

I would have a million questions only she had the answer to. Ones I couldn't even think to ask yet. She was our whole family history, even more so now that all our photos and records were gone.

There were also different things that I didn't want to remember but knew I would anyway. How scared she was when she'd get a shooting pain through her back, the viselike grip that occasionally took hold of her upper chest. How sometimes she would start throwing up and then not be able to stop and would be too tired to drag herself from the toilet back to the bed, only to have to come back and throw up again in a few minutes. She laid down on the warm bathroom floor next to the toilet, horrified by her stained nightgown but too exhausted to put on the new clean one I'd brought her. I'd sit down next to her and put my hands on her back, give her another anti-nausea pill, and look at the bones protruding from her shoulders, her hips. How she would announce, in the darkest depths in the days after a chemo infusion that she was definitely done, that she couldn't live like this, that she wanted it to end. And then, a few days later she'd have a good morning, bouncing out of bed at 7 a.m. and cleaning the house and ordering more oakleaf hydrangeas to plant.

Hope is like this. A trickster that transforms itself all the time, expanding to fill the space it's given. First you hope that the scan or the blood work doesn't turn up cancer. Then if it does, you hope for the good kind. If it's not the good kind, if it's a worse kind, then you hope it's contained or operable or responds well to treatment, that the tumors shrink, the blood work improves. If those things don't happen, then you hope that at least things don't get worse. If they do anyway, then you hope for the best possible version of worse. On and on, just like this. As hope—once big as the sky—gets ever smaller until eventually it's gone. It happens quietly, as if hope had slipped out of a dinner party early, while everyone was busy talking. When you finally notice it's not there, it's sort of too late to wonder when it left.

That is what happened to us. January turned to February, March to April, April to May. I tried to swallow my despair as well as my frustration over living with Josh in a small room above the garage, of trying to cook our meals in a microwave in our makeshift spaces, washing dishes in the shower, while we and Mom and Sam waited for Jake and Alice's new house to be finished so we could move into theirs and finally have a kitchen of our own. But also, and even though they were only a hundred yards away, we missed them. As a firefighter, Jake was an essential worker with frequent Covid exposures, so we were quarantined from him and Alice and the boys because Mom was so vulnerable.

In early May, Josh left for salmon season in Alaska. He was running a salmon cannery now in the tiny Native Alaskan village of Larsen Bay, on the northern coast of Kodiak Island, a bush flight away from a grocery store, paved roads, and most everything else resembling a "town." Usually I'd go with him and we'd spend the duration of the summer living in a small house surrounded by raspberry bushes that I had to fight the bears for. But now Josh would be going alone and he'd be there till September. A five-month eternity.

"I'm sorry. I don't want to go," he said to me on the curb at Burbank Airport, muffled behind the plastic gray respirator with the round pink filters I'd made him wear. When I got home I got into bed and sobbed. The salmon didn't care about our puny sorrows.

Mom's tumor marker at her next test crept back up a bit and her liver panel was incrementally worse. I knew before she did. Managing her stroke risk and her symptoms was a full-time job because they changed constantly and new things needed to be tried all the time, dosages played with, new meds to treat the side effects of the other meds. Constipation, nausea, occasional shooting pains that took her breath away and then vanished, duller, throbbing pains that didn't. Her next scan was still a month away, but this was not a good sign.

I went into her bedroom where she was lying on her bed reading Joy Harjo's latest book of poems, *An American Sunrise*.

"Lar," Mom said now, looking up from the page she was on, "listen to this. 'I sing my leaving song. I sing it to the guardian trees . . . I will sing it until the day I die.' "

Three

Santa Paula, California, June 2020

In late June, Alice and Jake finished their house and we moved into their old one. Mom was thrilled. But then her blood work showed the chemo had definitely stopped working. I made her a strawberry smoothie and carried it to her bedroom.

"Hiya," I said, "I think we should talk about what you want."

"Definitely not oatmeal. Don't tell Sam but I think the way he makes it is disgusting."

"Not for breakfast, I mean like 'want want.' Out of the rest of your life—the time you have left. You are still in charge. Even if it doesn't feel like it."

This was her chance to do things differently than Dad had. A chance for all of us. I would do anything to make sure that, this time, no one was left wondering if they'd disappointed her or messed up. Her wishes would be clear and ours would be too. We would acknowledge her dying in a way Dad hadn't been able or hadn't wanted to. We'd learned from our experience with him. There was no way I was going back.

She was quiet a moment.

"I want to feel like myself again."

The one impossible thing. It gutted me.

"What else?"

She said she wanted to get the whole family together one last time, for a week. I told her I'd make it happen. Only it was harder than I thought. The pandemic was raging, and the ranch was still a construction zone with one spare bedroom. Perhaps the responsible choice would have been to stop there. To invite our loved ones to come and camp out, or to scratch the whole thing. But Mom had saved for her retirement. For years, she'd scrimped, and chastised me for spending money on things she thought were frivolous: Bay Area rent; cooking in my "nice clothes"; buying larger plants at the nursery instead of seedlings; ordering organic turkeys for Thanksgiving. We could save the money she'd put away for retirement. Maybe one day we'd wish we had. But getting everyone together one last time was the one thing Mom really wanted. The cost of *not* doing it felt more expensive. So we made a plan to go to a private ranch in Wyoming. If our luck held, we'd spend a week: Jake, Alice, their boys, all of Sam's daughters and their partners and kids, Josh, and me.

The Magee Homestead had individual cabins, fly-fishing, horseback riding, and a hot tub with views of the Bitterroot Mountains. Looking at the photos on their website, I could almost smell the cottonwood buds. Mom tried to back out a dozen times, saying she was too sick to travel and that she wouldn't be able to do any of the activities, so why bother. Sam and I worked hard to convince her otherwise, appealing to her higher self, the one who knew that she wasn't defined by what she could do but by who she was. "Lynn, it's okay if you do nothing but sit by the creek and talk with us," Sam said. Sometimes she agreed but mostly she was in mourning. She may have been slowly accepting her own impending death, but she hadn't made peace with being the kind of person who couldn't go fishing. And who could blame her? She went from perfectly healthy to dying in a matter of months.

We'd scheduled what we thought might be her last chemo infusion for three weeks before we left so the drugs would be as far out of her system as possible. We stocked up on pain and anti-nausea meds. I prayed in my secular way that we'd all get to Wyoming safely and without Covid. We mailed everyone face shields and respirators. Arranged for Covid tests. And still I worried. About our virus risk but not just that. It was late July, peak fire season—what if Jake was sent out on a fire and couldn't come? The worrying about this was easier than sitting back and watching Mom waste away. Which is what was happening. No matter how many smoothies Sam and I made for her, she was losing weight precipitously. I knew this couldn't go on for long. She would die of starvation before she inevitably went through liver failure. But how much time did we have? No one could say for sure.

Before we sent the final deposit to the ranch, I had a phone call with the staff. I wanted to be honest about what we were doing and make sure they'd be able to handle it. "Just so you know," I said, "this is a memorial service for my mom. Only she'll be there." There were a few beats of silence and I pictured them raising their eyebrows at one another under their cowboy hats. Jeremy, the proprietor, spoke up. "It's a first for us for sure, but we will do anything and everything we can to make this as meaningful as possible for you all."

We decided that Josh and I would do something of a marriage ceremony while we were there too. So Mom could be there. The ranch put me in touch with a florist who could make a bouquet. Instead, I asked for a ring of flowers to put on the brim of my hat. Mom chose a turquoise bolo tie of Dad's for Josh to wear. Our ceremony would be a blessing for Mom and a marriage ritual for Josh and me.

I tried not to get my hopes up. Josh's company, like a few different commercial fishing operations that depended on people working and living in tight quarters, was having Covid outbreaks. Since Josh was so trustworthy, he'd been sent to Anchorage to oversee his company's new testing and quarantine procedures. I begged him to be careful. Not only did I worry he'd get sick but I also knew that if he had a known exposure the Alaska Department of Health would put him in a mandatory two-week quarantine and he'd miss the trip. "Please, please, please," I pleaded, "be extra careful the two weeks before you leave." But two days before Josh was set to fly out, one of his colleagues tested positive, and the contact tracer assigned to his case put Josh in quarantine. He'd be locked inside an Anchorage hotel room for fourteen days. He would not be part of our ceremony for Mom. There would be no wedding ritual for us. I'd be doing this alone. I was so angry I could barely speak to him. Unfairly or not, I wished he'd been more careful. I hadn't been able to talk to him for a couple of days. But now that we were actually at the ranch, I felt my heart soften. I was still mad but more than that, I felt sorry for him for missing this.

Our days at Magee felt enchanted. At least once an hour I wanted to stop time and hover, looking at us all together, saying: *Remember this. Remember this. Remember this.* After a scary first night when Mom's head hurt so much that she thought she was dying (it turned out to be a reaction to the altitude, treatable with steroids that our friend Phil asked a local physician to prescribe), she took a half a Ritalin to counter the fatigue of her disease and it worked wonders. Or maybe it was just her will. Whatever the case, she rose to the occasion of our week together like we hadn't seen her since she'd gotten her diagnosis. She went horseback riding and fishing and out on the UTVs to explore the ranch. She swam and did a performance of "Ladies of the Elks," an imaginary radio show she used to do for Jake and me on our long road trips to the cabin in Oregon. We made a sign-up sheet and one by one, Mom met with each of us, to say what she wanted to say and give everyone something. It was a little wooden box she and I had gotten engraved with each person's name and a phrase she wanted us to remember: *Don't forget to see the beauty in everything and everyone*. Inside, we put an owl pellet—one of Mom's favorite things, a mass of undigested food the bird spits up. She was always searching the ground for them, knowing that even a regurgitated mass of yuck could be a kind of miracle if you looked close enough. All you needed was a pair of tweezers to dissect it with and you could find an entire mouse skeleton, or at least a small skull.

If I was being honest, that's what we were doing here. Not going through undigested bird schmutz looking for treasure, but trying to find something good, maybe even beautiful, in the ugliness that is terminal illness, the terror that is dying before you want to.

On our second to last night we got dressed up, me in my white linen outfit for the wedding that wasn't to be. The kids wore matching cowboy hats, even Toby and Reggie, Sam's daughter Kate and her wife Maureen's baby daughter, whose hats were barely bigger than grapefruits. I saw Mom walking to meet us and could tell she felt beautiful. Her eyes were bright as she held Sam's arm, coming across the bridge over the creek. My joy at her joy was a leaping dog.

We drove out to a rustic camp on the Platte River, a surprise location the Magee staff had told me would be perfect. The late-afternoon light was buttery on the swaying grass and stands of rustling aspen and cottonwood trees. The surface of the river was broken only by the rings of rising trout. One of our guides, Clayton, stood along the shore casting his fly line in perfect eights toward the setting sun. A snapping bonfire burned in the center of a ring of benches. Freshwater pelicans flapped past overhead. A few hundred yards away I could see a rustic wooden deck jutting out over the river. On it, a long table was covered in glass jars of wildflowers. The smell of burning hardwood and sizzling steak carried on the breeze.

Eventually we walked down to the river's edge and stood in a circle in the tall grass. Sam asked us to hold hands. Wilder wriggled free and laid in the grass. Benny was serious, holding on to me tightly. Something holy settled over us like a net, holding even the babies still. "We are a family," Sam said, choking a bit on the words. "And we will always be a family. This will always be our family." Mom was crying. She took a deep breath. And one by one looked us each in the eye and said how much she loved us, saving Sam, then Jake, "my number one son," and me for the end.

"Lar, if you have even ten percent of the love I've been lucky to have in this lifetime it would be enough. I wish for you all that and more. I wish for you everything."

I couldn't stop crying. My tears were a river running straight into the Platte. And not just the Platte but the Umpqua. Not just the Umpqua but the Amazon. Not just the Amazon but the Chama. All the rivers I'd ever loved. And the oceans too. The Pacific. The Atlantic. The Bering Sea. The last ceremony I'd attended had been the Blessing of the Fleet with Josh, up in Seattle. I could still remember the priest's words: "Say to the waves, 'Peace. Be still.' You hold the human heart in the hollow of your hand . . ." That is how I felt now, like we were being tossed in waves so big I couldn't see over them. I pictured Dad in his surgical mask, his gloved hands reaching for a pulsing heart, and tried to gather my courage.

It was my turn to lead the blessing now. I tried to channel my friend Emily, a clinical chaplain who came to my writing workshops and who loved palliative care. We'd gone out to lunch once and I'd asked what seeing so much death and dying did to a person.

"Well, I go to Trader Joe's around dinnertime," she said.

I raised my eyebrows.

"It's really busy, and if I've had a hard day I like to stand by the tower of bananas and look at everyone around me doing their shopping. One by one, I look at each person and say silently to myself, 'You're alive! You're alive! We're ALL alive!' "

We laughed so hard then and I'd understood that a busy Trader Joe's was her version of the hourglass, the ticking clock, the hanging axe. Maybe all of us had one. You don't just shake death off like a wet dog after a bath. No. You can use it like an alarm clock to wake yourself up, and other people too.

Emily had a stole she sometimes hung around her neck while she did holy things. I'd seen inside and stitched there in gray-brown letters were the words PAX VOBISCUM + NOLI TIMERE. Peace be with you and be not afraid. Yes, I'd thought, writing out my blessing the day before. That's what I needed.

Now I was clutching a sheaf of printouts, looking around this circle of people I loved most. I told them this was the first real blessing I'd ever written. The only one that would ever matter, though I didn't say that part out loud. Instead, I asked Mom to stand in the middle of our circle and handed everyone a copy of the blessing. I explained that we would go around, taking turns saying each line till we reached the end. Mom could look at each of us as we spoke. The last line we'd say together. I asked Sam to start.

"May you feel how much we love you," he said, looking up at her from the paper, tears streaming down his cheeks. Mom's shoulders shook.

"May you understand how much you have taught us," said Sarah.

"May you know how much we have learned," Kate said.

"May you understand that you are a gift to us and to others. Even butterflies. Even bees," said Maureen.

"May you feel as sacred as we hold you dear," said Nancy.

"May our memories of you be a blessing that makes us laugh and sustains us," said Jake.

"May you give us the strength we will need to live without you," said Alice.

"May you know that you will never be without us," said Nancy's husband, Omar.

"May your next adventure be the most incredible and may you be there waiting when we get there too," I said.

"May you never wonder how much you matter," Sam said.

"May you know you always will," said Sarah.

"Peace be with you and be not afraid," we all said together, and cheered.

Four

Santa Paula, California, August 2020

Mom was buoyed by the trip to Wyoming and all she was able to do there, so when she came home she started a second-line chemo treatment we hoped would buy her more time. After his quarantine was up, Josh flew down to the ranch to spend a week with us. Mom was in good spirits and felt well enough to take us to the nursery to buy Josh his first tree to plant on the ranch. Josh chose a small pistachio but when we got to the checkout and Mom saw the price, she got annoyed. There were an awkward few moments as Josh stood there offering to put it back, but we took her surly frugality as a good sign. We made a plan to get married the third week of September, when salmon season ended and Josh was back for good. Mom promised she'd do everything she could to stick around for it.

Just a few weeks later, I wasn't sure she'd make it. Every day Mom looked thinner, more like an anatomical illustration than herself. And then one afternoon she announced she wouldn't be doing another infusion. She was done and she meant it this time. I was monitoring her liver function closely because as soon as it started to turn, her plan was to take her right-to-die medication. She'd picked it up with Sam at UCLA and gotten a briefing in the hallway outside of GI oncology, where they were handed a printed sheet of instructions and a heavy jar of medication in a folded paper bag. She put the bag in the linen closet next to a stack of clean sheets.

I saw it there whenever I went in for another pillowcase or to get her heartburn medicine and I thought about Dad's old pill bottle. This time I knew exactly what was coming, but that didn't change how badly I didn't want it to. So I tried to distract Mom with wedding plans. My most stylish friend, Shoham, helped me pick out a bunch of potential outfits on sale and we did a fashion show with Cath, Leyla, Alice, and Mom on the patio off their bedroom. I wanted her to help me choose what to wear.

The hawk showed up the next day. It was a Cooper's hawk, a small bird of prey that mainly eats other birds, with what looked like a broken wing. Jake saw it first and thought it might have flown into one of their windows by accident. He called the Ojai Raptor Center, which said we should wait for the bird to get tired and hungry and then try to capture it and bring it in for treatment. Mom and I were putting away plates in the kitchen when I heard rustling by the back door. The hawk was crouched a few feet away, between two baby boxwood bushes. One wing was bent at an odd angle, but the hawk's eyes were bright and fierce, taking me in. I'd never been so close to a hawk before.

I pulled some raw chicken out of a large Costco pack and threw the bird a hunk. It flapped backward across the ground, startled and wary. But I knelt down, waiting quietly, and soon the bird hopped back and snatched the meat, tearing at it hungrily with its small sharp beak. When the bird finished it looked at me with what I swore was a question. "Okay, okay," I said, and went back in the kitchen for more.

I know I was supposed to be letting the bird get weaker so it could be more easily captured. But I couldn't look at that powerful creature and let it waste away. So for the next few days, I wouldn't see the hawk till it saw me, moving around the yard or washing dishes at the kitchen sink, and then I would toss it some chicken.

On one of those afternoons Mom and I were in the room we were making into an office. She was filing paperwork she'd been organizing for weeks, trying to get all her affairs in order. We often marveled at how much bureaucracy it took to die.

"I think the hawk is here to take me to the other side," she said, looking up from a stack of invoices.

"What if it's just a hawk, Mom?"

"It's not," she said. "It's Dad. He's here to get me."

I wanted to argue but I couldn't. I remembered what Michelle's dad had told me, back on the Navajo Nation all those years ago, that eagles carry prayers to the heavens. Maybe this hawk *was* Dad. Birds of Pray. A wish made visible.

"Lar," Mom said, changing the subject, "did I tell you we found a bucket of honey yesterday?"

I thought we'd lost it all in the fire. Every single jar.

"No," she said, "it survived because it was in the shed. I'm thinking of putting it in the driveway."

This was Mom's trick for getting our honey to de-crystalize. The heat from the asphalt seeped into the bucket, gently turning the crystals liquid so the honey was easy to pour into jars. A five-gallon bucket would be enough to last a few years if we were careful.

There is something I wish I'd said to her then, about bees, but I hadn't learned it yet.

The ancient Egyptians used honey for more than their prescriptions; the insects also showed up in holy texts. On one papyrus it was written that when the sun god Re (or Ra) cried, his tears fell to the earth and became bees that made honey for the people.

Life from grief. Pain into sweetness. Sorrow into medicine.

That night I lay in bed, naked with the sheets and blankets kicked off, sweating. It was over ninety degrees inside, even though it was after midnight. Through the open window, I heard a chirp and sharp whistle. The hawk! I knew its sounds well now, the dragging-hop through the dry leaf litter. But there was something else too. A heavy plodding and what sounded like a mammal scream. Something, or someone, was trying to kill the hawk. I could hear it trying to get away in the dark. I jumped out of bed, naked, and ran down the stairs to see what I could see. But as soon as I stepped outside everything immediately went quiet. Whatever it was knew I was there. I started back up the stairs but heard the hawk cry again. The tussling was in the dry leaves under the pomegranates, up the embankment from where I was standing. Of course that's where the hawk would be hiding at night; unable to fly into a tree, the thick bushes would provide some cover. I heard a high hiss from whatever was going after it. My heart was in my throat, my pulse thudding. I looked around for something to throw but there was only a big metal shovel with a long wooden handle leaning against the side of the garage. I slammed the metal end down on the blacktop again and again. I felt the clanging up through my arm, into my teeth. "Leave the bird alone!" I screamed toward the commotion. "Get out of here! Get!" I banged harder. The hissing stopped. And soon the rustling did too. It was silent. I looked down at my feet. Felt, for the first time, the night air on my bare skin. I heard a barn owl call down by the creek, the sound of crickets. I went back to bed. An hour later, though, I woke up again. More hissing. A hawk's cry. Again I went downstairs, banged the shovel, and screamed into the dark. This time, I wore my boots and went charging into the thick wall of pomegranates. I could feel the branches tearing at my hair, my skin. I didn't care.

The hawk couldn't die. Not yet.

I pictured Mom in her bed on the other side of the house. Her reading glasses folded on the table next to her, on top of the little book Jake and I had given to her for her birthday, a list of things we loved about her. I hoped she'd sleep through all this and wake up, by some miracle, feeling like herself and tease me about how I'd been worried about her for no reason. We needed more time. I had so much more I wanted to know. Why hadn't I paid better attention in all my years watching her make granola. And persimmon pudding. Why hadn't I recorded every conversation we'd ever had. I'd felt like a hoarder these last months. Like the videos of people stockpiling toilet paper back in March and April. Only it was her I wanted. More her. It's all I ever wanted. Even when I had her.

In the early spring, when she still had energy, in between infusions, we walked around the ranch. One day we were on the hill by the new baby avocados we planted to replace the ones that died in the fire.

"You have to look tree by tree," she said to me, motioning down the row.

"It's not enough to look at a block from the outside. Because individual trees have their own soil, microclimate, nutrient problems. They can be feet away from one another but have entirely different needs."

In our family, in addition to taciturn pets, trees were our love language. We planted something to mark every milestone, especially births. There are Laurel's avocados. And Jake's lemons. Benny's block of trees and Toby's baby avocados. They aren't ours in the traditional sense because you can't own trees. Not really. "Having" in most cases isn't the same as "owning." It's that we and the trees were planted at the same time. In the same ground.

We would plant trees for Mom's death too, of course. We just hadn't talked about it yet. Sam quietly ordered some more magnolias and two big redwood saplings. Antonio moved our old wooden teak bench to a spot up by the new water tank, below the oak tree where the swing had once been, and laid irrigation line so we could get water to the saplings once they went in the ground.

The morning after the hawk was attacked, I was outside filling the hummingbird feeder when I heard rustling again, just a few feet away. The bird was under a lemon tree looking at me expectantly.

"You made it!" I shouted. And ran inside for its breakfast.

That night I lay in bed, dressed this time in case I had to fend off a predator, my rubber boots waiting at the door. But it was quiet.

I woke up the next morning expecting the hawk to appear like it usually did when I started moving around the house, but it never showed up. I went into Mom's bedroom to tell her I couldn't find it and I saw her. Hands crossed in her lap, sitting up in bed. Resolute.

"I'm ready, Laurel. I can't do this any longer."

I wanted to scream. I wanted to raze the trees. To beg her to stay. But I didn't. I just said "Okay."

Five

Santa Paula, California, August 2020

Mom was impatient. Later Jake and I joked that she treated dying just like she treated every trip to the airport. She'd tell us to be ready, bags packed by 7 a.m., but at six forty-five she'd be idling in the car wondering why on earth we weren't there yet. When she made up her mind, it was done. And if she wasn't early, she was late.

But Jake, Alice, and I protested. What if she waited one more day?

"No," she said.

What if I promised to control her pain better today? Called her team at UCLA? Got stronger meds?

"No. It's time."

The earth in my chest shook and cracked open. I wasn't ready but I would never be ready.

As if she could tell what I was thinking, she said, "We will never have enough time, Laurel. There was never going to be enough. No matter how much we'd gotten we'd still want more."

She was right.

What followed is a bit of a blur. I finished reading her a draft of this book. And I know she called her friend Myrna, but when I asked if she wanted to speak to anyone else she loved, she shook her head. It was too hard. Impossible, really. But I asked if we could call Josh to say goodbye. The connection from remote Alaska had a bad delay but she spoke and he listened. "Take care of my girl," she said. "I know you'll find your way here, even more into everybody's hearts. You will find your spot among the trees and the hawks and whatever else. I know you will, Josh. I know you'll be a valuable piece of the ranch. And I know you guys'll have great fun. I know you're going to have arguments too. But I know you'll work them out because of who you two are. I just wish I wasn't going to miss it." She told him how much she loved him, how she'd never known anyone like him, and asked if he could see salmon from where he was standing. He cried as he told her how much he loved her. And then, eventually, she said she'd let him go. As if he were the one leaving.

Jake, Alice, and I gave Mom and Sam some time alone. We took the bag of medication out of the linen closet and read the instructions standing in the kitchen, the same instructions she'd made me and Sam practice a week before because that was the kind of thing she did. "Stir slowly but rapidly," she'd read aloud to us. A contradiction like so much of this experience. We'd laughed about it.

And then it was time.

"Lar," Mom said to me as I walked back into the room, "I want a lay-down hug. A really good one."

I got in bed next to her and wrapped my arms around her as tightly as I could without hurting her. She was a bird of bones. But still herself. A force. My tears were falling sideways, pooling in my ears, pain roaring in my veins.

"Yes," she said, "just like that," as I squeezed her.

Jake brought the medication into the bedroom in one of the bistro glasses we used for juice. She needed to drink it within a minute of it being made. I lit a handful of sage—the last of the leaves I'd collected before the ranch burned. We played Andrea Bocelli and then Bach through the speakers just like she'd asked. We looked at each other and at some point we stopped speaking. The sunlight poured onto the wood floor.

Someone had opened the French doors to her bee and butterfly garden. Each of us got on the bed with her. Mona, Jake and Alice's sweet blind pit bull, curled into a ball on the floor. We assured Mom we'd followed the directions. She reached out and I held the cup to her lips to help steady her hand. My fingers on hers. She drank it in three long gulps and lay back on the pillows. We put our hands on her feet, on her legs and shoulders. Within a minute or two she closed her eyes. I lay down next to her. So did Jake and Alice and Sam. We waited. We played more of her favorite music and then a version of the haunting "Eli, Eli" song we'd discovered on the recording of my bat mitzvah Alice had found.

> I pray that these things never end,
> the sand and the sea,
> the rush of the waters,
> . . .
> the prayer of the heart.

Over the next few hours Mom's breathing slowed along with her heartbeat but stayed steady, a metronome that didn't want to quit.

I looked down at her legs, so small now, next to mine. Both of us wearing jeans. She'd put on her favorite socks, green patterned with pink butterflies, to die in.

When it had been two hours, I pressed my hand to her neck to feel her pulse. Still steady. I thought about my old stethoscope, the one Dad gave me. It had burned in the fire, but I could still remember the sounds. *Lub dub, lub dub*. Mom's heartbeat was the first thing I'd ever heard. I wondered what she was hearing now. I hoped it was us, the birds in the bath in her garden, the songs she'd loved and chosen to leave with.

One morning, back in the spring, I'd gone in to see her and she looked so happy. When I asked what was up, she said she'd had a fantastic dream. "I was wearing my ranch clothes and had one of my ball caps on, my hair in a ponytail. I felt like me. And I was at the edge of a huge canyon with rocky red cliffs. I started walking down into it. I knew I hadn't chosen to go but I had to. And when I got to the bottom I saw the most stunning pool of water I've ever seen. I put a foot in and"—tears were streaming down her cheeks—"I knew that it was the source of all life. It felt so good. It felt like home."

I closed my eyes now and watched her take a few steps down a narrow trail, the river a ribbon far below. She stopped, looked back at me, and smiled. Above her, in the widening sky, a small hawk with striped wings dipped and banked on the thermals.

"I'll miss you with every breath I take, for the rest of my life," I murmured. "And then one day I'll be with you."

It took a while but eventually her breathing slowed, her heartbeat faint as moth wings beating. And then I felt for her pulse and it was gone. I looked at Jake and Sam. It was nearly sunset; the sky was a dozen shades of purple. A beautiful bruise. I noted the time, 7:32 p.m. And then we heard it. A chorus of coyotes, long and loud, from up on the hill or down in the creek. There were just so many, and they went on and on. Yipping and calling and howling. And then, underneath the racket, we heard two deep *hoooooo*s of a great horned owl.

"It's a greeting," Sam said. "They're welcoming her home."

Six

Santa Paula, California, September 2020

After Mom died, whenever I checked our mailbox there were packages addressed to her. The extra plates and wineglasses she'd ordered for the wedding, the tiny glasses we bought for the liqueurs I'd made from our apricots and plums all summer. Every time I opened a box I felt like I was being stabbed. Before she died she'd made me promise that Josh and I would still get married even though she wasn't going to make it. She assured us that she'd be there right beside us, watching. But now, frothing with pain, I didn't see how I could possibly do it. The date was three weeks away. I had a phone session with Judy and tried to talk it out.

"Laurel, you definitely don't have to get married," she said, "even if you promised your mom you would. It would be totally understandable if it was too soon."

She paused.

"All of this makes me think of something, though. There's a Jewish principle that dictates that between a funeral or a wedding, you're obligated to choose the wedding. Between life and death, you're obligated to choose life."

This sounded a lot like something my parents would say. Also, there was Dad's conviction that you always needed to do a nice thing after a hard thing.

And so, on September 26, just over three weeks after she died, I was in Mom's closet putting on the clothes she'd helped me choose. A pair of creamy silk pants, a tie-front white linen blazer, and a glittery pair of sandals I'd bought used. My favorite part, though, was my hat. It was a custom open-crown wide brim from a hatmaker in LA named Brandon whose mom had cancer too. Inside, on the leather band where he normally stamped people's initials, I'd asked for a phrase instead. PEACE BE WITH YOU AND BE NOT AFRAID.

My stepsister Kate helped me tie a long piece of tulle around the crown of my hat that flowed out behind me onto the ground. Around my neck I wore Mom's locket with the tiny hand-painted portraits of her and Dad on their wedding day, one of the few things she had taken out of the house during the fire. I wore her gold bee earrings too. And when I spun in front of the mirror watching the tulle flow behind me like a tail, I could almost hear them buzzing. I liked what I saw and wished twelve-year-old me could see her too.

We decided to have the ceremony at the top of the hill. At the base of one of my favorite oak trees, its trunk still black from the fire. When Sam and I came over the final rise, where the donkeys had loved to stand and survey their lands and where I'd escaped to nearly twenty-five years earlier on the day Dad died, crying in the sagebrush, I saw Josh. He was looking at me from under the brim of his own hat, the one I'd gotten for him in Santa Fe back in December as an engagement present. He looked gorgeous in his suit, western-cut brown wool that I'd found in a consignment shop a couple years before and bought without knowing if it would fit him. He wore a boutonniere that matched my bouquet, made of the white peacock feathers I'd been picking up all summer from our birds. He had tears in his eyes looking at me. Next to him was our friend Samin, whom we'd asked to officiate as soon as we'd gotten engaged. She was waiting, a huge smile on her face, her dark blue silk dress billowing in the wind.

Behind them I could see Sam's daughters, my chosen sisters Sarah, Kate, and Nancy. Josh's mom and dad, two of his sisters, his brother, and his brother's wife. Cath and her husband, Travis. Jake—in one of Dad's bolo ties—Alice, and my nephews. Wilder, who was four now, had taken his shirt off and was sitting bare-chested in the sun. All around them were more friends, family, and other animals whom I couldn't see but knew were there. The kids from Josie's Place, our leaders Pat and Andrea. All the grieving adolescents and teens I'd talked to who'd taught me it was okay to feel the bad stuff. Petra and Emerald and the other hungry women in the desert. The beavers and the doves. The men who'd disappointed me so thoroughly that I'd finally taken my hand off the flame. The swarming bees and the Diné sheep. Wendy and Caroline, my Thacher girlfriends. Connie. Shoham. The medical students and physician-writers who'd made me a teacher. Judy. Cedar and all the other good dogs and grouchy burros who'd loved me even when I let them down. I was walking up this hill for all of us, the fatherless daughters, the motherless sons. The orphans and parents forced to say goodbye before they were ready. Anyone who's ever tried to give up on loving because it hurts too much. We are legion. And we just need a chance.

I hugged Sam and went to stand with Josh and Samin.

"My goal today is to make everyone cry," she said, and laughed. Samin was a born minister. A holy woman. She began to read an excerpt from *The Book of Delights* by Ross Gay.

" 'What if we joined our wildernesses together? . . . That the body, the life, might carry a wilderness, an unexplored territory, and that yours and mine might somewhere, somehow, meet. Might, even, join. And what if the wilderness . . . is our sorrow?' "

"My question"—Samin said, in her own words now—"is what if the sorrows cancel each other out? We who love you have watched you two overcome the fear of loving one another, because it might mean you'd have to lose each other someday. You've faced your fears head-on and continue to show up and face them every single day. Because what else is there? What else is worth it? You've chosen love. You've chosen joy. You've chosen to join your wildernesses together."

Down at the house, we toasted with champagne and watermelon juice from the melons I'd grown the whole terrible summer.

Jake tapped his glass and said he wanted to make three toasts. One for Dad, one for Mom, and one that was his.

My breath caught. And I cried while he talked about how Dad would have loved Josh but that he might not have known it, and that Mom would have wanted us to savor every minute of our lives because we knew all too well that they're numbered.

Then it was Sam's turn.

Sarah stepped out from behind him. She was carrying a brown-and-white-painted pot with two gently curving spouts.

"This is a marriage vessel made by an artist in Acoma Pueblo," Sam said. "Your mom got this for you two as a wedding present so that you would always remember to drink from the same cup."

After the fire Judy told me that it was only the vessels we'd lost. I'd wondered then what happened when you didn't have containers for what you loved most. But now here was Mom, reaching out to give me one when I needed it.

We set the pot down and I heard faint strains of a trumpet coming from the other side of the house. Mom had one more surprise. We'd planned it together. It was Mariachi Camarillo, a local nine-piece family band, who were now walking toward us, single file, in matching navy suits with gleaming silver thread. Their eyes were smiling above their face masks and they fanned out playing "Como La Flor," the brass of their instruments reflecting the sunset. We danced and danced. The sun went down and we moved to the table, but we could barely stop dancing to eat. I begged Dominic, the band leader, to play another hour and he agreed. Connie and her partner, Faye, showed up carrying bottles of mezcal. I hugged them both tight and then ran back onto the grass, under the hanging lights Sam had strung up. Bats were darting to and fro now, having their own wedding banquet. Down by the creek the owls would just be waking up.

For the second time that day I thought of the kids at Josie's Place and the Dougy Center. And even though I'd never met her, I thought of a young girl named Ixchel that Pat had once told me about. After her first session, Ixchel said to her mom, "We can be happy-sad here!" That's how I felt now. How I wanted to feel forever. There is no such thing as happily ever after. There is only happily sad or sadly happy. And that is more than enough. The truth is that every heart's a phoenix. Being born and born again. That's what Dad held in his hands and what each of us needs to remember. It's never too late. Go. Now. Do it. Say the thing that scares you most. Even if it's goodbye.

Be not afraid.

Acknowledgments

Bravery is a group project.
Thank you to everyone who helped me understand.

Especially, the wise kids and parents of Josie's Place, Pat Murphy and Andrea Bass; the families and staff of the Dougy Center, including Donna Schuurman, Joan Schweitzer Hoff, Jana DeCristofaro, and Alysha Lacey; Jonathan Goldstein and *This American Life*; my *Pop-Up Magazine* family; the School of Lost Borders, Petra Lentz-Snow, Emerald North, and my fellow fasters, especially Afrose Ahmed and Adia Millett; the Thacher School; the Benally family and Rock Point Community School; Stanford Spiritual Care, especially Emily Linderman and Landon Bogan; Corey Arnold; Suzi Golodoff, Beatriz Dietrick, and the rest of my friends in Dutch Harbor; the incredible team at Magee Homestead; Bill Plested, MD; Amitav Ghosh; Jonathan Berek, MD; Chase Elder; Caitlin Swaim; Lauren Tabak; Jess Seitz; Kim Pierce; Jessica Lanyadoo; Emily Weinstein; Bryan Fisch, DDS; Judy Gold; Peter Robinson, Marilee Lin, Susie Caldwell Rhinehart, Lori and Cam Schryver, and the other good teachers who never tried to convince me of God's plan; Ann Hamilton and Michael Mercil; Myrna Golden; Kathan Glassman; Dan and Susan Pinkerton; David Stephens; Mark Lodge and Theresa Fenton and the Puako crew for the pilialoha; Josh Biddle, MD; BJ Miller, MD; Michael Fowler, MD; the bush pilots of Island Air, Ravn Alaska, Medevac Alaska, and Talkeetna Air Taxi for your smart decisions in bad conditions; Malia Wollan; Courtney Martin; Alexis Madrigal; the generous writers of the Notto; Susan and Jake Gillespie; Cheryl Strayed, for giving me a torch when I needed it most, also prosecco; the clinicians and other healers who cared for my mom, and by extension, me too: Zev Wainberg, MD; Megan Price; Sarah D'Ambruoso; Susanne Warner, MD; Joshua Rosenburg, MD; Michael Eselun; Jihad Warwar, MD; and Diane Haug; the physicians, nurses, and others at the Mayo Clinic, UCLA, Memorial Sloan Kettering, and Massachusetts General Hospital whose hard work and creativity kept my dad alive long enough for his kids to really know him. I wish I knew your names. You made all the difference.

Stanford School of Medicine's Medical Humanities and the Arts Program, the Stanford Department of Anesthesiology, Perioperative and Pain Medicine, and the Stanford Center for Biomedical Ethics have given me support and an intellectual home, especially the inimitable Audrey Shafer, MD; Ron Pearl, MD; Jackie Genovese; Christy Hartman; David Magnus; Holly Tabor; Gabriella Rivera, Vi Dang, Brian Bateman, MD, and Bryant Lin, MD. Thank you also to the literary physicians of Stanford, you help me more than I help you, in particular Shireen Heidari, MD; Adjoa Boateng, MD; Bill Meffert, MD; Alyssa Burgart, MD; Karl Lorenz, MD; Iris Gibbs, MD; and Yeuen Kim, MD.

My students, especially Pablo Romano, Candice Kim, Grace Li, Ben Teasdale, Noemie Levy, Dasha Savage, Ruth Marks Case, Arifeen Rahman, Jason Gomez, Jenny Tiskus, Julie Barzilay, Brandon Turner, Bonnie Wong, Marija Kamceva, Uriel Sanchez, Stephen Marcott, Maïté Van Hentenryck, Vongai Mlambo, Claire Rhee, Brian Smith, Rachel Ryan, and the many others of you, present, past, and future, who have written your names on my heart. You heal the world.

The Writing Medicine community, you are my one true congregation. Thank you.

I have received support from the TED Fellows Program and the

Rockefeller Foundation, including Pilar Palaciá and my cohort, notably Wizdom Powell and Rozana Montiel.

Priscilla Painton, Jonathan Karp, Hana Park, Anne Tate Pearce, and the rest of my team at Simon & Schuster, I am honored to be in your pack.

Barney Karpfinger, you will always be the one who made me a writer and I will always be the most grateful.

Cathy Jaque, thank you in every language.

Skyler Marshall, you are a superhero posing as an assistant.

Cristina Valdovinos, gracias por acompañarnos en este misterioso viaje. Le prometo que algún día aprenderé a orar.

Maria Barrell, Stefanie Warren, Brooke LeVasseur, Quinn Kanaly, Mandy Sonenshine, Auriga Martin, Brittany Sanders, Travis Keeling, Catherine Pinkerton Keeling, and Leyla Abou-Samra, you've been my love and my mirror for twenty-five years and counting. Thank you. Shoham Arad, Jon Mooallem, Wandee Pryor, Amy Standen, Chris Colin, Wendy MacNaughton, Caroline Paul, Rebecca Goodstein, Bonnie Tsui, Haley Howle, Rebecca Skloot, Pat Walters, Annie Brown, Doug McGray, and Carrie Donovan, you are my love orchard. I'm grateful to Chris, Mike, Marisa, Marija, Cody, Christina, Anthony, Lex, Sean, and the rest of the Maricich clan for inviting me in. Judy M., you are wisdom embodied. Antonio Aguilar, gracias por su dedicación a Los Perules. Estamos agradecidos por siempre. Phil and Jill Weinstein, you are my chosen ones. Samin Nosrat, "gratitude" isn't a big enough word. "Family" is. Constance Lee Hockaday, thank you. This book wouldn't be here without you and neither would I. Nancy, Kate, and Sarah, my sisters from another mother, we are always. Rob, I don't want to be in the crucible with anyone else but you. Not ever.

Alice, thank you for showing me how to love best and fiercely every day. Jake, this story has always been for you. They all are. Bennett, Wilder, and Toby, you're my heart. I hope this book doesn't embarrass you. But if it does, just know that it's less embarrassing than everything I will do to you once you're in high school.

Josh, I hate how much I love you. It scares me to death. But you are worth it. You have always been worth it. Thank you for running into the fire, and most importantly, for staying. I'm yours.

Mom and Dad, your love is the ink in my veins. If you're reading this, you know I'm proudest of being your daughter.

About the Author

LAUREL BRAITMAN is a *New York Times* bestselling author and the Director of Writing and Storytelling at the Medical Humanities and the Arts Program at Stanford University School of Medicine. She holds a PhD in Science, Technology and Society from MIT and is the founder of the global community of writing healthcare professionals, Writing Medicine, now in its fourth year. Her last book, *Animal Madness*, was a *New York Times* bestseller and has been translated into eight languages. Laurel lives on her family's ranch in Southern California with her husband, her brother and his wife, and their three sons. The family is still growing avocados and citrus commercially. She can be reached at laurelbraitman.com.